Logic in Theology and Other Essays

With a Sketch of the Life of the Author and a Catalogue of His Writings

By:

ISAAC TAYLOR

WIPF & STOCK · Eugene, Oregon

Wipf and Stock Publishers
199 W 8th Ave, Suite 3
Eugene, OR 97401

Logic in Theology and Other Essays
With a Sketch of the Life of the Author
and a Catalogue of His Writings
By Taylor, Isaac
Softcover ISBN-13: 978-1-7252-9666-4
Hardcover ISBN-13: 978-1-7252-9665-7
eBook ISBN-13: 978-1-7252-9667-1
Publication date 5/1/2021
Previously published by William Gowans, 1860

This edition is a scanned facsimile of
the original edition published in 1860.

CONTENTS.

	PAGE
ESSAY I.	
LOGIC IN THEOLOGY,	7
ESSAY II	
THE STATE OF UNITARIANISM IN ENGLAND,	71
ESSAY III.	
NILUS:—The Christian Courtier in the Desert,	114
ESSAY IV.	
PAULA:—High Quality and Asceticism in the Fourth Century,	153
ESSAY V.	
THEODOSIUS:—Pagan Usages, and the Christian Magistrate,	170
ESSAY VI.	
JULIAN:—Prohibitive Education,	199
ESSAY VII.	
"WITHOUT CONTROVERSY,"	223
SUPPLEMENTARY TO THE FIFTH ESSAY,	291
BIOGRAPHICAL SKETCH,	295
CATALOGUE OF THE AUTHOR'S WRITINGS,	299

THE reader is informed that a great part of the FIRST ESSAY in this volume appeared as an Introductory Essay to "Edwards on Free Will." The SECOND ESSAY, which first appeared in the *Eclectic Review*, October 1830, was reprinted at Manchester soon afterwards.

The other Essays—the THIRD, FOURTH, FIFTH, SIXTH, and SEVENTH—have not before appeared in print.

LOGIC IN THEOLOGY,

AND

OTHER ESSAYS.

ESSAY I.

LOGIC IN THEOLOGY.

Modern physical science has had its commencement, and has attained its present firm condition within a period of three hundred years. The philosophy which it has displaced had held undisputed sway during more than eighteen hundred years. In comparing the recent with the ancient scheme of natural science the contrast is not greater in regard to the contents, or the ascertained results of the one system, than in regard to those principles of reasoning and those methods of proof which have been admitted in each.

Throughout that long anterior period of imagined intellectual liberty, but of real bondage, the masters of philosophy believed, and they taught, that the human mind possesses, or may attain to, a sovereign comprehension of all things, real and possible, so that it may work out for itself a scheme of the world, material and immaterial, derived from its own conceptions; a scheme such that it shall furnish a true explication of all phenomena of the actual world.

This prodigious illusion—such we now think it—was already passing off from the mind of Europe, as a dark cloud, at the moment when Bacon, in formal terms, challenged it as a folly, and the parent of error. Since that time realities, one by one, have been coming into their due position in the room of dreams. This, with an allowance made for exceptional instances, may be affirmed concerning the physical sciences of this modern period.

In turning toward those regions of thought where we cease to be concerned with things palpable, visible, measurable, ponderable, a corresponding affirmation cannot be advanced, apart from exceptive statements, so large, that we may well doubt whether the affirmative side and the exceptive should not change places; or whether, in the regions of *non-material* philosophy, what we may affirm with truth is only this—that in *these* fields the antiquated Logic still holds its sway—a due allowance being made for instances in which juster modes of thinking have gained ground.

In proportion as the human mind is compelled to feel its dependence upon its instrument, namely—language, it is led, almost irresistibly, to expect far more aid from the logical collocation of words and propositions than these implements of thought can ever yield. Language, logically compacted in propositions, avails to give us the best possible command of the knowledge which we actually possess; but it has no power to increase that stock, even by a particle.

Nevertheless the advantages derivable from a well-compacted and a well-commanded stock of knowledge are so great—they are so inestimable—that it becomes difficult to avoid attributing to our logical methods an efficacy which does not belong to them. We believe ourselves to have *acquired* knowledge, when, in fact, we have done nothing more than bring our materials into available order. In truth, it may be granted that order is a positive gain in respect of materials of which we are likely to make no use while they lie scattered before us in confusion.

The imagined efficiency of logical methods for augmenting our stock of knowledge—for bringing us to know what otherwise we should not know—is still affirmed, and is trusted to, in the department of intellectual philosophy; nor can it be said that those vast advances of physical science, which have resulted from the adoption of a wholly different principle, have much availed to bring about a corresponding improvement on this side; for it continues to be believed that, by carrying the highest abstractions a step or two further than they have hitherto gone, the human mind may come to solve the problems of existence, and may master the mysteries of its own being.

In the region of religious speculation, or of abstract theology, various influences combine to strengthen this same confidence in the potency of formal methods of reasoning for the attainment of knowledge. Concerning these influences it is not proposed in these pages to make any inquiry; nor to ask what may have been their operation in distorting or disturbing the principles of a purely biblical theology. Instead of attempting a task so difficult, and of such wide range as this, we take up a single instance in which logical methods which are affirmed to be strictly demonstrative, and irresistibly conclusive, have been applied to a class of subjects in relation to which we are far from being dependent upon language, or upon Logic, and where genuine knowledge, as to its sources, and its materials, is within our reach—subjects which belong much rather to physics than to metaphysics.

An inquiry—properly physical—concerning the constitution of human nature, has come to be considered by theologians as their own, in consequence of its connection with the principles of the moral and religious life. Theology—that is to say, a mixed product of abstract speculation and of biblical teaching—has interwoven itself, has entangled itself, with what appertains to the philosophy of human nature. A disentanglement of the two is what may well be aimed at, as desirable.

SECTION I.

In modern times no instance of the misapplication of *mere logic* to the solution of a physical problem has been more signal, or has had so wide and lasting an influence as that of the "Inquiry into the Modern Prevailing Notions respecting the Freedom of Will." Jonathan Edwards has held his ground as a master in morals and theology, almost unquestioned, from his own times to these.

Should we think, then, to dislodge him from his position? We are far from wishing to attempt it. But what may be done is this—to accept, and to leave to its merits, the alleged demonstration of an abstruse dogma, and to set it off as a matter altogether indifferent to Christian belief, as it confessedly is so to the conduct of common life.

Philosophical writings are allowed to command a more grave attention, and to challenge a higher rank in literature than is accorded to works of imagination; but then it is their fate more often to fall into oblivion; or even if remembered and preserved, yet to be superseded, and to forfeit the honours they once enjoyed as canons of science. The reason of this difference is obvious; for in the one class of compositions an end is proposed, namely, to give pleasure to the reader—which may be attained in a thousand ways, and in the pursuit of which genius ensures its own success. But in the other class, where the discovery of truth is the single object, success depends, not merely upon the ability of the writer, but upon the good fortune also which leads him to choose the one right track, amid innumerable devious paths.

Works of science lose their credit, as such, either in consequence of the refutation and entire rejection of the principles they maintain; or they are gradually superseded, in the course of improvement, by better digested systems, founded on the same general doctrines. In instances of this latter sort the discoverers of certain great truths which have become the property of the intellectual commonwealth, though they still hold their titles of honour, are more often spoken of than read; or they are read only by the few who make the history of science their peculiar study.

Whatever may in the next age be the fate of the "Inquiry concerning Freedom of Will," it may safely be predicted that, at least as an instance of exact analysis, of penetrative abstraction, and of philosophic calmness, this celebrated essay will long support its reputation, and it may continue to be used as a classic in the business of intellectual education. If literary ambition had been, which certainly it was not, the active motive of the author's mind, and if he could have foreseen the reputation of his "Essay on Free Will," he need have envied few aspirants to philosophic fame. What higher praise could a scientific writer wish for than that of having, by a single dissertation, reduced a numerous, a learned, and a then powerful party, in his own and other countries (and from his own day to the present time) to the necessity of making almost a silent protest against the argument and inference of the book as unanswerable; and yet leaving them immoveably attached to their previous opinion. And then, if we turn from theology to science, from divines to philosophers, we see the modest pastor of the Calvinists of Northampton assigned to a seat of honour among sages, and allowed (if only he will forget his faith and his Bible) to speak and to utter decisions as a master in the schools.

It might indeed have been well if this devout man could have foreseen the consequences that have actually resulted from the mode in which he conducted his argument; for in that case he would not have allowed those who reject the Christian system to triumph, by his aid, over faith, as well as reason. He would, instead of abandoning the ground of abstract reasoning as soon as he had achieved the overthrow of the logical error of his opponents, have laboured so to establish the responsibility of man as should have compelled unbelievers, either not to avail themselves at all of his proof of universal causation, or to yield to his proof of the reality of religion.

The constitutional diffidence, and the Christian humility, and the retired habits of the American divine, forbad his entertaining the thought that he might be listened to by philosophers as well as by his brethren—the ministers of religion. Supposing himself to be writing only for those who acknowledged, as cordially as he did, the authority of Holy Scripture, he did not scruple to make up his chain of reasoning, indifferently, of abstractions and of texts. Especially in the latter portion of his treatise, he readily took the short scriptural road to a conclusion, which must have been circuitously reached in any other way. Just as these conclusions may be, they commanded no respect beyond the limits of the Christian community; nay, they excited the scorn of those who naturally said —If these principles of piety could have been established by abstract argument, a thinker so profound as Edwards, and so fond of this method, would not have gone about to prove them by the Bible.

Deistical and Atheistical writers, availing themselves eagerly of the abstract portions of the "Inquiry," and contemning its biblical conclusions, carried on the unfinished reasoning in their own manner; and when they had completed their work, turned to the faithful, and said —Quarrel not with our labours, for the foundations were laid by one of yourselves!

Notwithstanding this accidental result of the argument for moral causation, as conducted by Edwards, this treatise must be allowed to have achieved an important service for Christianity, inasmuch as it has stood like a bulwark in front of principles which, whether or not they may hitherto have been stated in the happiest manner, are of far deeper meaning than is any sectarian scheme of doctrine, and apart from which, or if they were disowned, the Christian community would not long make good its opposition to infidelity. If Calvinism, using the term in its modern sense, were exploded, a long time would not elapse before evangelical doctrine of every sort would find itself driven into the gulf that had yawned to receive its rival.

Whatever notions of an exaggerated sort may belong to some Calvinists, Calvinism encircles or involves great truths, which, whether defended in scriptural simplicity of language or not, will never be abandoned while the Bible continues to be devoutly read; and which, if they might indeed be driven out of sight, would drag to the same ruin every doctrine of revealed religion. As much as this might be affirmed and made good; although he who should undertake to say it were so to conduct his argument as might make six Calvinists in seven his enemies.

Yet few would affirm that the treatise on the Will is itself complete, or that it is not open to reasonable objection on the part of those who refuse to admit its conclusions, or that it leaves nothing to be desired in this department of theological science. Edwards achieved his immediate object—that of demolishing the Arminian notion of contingency, as the blind law of human volitions; and he did more than this, for he effectively redeemed the doctrines called Calvinistic from that scorn with which the irreligious party, within and without the pale of Christianity, had been used to treat them; and there is reason also to surmise that, in the reaction which has counterpoised the once triumphant Arminianism of English divinity, the influence of Edwards has been greater than those who have yielded to it have always confessed.

But if the "Inquiry on Freedom of Will" is to be regarded as a scientific treatise, then we must protest against that mixture of metaphysical demonstrations and scriptural evidence which runs through it, breaking up the chain of argumentation, and disparaging the authority of the Bible, by making it part and parcel with disputable abstractions.

But besides the improper mixture of abstract reasoning with scripture proof, the reader of Edwards will detect a confusion of another sort—less palpable indeed, but of not less fatal consequence—as to the consistency of a philosophical argument—a confusion which holds intellectual philosophy far in the rear of the physical sciences. This error is that of mingling what is purely abstract with facts belonging to the physiology of the human mind. Even the reader who is little familiar with abstruse science will often be conscious of a vague dissatisfaction, or latent suspicion, that some fallacy has passed into the train of reasoning, although the linking of propositions seems perfect. This suspicion increases in strength as he proceeds, and at length condenses itself into the form of a protest against certain conclusions, notwithstanding their apparently necessary connection with the premises.

The condition of purely abstract truths is, that they might be expressed by algebraic or other arbitrary signs, and in that form made to pass through the process of syllogistic reasoning; certain conclusions being attained which must be assented to independently of any reference to the actual constitution of human nature, or to that of other sentient beings. Abstractions of this order stand parallel with the truths of pure mathematics; and it may be said of both that the human mind comprehends their properties and relations, and feels that the materials of its cogitation lie within its grasp, and need not be gathered from observation.

Not so as to our reasonings when the actual constitution of either the material world, or of the mental, is the subject of inquiry. When an argument relates to the agency and moral condition of man, nothing should be taken for granted, or allowed to flow in the stream of logical demonstration, which at best is questionable, or which, whether true or false, should be stated as simple matter of fact, and by no means confounded with those unchangeable truths which would be what they are, though no such being as man existed.

But owing to the abstruse nature of the subject, and to its not being susceptible of palpable proof, problems belonging to the science of mind have commonly been attempted to be solved on this principle of confounding the abstract with the physical.

In the case of our availing ourselves of the reasoning of a writer like Edwards, it behoves us to take heed that we do justice at once to him and to ourselves; to him, by not imputing to him, *individually*, a blame which belongs in common to metaphysico-theological writers of every age—and to ourselves, by yielding our assent to his argument only so far as it is purely of an abstract kind, and holding ourselves aloof from conclusions which involve *physiological facts* which either were not considered by the author, or perhaps were not known to him.

Of what sort, we may ask, is the inquiry concerning human agency, free will, liberty, and necessity? In other words, to what department of science does the controversy belong, and on what ground is it to be argued? And further, it may be asked, at what points does the subject touch the constitution and the movements of the human system, individual and social? or in what sense is it a *practical* question?

Unless, for the sake of an inference (soon to be mentioned) it might well be deemed unnecessary to assume, as at all a reasonable supposition, that the ordinary interests of life are liable to interference from abstruse problems of any kind—such, for instance, as are propounded in the controversy concerning liberty and necessity. There have indeed been seasons during which an interference of this sort was imagined to be proper; and it may also have found more indulgence than was due to it within the circle of German philosophy; but at present the force of common sense is too great, and the credit of abstract speculation is too small, to allow room for questions of this order. Or, even if it were otherwise, the supposition of a practical consequence belonging to the problem of moral causation would stand discharged by the leave of even the most resolute impugners of common sense, who, not only in their personal conduct, but by explicit admissions, excuse themselves and others from paying any more respect to such speculations than what is thought due to the paradoxes of those who abound in learning and leisure. "When the Pyrrhonian," says Hume, "awakes from his dream, he will be the first to join in the laugh against himself, and to confess that all his objections are mere amusement, and can have no other tendency than to show the whimsical condition of mankind, who must act, and reason, and believe; though they are not able, by their most diligent inquiry, to satisfy themselves concerning the foundation of these operations, or to remove the objections that may be raised against them."

Yet let us for a moment admit the supposition that doctrines such as those of the Pyrrhonist have a claim to be listened to before men can, with reason or consistency, either proceed to transact the business of life or accept as certain any system of belief, religious or philosophical.

Let it be allowed, then, that the unsolved problem concerning the alleged liberty of the human mind, and its exemption from the stern conditions of physical causation, does affect, or ought to affect, not only our religious opinions, but also our notions, feelings, judgments, and conduct in everyday life.

That we may give every advantage to this supposition, and may exempt it from entanglement with those recent theories of human nature which Christian men must reject, we consent to take our doctrine of moral causation from the "Inquiry concerning Freedom of Will."

Let it be granted that Edwards is quite successful in those sections of his essay in which he labours to prove that the doctrine of necessity, as held by him, perfectly consists with all true notions of virtue and of human accountability; nay, that there neither is, nor can be, any virtue in the universe which is not founded upon this moral necessity, as set forth by this Christian philosopher. Consequently, the prejudice against this doctrine, as if it might favour fatalism, and so were of dangerous tendency in morals, is unfounded.

This allowed on the side of Edwards and his argument, then we must ask leave to advance a step on the other side, as thus:—We are supposing the case, not of an acute and accomplished logical reader, but of an intelligent and fairly-educated man, competent to understand whatever in our best writers is indeed intelligible, and who reads what he reads for his personal improvement, and not as if he were about to pass an examination upon it in his college. This is just the case of nineteen out of twenty, or of ninety-nine out of a hundred, of those who read such works as Butler's Analogy, or Hume's Essays, or Jonathan Edwards on Free Will.

Now, such a reader of that essay as we have described, is likely to reach its last page with a mixed feeling, which he might thus express:—I cannot deny that this acute reasoner carries his point; he *is*, he *must* be right; for where can I find a break or a weak place in his chain of reasoning? I may then dismiss any misgivings that have haunted me in the perusal of the essay, and resolve to take to myself the author's doctrine of moral causation, as being a sure inference from admitted axioms.

But of what sort are those misgivings which we imagine to have haunted the mind of an intelligent reader of Edwards' Essay? They are, we think, such as these. He feels that this firmly-jointed chain of demonstrative reasoning is Logic, but is not fact; and that, whereas what the argument professes to have to do with is—human nature—that is to say, the actual constitution of a being who thinks, feels, and acts in conformity with the laws of his structure, intellectual and moral—the strength and force of the author's reasoning consist in the due dependence and the artificial sequence of propositions, that is to say, of collocated words and phrases, beneath which *the matter of fact* is tacitly assumed, or is concealed and put out of sight. This irrefragable argument resembles, in its mode of reaching a conclusion, those ingenious paradoxes in which things the most absurd are made to appear incontestably certain.

Unexpressed misgivings such as these, which we suppose to trouble an intelligent reader of the Essay on Free Will, might wear themselves away after a time, and leave him at ease as to the soundness of the author's argument; but in the course of his discursive studies he is startled by the discovery that Jonathan Edwards, the Christian theologian and the devout Calvinistic teacher, has been hailed as a master in philosophy, and a powerful coadjutor by the chiefs and apostles of modern unbelief, and even of atheism. As he follows the course of thought in England, America, France, Germany, during the last hundred years, he finds this Christian writer travelling in company with the latest of the modern champions of materialistic pantheism, upon the same road!

At this point his first vague misgivings are supplanted by deep-felt apprehensions or alarms; and, if he be a Christian man, he doubts whereunto he shall be led while yielding himself to the guidance of a logician whose demonstrations, though irresistible, are welcomed by the preachers of impiety. There must then be a fallacy somewhere in this chain of reasoning; but he will believe it to occur lower down in the chain than where Jonathan Edwards concludes his argument. With some such undefined and saving belief as this the intelligent Christian reader resolves to make himself contented. Pantheists, materialists, atheists, in availing themselves of the hard logic of this Christian writer, have no doubt committed a robbery, or they have inserted a fallacy of their own, and have drawn from it a mischievous inference which he would have abhorred.

In this manner such disquieting thoughts may be put to rest; but a consequence ensues which is not of the less ill influence because it creeps upon all minds, silently and unperceived. What is it, then, that, in such cases, takes place in the minds of intelligent and fairly-educated persons—the mass of an instructed Christian community? We shall attempt to give some answer to this question; and let it be understood that, throughout this argument, we quite exclude whatever may attach to the narrow prejudices or the misconceptions of the uneducated—religious or irreligious. We have in view the taught, the reflective, the rightly-minded, among our Christian communities.

SECTION II.

Everything within him—his intellectual and his moral consciousness entire—contradicts, to a man of sound mind, the paradoxes of fatalism. When he is told that causation is all of one kind, that there are in the universe no causes but physical causes, that there is no meaning in the word Liberty, that the distinction between virtue and vice is an illusion or a prejudice, and that it is absurd either to praise or to blame the actions of men; —when doctrine like this is advanced, it meets its merited contemptuous disregard, or abhorrence, from every mind that is not incurably sophisticated or debauched.

All things contradict monstrous paradoxes of this order;—the instincts of reason and of the moral sense, the very structure of the social system, the procedures of law and political society, all proclaim and affirm a contrary doctrine. The man who in his closet may for an hour have lost his grasp of common sense, while he has listened to sophistries of this kind, recovers his position, and regains his hold of reason the moment when he takes his place anew in the domestic circle; or if this means of intellectual restoration were not enough, his recovery will be secured by his return to the business and the responsibilities of the external world.

All may now seem to be set right;—and so it would be if we always dealt equitably with our feelings and states of mind at different times; but it is not so: a doubt or a distrust which, if valid at all, must take effect alike upon two or more objects, or interests, or persons, is perhaps thoroughly cleared up and discharged from our thoughts in its bearing upon one of them; but it is left, as we may say, to hover over or to beset another of them. This should not be; but among the incoherences that attach to our human nature this is one. We do not always make thorough work in putting our own minds in order: perhaps very seldom do so.

It is certain that whatever we affirm to be the constitution of man, as to his volitions, whatever may be the conditions of that liberty which he believes to be his prerogative, it is the same in all its applications. Man is free, or he is the passive creature of physical causation in all things alike. He is not free in one sphere, or one department of his daily life, and necessitated in another department; he is not blameworthy and praiseworthy and responsible six days of his life, and not so one day in every seven; he is not rewardable and punishable on the exchange or in the market, but not so at church. He must consent to be dealt with, and he must deal with himself, at all times, and on all occasions, on one and the same principle. Whatever sense we attach to the abstract terms Liberty and Necessity, this same sense must be adhered to—Sunday and Monday.

But now, if we are accustomed to give strict attention to our states of mind, or feelings, at different times or on different occasions, we shall be compelled to admit that something far short of this even-handed dealing with ourselves is often allowed to have its course. A man who would think himself insulted if, on the broad ways of common life, he were accused of adopting the principle of fatalism or physical causation, as professed by the atheistic materialist, goes home to his study, spends his hour of listless musing with some writers of this class, and yields himself, in respect of his abstract moral and religious belief, to this very principle. He is a convert in his closet to a doctrine which, if imputed to him out of doors by another, would imply that he is fool or knave.

What ensues, then, is this:—Thoughtful men fall into the usage of supposing that human nature stands related to two worlds—the world of common life, and the world of moral and religious feeling—on two different and contradictory principles, or according to two independent and discordant systems of law. Under one of these systems he entertains a lively and efficacious sense of responsibility and duty. God forbid that he should fail in any of its requirements! But under the other of these systems his convictions have become confused and vague, his notion of responsibility has entangled itself with ambiguous abstractions, his sense of duty has lost its vivacity, the moral feeling has suffered paralysis: in a word, so far as his morality connects itself with his religious belief, he is a feeble creature, an invalid.

If then we are required to say what we mean in deprecating the intrusion of Logic upon the ground of Theology, this is our meaning:—We deprecate the trusting ourselves to the certainty of wordy demonstrations in instances in which these methods of argument, while they avail nothing for the discovery of truth, give encouragement to that besetting illusion which impels us to divorce morals and piety from their due companionship with the motives and energies of common life. It is this parting off of the one from the other which so much perplexes the Christian moralist, who finds it often a task beyond his ability to give vividness and reality to the feelings of men when he would awaken in them the sense of obligation in matters of religion.

Just in proportion as fatalism, under any of its phases and disguises, is shown and felt to be untrue in human nature, so much the greater reaction will have place upon morals and piety, so long as, upon this undefined ground, it keeps its position at all. This fact should be well understood, for the contrary might seem the more probable consequence: it might be conjectured that, when a healthy and vigorous mind disabuses itself, as by a convulsive effort, of the paradoxes of fatalism, as related to common life, it would dismiss them altogether from its consciousness, and resolve to be ensnared no more in the same manner. This, however, is not always, nor perhaps often, what takes place.

It is common to human nature (we need not here stay to inquire why) to throw itself off from the familiar ground of proximate and intelligible causes, and to seek such as are abstruse, difficult, and ultimate, whenever it is agitated by undefined and powerful emotions. We have in this fact one of the sources of superstition; and as it is in a sense true that fear is the mother of the gods, so, in a sense, it is also true that anxiety, despondency, and the impatience of pain and sorrow, are teachers of metaphysics. It may be doubted whether certain profound speculations would at all have suggested themselves to the human mind, if life had been a course of equable prosperity. It may be questioned whether the inhabitants of worlds unvisited by evil—how large soever their intelligence may be—have ever thought of asking, What is virtue? or, What is the liberty of a moral agent?

The conflicts of hope and fear in the heart, and the assaults that are made upon hope by the scepticism or the mockery of those around us, impel us naturally, yet unwisely, to throw up the good and proper evidence which, though it be simple, and intelligible, and sufficient, does not open to the mind a depth profound enough to give room for the mighty tossings of the soul in its hour of distress:—The only testimony or proof that is strictly applicable to the point in question is thoughtlessly rejected; and in an evil moment we transgress the limits of safety and of comfort, and pass from the φυσικὰ to the μεταφυσικά. When this unhappy mistake has been committed, two courses offer themselves;—the one is to beat up and down through the regions of night whereupon we have entered, until we find, or fancy that we have found, solid footing, and discern a glimmering of light: —the other course is, by a buoyant effort of good sense, to spring up at once from the abyss, and effect our return to the trodden and familiar surface of things.

The process is a frequent and familiar one, which leads the mind to reason on *important occasions* in a manner which it shuns as absurd in parallel instances of a trivial sort. The man who loses his footing in the street, and besmears a new suit with mud, makes mirth of the simple accident. But if, when he is on his way to accomplish some momentous purpose—to make a fortune or to rescue one—he falls and breaks a limb, and, as the consequence, irretrievably forfeits the only auspicious moment of his life, he then looks at the *philoso-*

phy of the mishap; and, as he lies on his couch, meditates and reasons concerning Fate and Providence until he has bewildered his best convictions, and, in the gloominess of his sorrow, has persuaded himself that there is no heavenly superintendence of human affairs —that chance is mistress of the world; and at length he concludes that forethought, prudence, and activity, not less than faith and piety, are a specious folly. Perhaps he resolves henceforward to pursue nothing beyond the sensualities of the hour. Nevertheless, this same man, whom calamity has thus taught to be a metaphysician, adheres still, on all trivial occasions, to the maxims of vulgar good sense; his philosophical principles he takes up and lays down, according to the magnitude or the insignificance of the business in hand, and is not consistently sage or simple through the course of a single hour. He would deem it a folly to attempt to avoid the destined track of a bullet that is whizzing through the air; and yet he flinches from a splash of dirt! But should he not remember that the very same awful fate that rules the flight of leaden bullets, presides, not less arbitrarily, over the whirling of straws, the drifting of dust, and the projectile curves of mud?

Fatalism, in any of its forms, has, we suppose, been driven off from the road-ways of common life, and has been rebutted in its attempt to interfere with the energies of the day; nevertheless it has not been logically refuted: it holds its ground as a theory of the universe. Logical philosophers, and along with them logical theologians, affirm that hitherto they have not been overthrown in argument;—the vulgar turn away from their teaching; but all who *think* assent to their doctrine.

What happens, then, is this—that intelligent and

religiously-minded men, listening to this boast, silently yield themselves to it, and with an unquiet feeling bow, in their religious meditative hour, to the monster tyrant that affirms his right to hold sway in the spiritual world.

Thus it has happened that the momentous interests of the future life, as set forth by Christianity, because they profoundly move the soul, lead both the defenders and the impugners of a documentary religion aside from the only pertinent inquiry—Are its facts duly established, according to the ordinary maxims of testimony, while they discuss controversies to which religion is related only in common with the most familiar movements of social life. Let philosophers deny, if they please, the existence of a material world: but why should the teachers of Christianity, rather than any other class of men, come forward to oppose the paradox? If that paradox has, in fact, any meaning at all, or if it carries any inference which men ought to listen to, then should lawyers leave their courts, as well as divines their pulpits, and merchants their markets, and physicians their hospitals, to join in the debate. If *any* persons are interested in this abstruse question, *all* are so alike—demonstrably all are interested in one and the same degree. Or let philosophers turn about and deny the existence, not of the material, but of the immaterial world. All men, in this instance, as well as in the other, and all human interests, duties, functions, hopes, and fears, are either alike concerned in the refutation of this dogma, or may alike, in their several circles of practical activity, look upon it with indifference. Or again, let philosophers affirm that an iron fatality—an immoveable sequency of physical causes and effects—rules the world.

If there be *any* practical inference whatever—any inference which demands respectful hearing—attaching to this doctrine, then that consequence *bears evenly* upon all activities, upon all motives, upon all reasons of conduct, upon all calculations of futurity; and should either be allowed to arrest the entire machinery of human life, or should be utterly forgotten and neglected, whenever men are called to act and feel as rational and moral beings.

It enters into the definition of metaphysical problems —that they are *universals*. To bring them, therefore, down upon one class of instances, to the exclusion of other instances, is an enormous solecism. To single out Christianity from the crowd of human affairs and interests, and to assail it, so singled out, with alleged demonstrations which, by their very nature, are equally true of all things, or false of all, is the same sort of proceeding, as if a mathematician, after demonstrating the properties of the triangle, were to apply his doctrine only to such triangles as are formed by the rafters and joists of a roof.

Those who at the present time would avow themselves as, in the main, the disciples of Jonathan Edwards, and affirm that they regard the "Essay on Freedom of Will" as an exhaustive argument, leaving nothing to be desired on that side, will protest against the unfairness of the attempt to give him his place among fatalists, or to admit that he has given any occasion of triumph to modern materialists, pantheists, atheists.

If on the present occasion we consent to this challenge, which brings an eminently devout man over to a position among the enemies of all belief, we must do so on the ground of reasons such as these following:—

The extreme form of philosophic fatalism is that

which explicitly, and without disguise, affirms the distinction between physical and moral causation to be imaginary—an illusion—a vulgar prejudice. This dogma has perhaps never been conveyed in simpler or more intelligible terms than in those—often quoted—of Diderot:—" Regardez-y de près, et vous verrez que le mot liberté est un mot vide de sens; qu'il n'y a point, et qu'il ne peut y avoir d'êtres libres. . . . . . Le motif nous est toujours extérieur, étranger, attaché ou par une nature, ou par une cause quelconque, qui n'est pas nous. . . . . Mais s'il n'y a point de liberté, il n'y a point d'action qui mérite la louange ou le blâme; *il n'y a ni vice, ni vertu,* rien dont il faille récompenser ou châtier. . . . . . Il n'y a qu'*une* sorte des causes à proprement parler; ce sont *les causes physiques.* Il n'y a qu'une sorte de nécessité, c'est la même pour tous les êtres."

Recent writers, whom we need not cite, not intending to enter into controversy with them, have laboured to conceal the offensiveness of this doctrine, and to render it less repugnant to the reason and consciousness of the mass of men, by means of elaborate and ingenious mystifications; all which, however, when given in the fewest words, can mean nothing less, nothing else than this:—Human actions are as "the circumstances" and "the disposition;" and this disposition, taken at any moment of a man's life, is the product of an antecedent series of circumstances, interior and exterior—animal, and, as we say—moral, which have wrought together to make him what he is. This doctrine, whatever may be the softening or the glozings that are attached to it, we must take leave to speak of as identical with that professed by Diderot, and cited above.

Now, let everything be granted to the full that can fairly be affirmed on behalf of the author of the " Essay on Freedom of Will," for the purpose of bringing him off clear of any association with writers of this atheistic class; let it be said that this Christian divine opposes himself strenuously, and triumphantly too, to the irreligious doctrines of the fatalists; that if the completeness of his exculpation of himself in this behalf is not perceived and admitted, the fault is attributable to the reader's own confusion of mind, and his inability to understand an abstruse argument: grant all this, or more, and yet the fact stands before us that a large proportion of persons—the intelligent and the educated, who may have read the essay, and who, at the moment when certain portions of it are under the eye, believe themselves to apprehend the author's reasonings and distinctions, quickly lose what they thought they had held, and relapse into an intellectual condition of a very ambiguous sort. Question them categorically, and they will say, "Edwards is no fatalist;" but ask them to give you the grounds of the distinction which they draw between his doctrine and that of Diderot, and they would acknowledge themselves perplexed; they would have recourse to the book itself, if at hand, and show you the page on which you may read for yourself the author's exculpatory averments and distinctions.

Distinctions of an abstruse kind, which are not understood without an effort, and which few minds can retain for any length of time, may abundantly suffice for *some* purposes, but they prove themselves to be wholly insufficient in relation to other purposes; as, for instance, in relation to the agencies and energies, the obligations and the requirements of everyday life, a very little of argument may be quite enough to save a sound mind from its entanglement with the paradoxes and the sophisms of the fatalist. But it will be quite otherwise when the same mind, the same healthy good sense, falls in upon itself, to contend, as it may, with the very same paradoxes and sophisms, thought of in their bearing upon the first principles of morals, and upon the elements of abstract theology. In *this* dim region, and on *this* ground, the man, well taught and thoughtful as we suppose him to be, finds himself grappling in the dark with an adversary whose power to injure him may be greater than he thinks.

The religious man, struggling with giant doubts that threaten the very life of his soul, will find himself every day less and less able to draw comfort or confidence from nice distinctions or subtile demonstrations, such as those are which had availed—as he thought—to rescue the argument of Edwards from its apparent connection with the fatalism of pantheists and atheists.

We come round again, then, to our point, and affirm that, when Logic interferes with Theology, it may do more harm than those think of who resort to it as a means of advancing our religious knowledge. But it may be said, If Logic be valid, and if its results are demonstrably certain, who shall stay it in its course or repel it, as if it were an intrusion? If logicians can so establish their position in any department of human thought—if they can so fortify themselves there that we cannot drive them off from their ground—who is it that presumes to find fault? The master of Logic, Aristotle, has taught his followers to be fearless, if only they adhere to his methods of assault and defence.

And how fearlessly did this mighty reasoner, who

wielded so long the iron sceptre of a wordy despotism, affirm things to be, which are not! The instances are familiar to every one who is conversant with the history of philosophy.

What we mean by Logic, when we thus deprecate its interference with Theology, is the attempt, by the formal collocation of propositions, to reach conclusions in matters where the unknown is involved, and is commingled with what is known to us, either as matter of consciousness, or of observation and experiment. We ask leave here to bring in the aid of an illustration, not intending to push it further than shall seem fair.

"It has lately been surmised by some adventurous spirits among us that great, nay, incalculable effects of a mechanic sort may be drawn from—who shall believe it?—the employment of the vapour that arises in bubbles, as we know, from the surface of water on the boil. But that this strange surmise is without foundation, and that the hopes vainly built thereon shall turn out to be nothing better than a bubble, may easily be proved, and may be made evident to all men's understandings that will give heed to the reason of things, as shall now be shown.

"Let us first ask what this vapour or steam is whereof we are now to speak, and from the action of which such great things are expected to come. It is, we are told—and we are willing to grant it—it is the offspring of the combination of two elements, namely, fire and water. But now, before we inquire concerning the inherent properties of either of these elements—separately, we wish this only to be granted to us—and it is an axiom manifestly certain or self-evident, and which, we suppose, none will call in question who retain the faculty of reason, and it is this—that there will never be found, in the sum or product of two quantities or matters of any sort, more than is contained in the two separately estimated. To imagine the contrary of this axiom were the same thing as to say that two and three put together make seven, or any other number. Certainly, we need give ourselves little pains for establishing what is so manifest.

"Now then we come to a more particular inquiry concerning the nature of these two elements—fire and water. We take, first, this last. In comparison of the three elements, fire being now put out of view—(there *are* only *four* elements, as we well know, for the notion of a *quintessence* is a mere phantasy)—water is the weaker of the three; in respect of earth, it is weak and unstable; for let but an infant apply a finger to its surface and it forthwith gives way, or yields itself to so feeble a motion. Moreover, under the rays of the sun, itself utterly vanishes and ceases to be; and that, in respect of air, water is the weaker of the two, we may either rest satisfied in that testimony which speaks of 'mighty winds,' or we may appeal to the experience of men in such instances as these:—say that water has gotten possession of a goodly garment, thoroughly sodden thereby; now, let only this same garment, whether it be cloak or sheet of any sort, be hung up in the way—not of a mighty tempest, but in the course of the gentlest breeze or current of air: what happens in this case is this—that the stronger of the two, namely, air, drives forth and dislodges the weaker, namely, water, so that in a short space of time this cloth or garment is found to have changed masters; for water hath confessed its feebleness in respect of air; else how can we believe that it would so soon, and without noise, have abandoned what it had taken to itself, unless, indeed, it were conscious of its impotency as compared with its rival? Let this instance then suffice for proving our first point—namely, that water is a creature weaker than the other elements; for we need not argue its weakness as compared with earth.

"But now as to fire—the other ingredient of vapour or steam, as we are told. Some men will be ready to affirm that fire is indeed of a most powerful nature, and so we grant it to be in a certain sense; but let us consider of what sort or quality is that power as to its metaphysic nature. We say it is of that sort which is proper to a nature which, more than any other known to us, is hungry, indigent, exigeant, and negative. How else is it that men have come to speak of fire with dread, calling it, and rightly so, the 'all-devouring element?' Of so hungry a nature is this element, that it is ever crying 'Give, give;' and never does it rest content until it hath eaten up, and swallowed with greediness, all things near it, short of the very hardest matters, such as rocks, which it hath no stomach for. Fire is much like those sturdy beggars who, meeting men on the highway, ask alms, but, if denied, will take by force all that a man has, to the last rag. Who is it then, things being so, that shall think to seek for aid and help in any great work from that which, of all things known to us, is itself the most in need, and which itself actually dies and comes to nothing, or to pale ashes only, when it hath quite finished its meal?

"We may then quickly sum up this controversy, and shall appeal to the common sense and experience of men in thus concluding, that this expectation, entertained by certain overweening men, that, by conjoining the weakest of the four elements with that one which is the most greedy and indigent of the four, they shall be able to further their mechanic devices—is a great folly; and sure we are that the hopes which are built upon any such fanciful notion as this, contrary as it is to the common sense of mankind, shall turn out to be much like that whereon they are founded, namely, mere vapour or smoke, to the dismay of these dreamers, and the merriment of sober men that are lookers on."

Of such quality as this was a large proportion of the reasonings of past times, and not a little of these times. But what should have been the treatment given it? Not surely to attempt a course of counter-reasoning, resting upon the same ground of imagined analogies, and of verbal antitheses;—but an immediate appeal to facts. Is there any mechanic force in steam?—Try.

In any instance of a controversy concerning matters in relation to which an appeal to facts, or to direct evidence, or to undoubted experiences, may be made, this same mode of determining problems is, of course, to be resorted to. But is this the case in the instance of the ancient controversy concerning the liberty of human volitions? We might think it warrantable to assume as much in reading the noted "Essay" of Jonathan Edwards; for in almost every section he makes an appeal, more or less direct, to the experience and consciousness of men. But then, in those elaborately-compacted paragraphs in which he labours to drive his opponent into some glaring absurdity, his antithetic propositions are little better than compages of words—carrying with them a great weight of apparent meaning; but, for finding the real value of which, we must go down into the depths of the relationship of mind and matter, in the animal structure, and in human nature, especially. These ever-recurrent phrases, about the "Will" and its conditions, the bandying of which from side to side makes up a nine-tenths of the essay, assume the very matter in debate. The demonstration is indeed irresistible, if only we are willing to let pass these wonted phrases, unexamined, and to refrain from inquiring concerning their correspondence with the structure of human nature. But if human nature, and if its inner constitution be in question, then it is not formal Logic that can avail us for the solution of the problem, even to the value of a straw.

Within the compass of this often-repeated half-dozen of phrases, about "the Will" and its "determining motives," there are embraced the profoundest mysteries of the universe of intellectual and moral life. Say that these are mysteries which will ever defy the scrutiny of man: be it so: but this is certain, that questions of this order are only involved in greater perplexity when treated in any such manner as that which is attempted by Jonathan Edwards. We may amuse ourselves with seeming demonstrations in this style, as long as we please;—we may, as above supposed, show it to be absurd to look for mechanic force in the bubbles that play on the surface of boiling water: but let us look to the doings of the steam-engine, and be sickened of nugatory wordy reasonings about "the nature of things." Or we may prove it to be absurd to talk of any sort of liberty in the universe of thought and feeling which does not resolve itself into an eternal series of physical causation. We may do this, and then find ourselves held in the relentless grasp of that pantheism which worships eternal law as the parent of all things: —we may do this, and then find that our only means of escape from so terrible a despotism is—the irresistible consciousness of a life within us which is altogether of another order.

SECTION III.

But if Logic—the Logic of words and propositions—may not help us in physical science, or in making known the constitution of the material world, may it not yield its aid in determining those controversies that have arisen among Christian men concerning the meaning of holy Scripture?

Logic will indeed help us when the terms and the propositions in which it deals contain only such notions as lie within the grasp of the human mind; but not at all when disputation arises concerning things that are occult, or that touch upon the infinite and the unseen. Not indeed as if *such* controversies may not be determined in a manner that is satisfactory to ingenuous minds; but then this desirable consummation must be sought for altogether on another ground.

A Logic that is more exact may easily be made to demolish, or drive off from the field a Logic that is less exact. Coherent reasoning triumphs easily over incoherent reasoning. Jonathan Edwards floors Whitby and the Pelagians. Calvinism is a more compactly-jointed system than Arminianism: and therefore it holds its ground boldly as opposed to its adversary. This may easily be granted, and then the two questions return upon us—How does each stand related to the constitution of the human mind? and how to the testimony of Scripture? Neither of these questions finds a solution in those writings of the last age, or of earlier times, which have treated them as if determinable in scholastic style. We speak now of the controversy between Calvinists and Arminians or Pelagians, as a *biblical* controversy simply, and we remit the consideration of it as related to the philosophy of human nature.

The fruitlessness of any such method of conducting a biblical controversy might well be argued from the instance of the "Inquiry Concerning Freedom of Will :" the acknowledged superiority of this treatise to works with which it might properly be compared—a superiority confessed by philosophers as well as by divines—and its exemption from the besetting sins of polemical literature, point it out as an unexceptionable instance. Yet, what has been the result? A signal service has been rendered by it to the cause of certain momentous truths; but this service has accrued indirectly; while it has failed to bring the controversy between Calvinists and Arminians to an issue. The metaphysics of Edwards demolished the metaphysics of Whitby. This was a matter of course; for the *philosophy* of Arminianism could not endure a rigid analysis. Moreover, the metaphysics of Edwards has availed to impose a degree of respect upon the flippancy of philosophers. But then —not to insist upon the fact that the "Inquiry" has become almost the text-book of infidelity—it has not brought the abstract argument home to the purely theological difficulty. It has left things where they were in this respect, only with the disadvantage of suggesting a tacit conviction—that what Edwards could not effect can never be effected. The apparently incompatible propositions may therefore be affirmed, that, while he, as the champion of Calvinism, has achieved a victory, and has driven his antagonists from their ground, he has perpe-

LOGIC IN THEOLOGY. 39

tuated the religious difference by the mere fact of having failed in his attempt to compose it. Is it, then, to be desired that a second philosophic Calvinist should undertake the task of convincing Arminians by scholastic Logic, and so of bringing them to a cordial acquiescence in the meaning of certain portions of the Scriptures? Surely not.

An accordance among Christians in matters of belief must be the result, not of the perfectionment of abstract theology, but of a better understanding of the structure and intention of the document of faith, which, unlike any other writing, is at once the work of human minds, and not less absolutely the work of the Divine Mind. As a human work—as a collection of ancient treatises, letters, and histories, composed by almost as many authors as there are separate pieces—it is confessedly liable to the ordinary conditions of other ancient literature; and not merely to the *critical*, but to the *logical* conditions also that belong to the products of the human mind; and therefore when interrogated in relation to *certain abstract positions*, derived, *not from itself*, nor known to its writers, but from the variable theological systems of successive ages, it will yield not a few apparent contrarieties.

But the Scriptures claim no respect as authorities in religion, unless they be received as, in the fullest sense, a Divine work. As such, they must have their peculiar conditions; and these (or the most important of them) spring from the fact, that they contain information, explicit or implied, concerning more systems of things than one, or more orders of beings than one. But then this genuine information consists just of those portions, or fragments, or segments, of such systems, or of such series of causes, as involve practical inferences, important to the special purpose of restoring men to virtue. It must follow that the harmony of these disjointed portions will never come within the range of the methods of human science; for human science is drawn from *one system only*, and is *imperfect*, even in relation to that one system.

Illustrations are always more or less faulty, and yet they may serve a good purpose when advanced simply as such; and are not urged as if they were proofs or arguments. Let it then be supposed that, to a number of intelligent persons, instructed in at least the elements of mathematical science, there were to be given—not a diagram or description—but some of the distinguishing, and some of the most recondite properties of the three conic sections—the ellipsis, the parabola, and the hyperbola; and let it be demanded of them, not only to find curves possessing precisely such properties, but to find one regular and simple figure which should contain the three harmoniously upon its surface. Now it must be granted, as hypothetically possible, that some one of these persons, either by a happy accident, or by force of his intelligence, might at length produce the cone, and demonstrate upon it the several properties of the theorem. But, to make our illustration complete, it should be supposed that no such figure as a cone had ever actually been seen or thought of by the persons to whom the problem is given. What then would be the probable event? May we not assume it as likely that each individual, attaching himself at the first moment to the properties of some one of the three propounded curves, and giving his attention exclusively to its peculiarities, and succeeding, perhaps, in the attempt to

LOGIC IN THEOLOGY. 41

reconcile these separate conditions among themselves, would be inclined to impugn, as *necessarily false*, those processes by which his companions were finding the other two curves; and, being satisfied as to the soundness of his own reasoning, would deem that of his friends absolutely irreconcilable with it. And so it must seem until the one true harmonizing figure is actually produced.

And yet how soon might a fierce controversy arise among the perplexed inquirers! How soon would there take place a separation of the partisans of the ellipsis, the parabola, and the hyperbola! The friends of the first of the curves would think themselves justified in denouncing the hyperbolists as extravagant heretics; while these, and with exactly equal reason, would hold in contempt the timidity of the ellipsists. Meanwhile, the parabolists, much admiring their own moderation, and not doubting that it was they alone who held the happy middle-way upon which truth loves to walk, and hence believing themselves qualified to act as mediators between the extreme parties, would gravely say much that was very plausible, and exceedingly well intended; but they would not, in fact, advance even a single step toward a true conciliation of the difference;—for this simple reason—that they are just as far as their companions from knowing the actual principle of explanation. The parabola may *seem* to be, but it is not in fact, or in any degree, a *reconciling truth* between the ellipsis and the hyperbola; for, in truth, the ellipsis and the hyperbola are not at variance. Meantime the controversy, although it tends to no satisfactory issue, is producing these two ill consequences (not to mention the excitement of bad feelings among friends) namely, that those of the company whose temper was the most calm and sceptical would be haunted by troublesome suspicions, as if he who had proposed the problem had made sport of the ignorance of all, by affirming things that are strictly paradoxical and untrue. And then the bystanders would almost certainly learn to treat the whole affair —the problem, its propounder, and the factions—with contempt. But we suppose that at this instant the propounder of the problem enters, and forthwith extinguishes the feud by the production of the cone!—all contrarieties are at once reconciled; all suspicions are dispelled; and eager dogmatists of all creeds are put to the blush!

To defend the propriety of this illustration in all its parts would be idle. It is enough if it throws any light upon the assertion, that the Scriptures, *because they are true and divine*, and because they propound separated parts, properties, or relations of systems not known to man, will for ever baffle the attempt to reduce their testimony within the completeness and rotundity of human science. If it be so, it must follow that metaphysical reasoning, how exact soever, is not to be looked to as the means of adjusting biblical controversies. That it may *seem* for a while to do so is granted; but the specious conciliation is either the mere confounding of an antagonist by force of superior logical strength, or it has been effected by *constraining* adverse portions of the scriptural evidence.

SECTION IV.

In every argument or inquiry concerning the constitution of the material world, and especially concerning the structure and the functions of the living world, vegetative and animal, it is unavoidable that the terms and the phrases therein employed, and which are recurring in every paragraph, should be made to embrace something which is known, commingled with something, or much, that is unknown. For this inconvenience there is no remedy. When we speak, for instance, of those energies of vegetative life in virtue of which the plant secretes its several juices or its solids, the sap, the gum, the resin, the woody fibre, the seed, the pulp, we note certain facts, but we suppose very much more. In the use of language for noting and conveying what we know as to exterior facts, we are aware of the risk we incur at every step, which is that of imagining far more than we know, and of allowing our ignorance to cloak itself in the ambiguities of speech.

No great mischief, however, ensues, in such cases, in the modern mode of discussing the subjects of physical science, so long as we keep an eye upon this source of error, and take care to disengage ourselves frequently from its consequences. The fault of our predecessors in philosophy was this, that they did not do so, but, on the contrary, allowed themselves to believe that, so long as their Logic was rigidly exact, all must be right. In adherence to the better usages of modern physical science, we learn to distrust all reasoning concerning the laws of the material world, in conducting which it becomes manifest that the terms we employ are coming to include a too large proportion of the unknown—larger than it is safe to allow them to carry. In such cases we abandon our Logic, and throw ourselves anew upon facts, by the means of enlarged observation and of reiterated experiments.

We need not stay here to adduce instances in illustration of practices that are familiarly known to those who are conversant with any department of natural philosophy. The application of these same methods to subjects belonging to intellectual and moral philosophy is not difficult, nor is it fairly questionable. Take the case now before us, of the conditions of moral causation attaching to the volitions of beings like ourselves, or, in other words, the question of " Freedom of Will." We might gather our set of terms and phrases—the verbal staple of this ancient controversy—from any page of the essay just now in view.

At once it is felt by every reflective reader—and it will be granted by every such reader who is not wedded to some controversial doctrine—that these words, and these constantly-recurrent combinations of phrases, and these often-repeated propositions which pass under the eye unexamined, do, in fact, stand representative of impenetrable mysteries in the structure of human nature and of animal nature, in all orders. The page or the paragraph offers to the eye—or say to the reason—a due catenation of affirmative or negative sentences; there is the proper antithesis, and then comes the looked-for conclusion, and then the alleged absurdity of any contrary supposition:—all looks well, so far as words can avail to carry us within the veil of the temple, and give the foot a place in the adytum of intellectual and moral life. But to how small an extent is this entrance, in fact, obtained by any such nugatory means?

There is, indeed, a lower level of animal existence— the very lowest—in relation to which the Logic of writers like Jonathan Edwards may be admitted to be sufficient, or adequate to the facts; at least in following it there is heard no loud protest uttered in contradiction of it. But it is far otherwise as we ascend upon the scale of life, for, at every step of this ascent the protest—the contradiction, becomes a degree more distinct; and by the time that we have reached the uppermost stage—even the platform of a fully-developed human nature—the world of high thought and of great actions, this contradiction, this protest, if it do not utter its voice as a thunder, yet so speaks within the soul of the man as that we accept it as a timely monition from God.

One might well be amazed in finding that some half-dozen or more of phrases—to few or none of which a distinct meaning can be attached—when worked upon in pedantic style, and handled, this way and that way, in apposition and in opposition, and in artificial sequence —are trusted to as means of laying open the structure of human nature!

In following upwards the scale of mental development we find, as we go on, first, faculties or powers of wider grasp and greater force, and *then*, and as the result of these, a far more intricate interaction of faculties, so that the ultimate products are such as immeasurably surpass, in quality, and in quantity, and in complication, any with which we had become acquainted among the lower orders of the animated world.

But now the ancient and scholastic practice of treating all questions of human nature abstractedly and metaphysically has induced the belief that volition in man is simple or uniform in its mode of springing up in the mind. Yet if the real world of sentient and voluntary beings is looked at, it will at once be seen, first, that each species has its peculiar conditions of volition, and that volition in each species results, at different times, from very different internal processes. It would appear, then, to be the natural course to look out, first, for the simplest instances of volition, and then to ascend from them to such as are complex, and therefore not so readily analyzed. This order of investigation directs us to the inferior classes of the animal community—it being probable that, in observing a less complicated organization, we shall become qualified to dissect that which is more so. For we may fairly presume that the more complicated orders take up into their mental machinery certain elements that have been imperfectly developed in the lower ranks of existence. It is on this presumption that we avail ourselves of the fruits of observation gathered from the movements and habits of inferior species. For it is only by a reference to our own consciousness that we learn to interpret such facts; and this interpretation presupposes the homogeneity of the primary elements of sentient existence. If a pure intelligence, or a simply rational essence—wholly destitute of all appetite, emotion, imagination—were to descend into this world of hungry, thirsty, passionate, irascible, and pleasure-loving beings, it would find itself utterly at a loss in endeavouring to comprehend movements which it witnessed. That is to say, having no participation of the elements of the animal and moral nature, it would want the glossary of mundane life, and would possess no means of interpretation:—all it saw would be a riddle.

But this is not the case when man looks around him upon his fellows of inferior rank; for possessing, as he does, every element of animal and moral life, he discerns few operations which he does not at once know how to translate into the language of his own nature; and thus he is qualified to philosophize as well upon the mental conformation of birds and quadrupeds as upon that of his own species. We say, he witnesses *few* operations that are unintelligible to him; but there *are* movements carried on, especially by the more minute tribes, and those that are the most remote from himself, which nothing in his own nature enables him to understand; they are facts that are not interpretable by consciousness, and accordingly we designate them by the term *instinct*, which has no clear significance beyond that which attaches to it as standing for a class of facts that are not understood. Such facts can afford us no aid in analyzing the operations of the human mind, and must therefore be excluded from our course of argument.

The inferior orders of conscious beings offer to our notice two or three distinguishable elements of volition, together with the rude commencements of another, for the full development of which we must look to the higher nature of man.

A proper test for discovering the elements of the mental conformation of any order of beings is afforded, *first*, by the educational treatment which common experience proves to be applicable to it; and *then*, by the emotions or sentiments which are excited in ourselves by its qualities or dispositions. In this method we employ, as if it were, a chemical agent for bringing to light a concealed ingredient. The dog is the subject of abundantly more education, and he is the object of more sentiment than the horse—not arbitrarily or accidentally so, but because he possesses more intellectual faculty, and more sensibility. His senses are eminently acute; his memory is retentive and exact; his passive power of acquiring habits is great; and, to complete his mental endowments, he is able, in a considerable degree, to hold in combination more than two or three connected ideas, and among them to select the proper inference from the antecedents. Thus qualified, he remembers his master's usages, he apprehends his master's operations, and he acts his part in accomplishing his master's intentions. And then, as a moral being, he is susceptible of so pertinacious an attachment to individuals, he has so much sense of duty and of honour, and is capable of so intense a wretchedness under the sense of ill-conduct and merited displeasure, that he becomes the proper object of correlative sentiments of affection, complacency, or displeasure in the human mind. The dog, in virtue of his individual dispositions, and apart from all sophistication or extravagance, is regarded with feelings which it would be as unreasonable to restrain, when so called forth, as it would be to bestow them, in the same degree, upon any other species of domesticated animals.

Nevertheless, the dog is limited in his range of mental faculty and of sensibility; and, in comparing his powers with those of man, we see the more clearly the foundation of that different treatment of which the higher nature is the subject, and we see, too, the absurdity of any physical doctrine which affirms the agency of men, of brutes, and of machines, to be one and the same thing. The dog, as he is not endowed with that inexplicable faculty which prompts the beaver to construct for himself a hut, or the white ant to erect a cathedral of mud, or the rook to weave for her family an aerial tabernacle, is not gifted with any reasoning power for attaining a similar result. If deprived of his comfortable kennel he will nestle in a corner, or edge himself into a rick; but he never attempts (though loose materials of all sorts may be lying about) to construct a house. Or, to exhibit the same limitation of faculty under another condition:—the dog may learn to take a penny to the shop, and to deposit it on the counter, and, with significant gesture, to demand his roll: but no education would teach him to understand the equity of the relation between two pence and two rolls, and three pence and three rolls; nor, supposing that he had dropped one of the pieces of money on the way, would he draw for himself the inference that he must, *therefore*, content himself with one roll the less. And yet a child would soon perceive these relations, and deduce the proper inference; or at least he would understand them as by a flash of intelligence, when explained to him.

The want, or at least the limitation of the power of abstraction, and of the comparison of complex relations, affects, in an essential manner, the moral constitution of these inferior species, even of the most intelligent of them; while, on the other hand, the possession of such powers confers upon man his responsibility, invests him with the anxious prerogative of being master of his destinies; and, in a word, transfers him from the present to some future system of retributive treatment.

The more sensitive species of animals, such as the dog and the elephant, enter within the pale of the moral system, or stand at its threshold—just as, in virtue of their sagacity, they enter within the pale of the intellectual system—by their susceptibility of emotions, which places them, to a certain extent, in communion with man, and renders them the objects of his moral sensibilities. This parallelism between the *intellectual* and the *moral* difference between man and the brute holds entire. Animals of the higher orders will do anything that comes within the range of association of ideas, or of the very simplest connection of cause and effect; but not more. And in like manner are they open to keen emotions of gratitude, shame, revenge; yet we soon touch the boundary of their moral capacities. The elephant has his emotions, and he is retentive of them; but he does not abstract the quality which has so strongly affected him from the act, or the person, to which it belongs; he is conscious of that difference in temper which distinguishes one of his keepers from another, and he treats them both accordingly; but he does not form a *separate idea* of goodness and malignity, much less does he compare such abstracted ideas with his own correlative emotions; and therefore he attains to no complex notion of virtue and of vice. As the consequence of this deficiency of faculty, the animal does not think of *his own* dispositions, or muse concerning his personal character, nor does he institute a mental comparison between his own behaviour or habitual temper and any abstract notion of moral qualities. *Therefore* neither the dog nor the elephant condemns or dislikes *himself*, much less does he conceive the idea of a better disposition, as an object of his ambition; and therefore he never attempts the work of self-education by repressing ill feelings, and by favouring the better.

Accordingly, self-originated reformation is not looked for from the brute. He may indeed be amended in his dispositions by *external treatment ;* he may also become more or less tractable in consequence of changes in his *constitution* or his *diet ;* but he never undergoes a change in consequence of a mental process—bringing abstract qualities into comparison, and allowing one of them to be chosen and followed, while others are hated and avoided. If it be asked on what ground we infer these deficiencies of internal structure in the brute mind, we reply, that the internal defect may fairly be implied from the absence of the proper outward results of the supposed faculty. In following even the most sagacious animal through his movements, in connection with new and artificial occasions, we catch him at fault precisely from the want of the power of abstraction: the internal structure, though recondite, is laid bare in such instances, and we cease to wonder that a being so deficient should not provide for his welfare by artificial means.

And the very same deficiency necessitates the permanence of his moral condition; and—knowing it—though we feel complacency or displacency towards the animal orders according to their dispositions, we neither assign to them the praise of virtue in the one case, nor impute to them the blame of vice in the other. The animal that does not observe proportions, that does not use instruments or construct machines, does not, for the same reason, attempt to remodel his own character; he does not, in any degree, educate himself. Virtue, vice, praise, blame, law, government, retribution, are conditions proper to the treatment of a being who, by his use of arbitrary signs, by his employment of complicated means, and by his manifold conversions of the powers of nature to his particular advantage, makes it evident that he possesses a faculty which, in connection with his moral sensibilities, renders virtue, vice, praise, blame, law, government, retribution, the true correlatives of his nature.

The sophism, therefore, which would *sever* virtue, vice, praise, blame, law, government, retribution, from human nature, contains an absurdity of precisely the same degree as that which would *attach* these conditions to the brute. It were a folly to look for arts and accomplishments among tigers, kites, sharks; and it is an equal folly *not* to look for them among men: it is an error of the same magnitude to deny that the being who builds, plants, writes, and calculates, cannot work upon his own dispositions, or, in other words, is not blameworthy, as to affirm that tigers, kites, and sharks might, if they so pleased, convert their natures, and become more amiable and less rapacious than hitherto they have shown themselves to be.

The conjunction of the higher elements of intellectual and moral being with the common ingredients of animal life is beautifully developed in observing the growth and expansion of the human mind from infancy to manhood. Nature, in preparing to bring upon the theatre of the world so noble an agent as man, steps back, that she may take the bolder leap, and reach a higher stage. Man, throughout the period of his infancy, is, as an agent, below his fellows in the animal world. It cannot be doubted that the perceptions of the human infant are more confused than those of the young of animals; and probably they amount to nothing more than vague sensations, conveying no knowledge of the external world: its instincts also are less *determinate* than those of other new-born animals; and the muscular force is a mere element, which remains yet to be developed. The development of this power seems to be effected by the constitution of an immediate connection between the muscular excitability and every sensation that affects the sensorium, whether arising from within or from without. In these movements there is no *volition*, there is nothing but the muscular contraction, as an immediate sequence of sensation. Thus are the muscles brought into play, strengthened, and taught to obey—instantaneously, the mind.

The distinction usually made between voluntary and involuntary muscular action is clearly founded upon a real difference. But then, when volition is declared to be a mental process, consisting of successive parts, a false supposition is suggested, as if movements that are not involuntary were effects of rapidly conducted deliberations and determinations. That complex process which, even in the adult, takes place only on occasions when antagonist motives are in conflict—as when prudential or moral considerations are wrestling with desires—is assumed to be the model of all the acts of the mind. But if we give attention to the preparation which nature is making in the first months of life for bringing the machine into full play, we shall be led to think that the main business of infancy is the formation of that habit of the animal system which places its movements in *immediate* sequence with the sensations and with the emotions.

Mobility, elasticity, promptitude, as the conditions of muscular action, get the start of the deliberative faculties; and they so possess themselves, by usage, of the animal and the intellectual being, that they hold through life their priority; so that, whatever power reason may at length acquire, man acts ten thousand times in the spontaneous manner which he learns in infancy, for once that he acts in the manner which metaphysical writers describe when they profess to analyze the process of volition. It is not until the power of locomotion has put the pupil of nature in trust, to a certain extent, with his own preservation, and when, as its consequence, he is brought hourly into new circumstances, that the first developments of reason may be observed. By this time the sequences of events fix themselves in the memory, and give birth to the expectation of like results from like antecedents. Then follow courses of conduct founded upon this expectation, and thenceforward—deliberative volitions; and thus it is that the mental machine is fast getting its wheels, one after another, into gear.

It would be curious, and perhaps instructive, to trace from its beginnings that expansion of the mind which imparts to it a deliberative power, and which constitutes man a voluntary agent, in the higher and proper sense of the term, and which, in its matured state, carries him to an immeasurable distance beyond the inferior species of sentient beings. In the nursery the hasty demands of appetite are arrested by maternal vigilance, and motives of another kind are placed before the mind, and antagonist considerations are urged upon its attention. Here, then, begins the process of complex volition; and at that moment the being sets foot upon a course that has no limit, and is translated from the lower world of animal life into the higher sphere of rational and moral existence. It is then that he is introduced to the community of responsible agents, and takes up his heirship of an interminable destiny.

Such of the desires as are sensual or selfish are constantly being brought into opposition, rendering the gratification of the one incompatible with that of the other: the two kinds stand in conflict for a moment, or more; and whether the final decision be better or worse, the mind is, by the mere contest, exercising its faculty of complex thought, and not improbably admits, during the moments of hesitation, other considerations of a prudential or moral kind, which, even if they do not prevail, yet enlarge the power of mental comprehension and comparison.

Where education does its work efficiently, the mind learns to obey the law of *real or rational connection*, in the place of that of simple suggestion, and it brings forward, like a faithful and intelligent minister, those considerations which properly belong to the occasion. This expansion of the mind makes itself apparent, in some cases, by the development of the inventive faculty; and the young mechanician, soon after the time when he has taken his place among responsible agents, is seen, in the exercise of the very same faculties of abstraction and of complex thought, to form conceptions of an end or design, and to select the fittest means for its attainment.

We should here notice that change in the sentiments of those around him which insensibly accompanies the early development of the mind. Even before this has taken place, the infant has made himself the object of complacency or of displacency, according to his original dispositions, or his individual character; and, before he is *blamed* or *applauded*, is loved, more or less, not only with a love of general benevolence, and not only with the instinctive parental fondness, but with a specific feeling of moral estimation.

This happens *before* the era of the unquestionable development of the power of self-government, and before the child is properly deemed praiseworthy or blameable, or is accounted to be amenable to law. But after this important change has taken place, a corresponding change is insensibly effected in the conduct and sentiments of others.

In the first place, particular actions are approved or blamed, on the principle that *now*, by the expansion of the faculties, it has become the law of his mental operations, that, in the moment of action, the several antagonist motives that should influence action, are, with more or less distinctness, present to the mind. The agent, therefore, is deemed to have made his choice, for the better or the worse, from among alternatives; and it were to degrade him from the rank to which he has attained to suppose that, like the inferior orders of the animal world, he did but obey a *single impulse.*

This is not all; for the agent is supposed to have made his choice, for the better or the worse, in this particular instance, according to his individual dispositions; and the action is approved or blamed, not only as an insulated fact, but as an indication of character. And then this character is the object, not only of complacency or of displacency, but of *approval* or of *blame*. The character is approved or blamed on the very same principle—differently applied, and further extended—which is the ground of the approval or blame of particular actions, namely, that the now-expanded faculty of the agent enables him, at once, to form abstract notions of moral qualities—to compare such notions with the sentiments they excite in his own mind, and in the minds of others—to institute comparisons between his own dispositions and the dispositions which he admires or condemns in others; and, finally, to make his personal dispositions the subject of a process of self-education.

That so much as this is presumed to be true by mankind generally, is shown by the three-fold treatment that is adopted with the view of amending the conduct and dispositions, as well of adults as of children. *First*, rewards and punishments are employed for insuring right determinations in particular instances of conduct. *Secondly*, it is usual to attempt to amend the dispositions and the character by an external management of the exciting causes of the various emotions, and passions, and appetites. These two methods are applicable, in an inferior degree, even to animals—to the horse, the dog, the elephant. But that which we name as the *third* method of treatment is exclusively proper to human nature; and its applicability rests upon the fact, that the human mind includes an element which is not granted to the brute. This is the endeavour to awaken in the mind the desire of reforming itself—that is, its habits and its settled dispositions. This differs from the second method— or the management of dispositions by external means; and it proceeds upon the known fact, that an introverted effort of the mind may, and does often, and under a great variety of circumstances, take place.

It is, we say, the usage of the human mind to make its own acts and dispositions the subject of its meditations, and these meditations enkindle emotions of the same kind with those that are excited by the view of similar acts and dispositions in other men;—and to these emotions is superadded a specific feeling, more intense than the first, and which borrows its force from self-love —becoming either complacent or displacent: in the latter case bringing with it emotions of shame, fear, and remorse. It is, moreover, proper to the human mind to conceive abstractedly of a mode of action, or of a style of character *better than its own;* and to assume that conception as a permanent object of desire. In consequence of such a desire, a tendency towards it, more or less strong and uniform, takes place. In this manner, amendments, reformations, and even complete revolutions of character, are every day occurring within the human system. It should here be stated that those deteriorations of character which are also continually going on within the same system do not come about by a corresponding process of the mind, or as the result of a conception of vicious qualities, and a consequent pursuit of them; for they arise from the unresisted progress of sensual or malignant passions, which, by indulgence, become at length paramount forces.

SECTION V.

Whether this faculty of reformation, which divides man from his fellow-sentient beings by an immense interval, must be regarded as inscrutable, or whether it admits of being separated into its components, is a question we may leave to be considered by psychologists: nor need it be determined in its relation to morals or religion, since the fact of its existence is admitted; and this fact is enough for any practical purpose. The intelligible principles of morals and Christian piety have no more connection with a scientific analysis than have the labours of the mechanician with a theory—could it be given, of gravitation.

But this power of introverted action, which, by emphasis, may be termed the excellence of human nature, is often absolutely dormant, just as the faculty of abstraction also lies dormant among barbarous tribes.

Moreover, it is exposed to much damage, and may at length be quite enfeebled, by a vicious course of life. Man may either lie inert, beneath the level of his proper destiny, or, which is a more melancholy case, he may *fall* below that level—he may revert to the moral imbecility of infancy; and he may sink further into an abyss, where he grovels hopelessly, and must be content to share sentiments of loathing with the hog or the hyena. Sad condition this of *necessity!*—miserable ruin and decay of the noblest structure!

It should always be remembered, that, if the actual condition of human nature be contemplated merely as a matter of physical science, it must be admitted to have sustained, from whatever cause, a *universal* damage or shock; inasmuch as its higher faculties do not, like the faculties of the inferior classes, work auspiciously, or in accordance with their intention; often—and in a vast proportion of instances—are they overborne, defeated, destroyed; while in *no instances* do they take that full, free, and perfect course which is abstractedly proper to them. We may, if we please, collate this physical fact with certain principles of theology, and may derive from the comparison a confirmation of our religious belief. But this is not a matter that is pertinent to our immediate purpose.

Every new power that is admitted into a complex machinery tends, of course, to multiply the variations of its movements, and so to render a calculation of those movements more voluminous or difficult; yet not to render them at all less *causal*, or in any sense fortuitous. But this general principle is open to some apparent exceptions; as thus—if the superadded power be of a commanding sort, it will simplify the movements rather than complicate them, and so bring them more within the range of calculation: instances may easily be adduced in which the agencies of higher and more complex natures are more simple and invariable than those of inferior beings. The mental machinery of the adult contains more movements, and is more complex, than that of the infant; for new faculties have come into play, the materials of intellectual action have been vastly augmented, and many susceptibilities have been quickened, which are non-existent in the infant. But while the actions of the infant from one moment to the next may defy calculation, the actions of the adult, though open to a hundred times more influences, are often simplified by the predominance of some one of them. Thus, a ruling passion, long indulged, *sets* through the soul like an impetuous current, and gives a high degree of uniformity to the conduct. Or a similar uniformity and simplification may result from the predominance of virtuous emotions. Or, again, that very expansion of the intellectual faculties which imparts the greatest *organic* complexity to the machine may, at the same time, when it reaches its perfection, restore to the operations of the mind the most absolute simplicity. Truth is one; and it is the glory and perfection of the intellectual nature to perceive that oneness; and in proportion as truth is so perceived, and is embraced, and is delighted in, the agency of the being will become so much the more simple, and *calculable*, and will lose its character of variableness. The same is true of the perfection of the moral faculties; and it may be affirmed, that perfection in all orders, and of all kinds, tends, with equal steps, towards simplicity, uniformity, and constancy.

And yet what, it may be asked, can be gained by

applying to *this* simplicity, or to *this* constancy, which is the very character of perfection, any term or descriptive phrase which, with equal or greater propriety, may be assumed to belong to the lowest orders of the animal world? There *is* a sense in which it might be so applied; but it must be an infelicitous and ill-omened perversion so to do. We gain, it is true, the conception of an awful goddess—stern in feature, inflexible in temper, and implacably despotic, who rules the universe, and who vouchsafes no other reply to supplicants, than the monotonous response—Whatever is, must be. Nothing is more infallible than the connection between perfect intelligence, and the perception of a truth presented to it. Who could wish to be privileged with a freedom from this sort of necessity? To whom can this kind of despotism be galling, or intolerable? Nor can any but the lost covet that other species of liberty which excuses us from the moral necessity of taking always the road of virtue. To be bound by this *necessity* is the true *liberty ;* and, in fact, at every step of our approach to the high ground of intellectual and moral perfection, do liberty and necessity merge and become identical; and he is the most free whose reason and whose volitions are the most invariable and uniform.

But this is the point at which it becomes urgently needful to make a protest against the inveterate practice of applying one and the same set of phrases to the most extreme instances—instances so extreme that the interval between them is immeasurably great. This source of confusion has had its rise in that controversial usage which has carried a subject belonging of right to the philosophy of human nature over to the side of abstract theology and of biblical interpretation. In this way it has come about that phrases such as those which are repeated on every page of Edwards' Essay—"the determination of the will,"—"the strongest motive swaying the will,"—"the choice which on the whole approves itself to the reason," and some others, are left to lodge themselves in the reader's mind, who believes himself to be logically safe when he applies them—now, to the thousand-and-one instances of actions that are spontaneous, instantaneous, instinctive; and now, to actions of the very highest quality, wherein faculties of reason and of feeling are combined in the production of a result which is a fit sample at once of liberty the loftiest, with determinations, or with infallibility the most absolute.

Of such long standing are those confusions which have sprung from the interference of Logic with morals and Theology, on this ground, that the only way of escape seems to be that of passing over entirely from the region where religious feelings and sectarian beliefs bear sway, to a region which is wholly exempt from any such influences; we mean—the sphere of purely intellectual action.

It is in this sphere that the human mind exercises and exhibits its powers with the most advantage, and it is here that it displays what are its proper forces. It is here that it gives evidence of its possessing a faculty of causation, enabling it to mark out for itself a path of discovery over the field of the material world. It is not that, on this field, the human mind is exempt from the influence of *motives*, or that it is in an impassive condition; for the impulses which here bear upon it are of the most vivid kind; yet they are such as take a broad bearing, imparting force at large to the intellectual energies, while they leave individual volitions to take their rise with absolute freedom.

It is admitted, or it ought to be admitted, on all sides, that the ultimate or *innermost fact* in the mental structure is wholly inscrutable; or that it stands on a level with those ultimate facts in physical philosophy which are held to lie hid beyond the reach of science:— these are the mysteries of the material world; and as to the world of mind, we assume nothing more than this, that it also has its mysteries—facts which, though they are not to be questioned, are not to be spread out to view as if more were known concerning them than is or can be known.

If so much as this be allowed, then our question is this, Whether, on the field of its intellectual activity, the human mind does not exercise its functions in a manner which demands an absolute distinction to be made between it, and any species of physical causation.

All things occurring in the material world—all events that are properly *physical*—may be traced up, in the order of time, to events, or to a state of things that is anterior to the moment of their occurrence. But is it true that in the same sense, or in any sense which is intelligible, all events in the world of mind are also to be traced upward, in the order of time, to events, or to a state of things that is anterior to themselves? We here assume the negative, and affirm, on the contrary, the strictly initiative activity of mind, and affirm this to be the distinctive prerogative of the *human* mind.

Those things that are anterior or antecedent to the state of the mind at any moment, or to any of its volitions, are such as these: there is the individual make, or, as we say, the idiosyncracy of the man—that which from birth, and under the lengthened influences of education, and all circumstances put together, has brought him to be just what now he is, in faculty, habit, and power:—then we are to take into the account the now-present circle of influences that attract the senses, or that in any way bear upon, incite, stimulate, or depress the mind, either enhancing its powers, or producing an abatement of their energy. In a word, we have before us—the individual man, and the circumstance; and both, in respect of the next ensuing volition, are antecedent to it; that volition being taken to be, or it is spoken of as, the effect of these two antecedent causes, or clusters of causes. It may be, moreover, that when this volition is considered as an effect or result of the two, we fail to trace what is due to each, up from the product to its cause.

But now let it be granted as possible, or as a case that is at least hypothetically admissible, that in the product there is found to be more—perhaps immensely more than we can, with any reason, attribute to either of the above-named antecedents. In the product there *is*, what was *not* in the causes, either separately considered, or considered in mass, or as the sum of the two. Instances of this very kind abound, and superabound in all departments of the physical sciences. The product is not only *more* than the sum, or than the multiple of the two above-named clusters of antecedents, but it is of a kind for which we must make search elsewhere than among those influences in respect of which the man is the creature of the conditions of his birth, education, and present circumstance.

We now take an instance.—That vast assemblage of conceptions and of beliefs which are embraced in the circle of the Modern Astronomy is an intellectual product—it is a result which has come out of the modern mind, and which at this time holds a place in all instructed minds into which it has entered by the ordinary methods of teaching. This modern astronomy may be, and it is, set forth and figured in books; and it is symbolized in those elaborate mechanisms and instruments to which itself has given birth, and which are its tools and its aids. But now this scheme of the stellar and planetary universe which we assent to as, in the main, true, and which we speak of without hesitation as conformable to the reality of things—this complex notion of magnitudes, distances, revolutions, perturbations—this GREAT IDEA of spheres, and of orbits, and of velocities, *whence* has it come, and *how* has it come, to fill the place which it actually occupies in the modern mind?

In answering this question we must not say, or imagine, that the modern theory of the universe has suggested itself to the human mind spontaneously, as if it were the obvious interpretation of what the eye is conversant with in surveying the midnight heavens. It is not the *visible meaning* of the things that are seen; for a supposition the very contrary of what is now known to be true in astronomy is that which the human mind has always spontaneously accepted. The diurnal movement of the celestial lamps from east to west has, in every age, been trusted and received as real, until Thought has laboriously revised, and has rejected these primitive suppositions.

Nor has the modern astronomy sprung out of that current of images which is ever flowing through the mind, and in respect of which it, for the most part, exercises no control. The human mind has not *dreamed* the astronomy which we now accept as true; it has not picked it up, as if it had floated down upon the meditative stream of unsought-for images.

But now has the modern theory of the universe, at length turned up in the evolution of an eternal series of chances? It is affirmed that the twenty-four or thirty letters of the alphabet, if thrown incessantly during millions of years, might come up in order, as a line of the Iliad; and that the chances of some other millions of ages would give us Homer entire! If then the universe itself may be the product of eternal chances, then why may not our modern notion of it have sprung also from the womb of eternity in the same manner? Who among us shall say he believes this?

We are now assuming that the modern astronomy *is*, substantially, *true*. Let it be imagined, then, that it has, at length, been spontaneously generated by the evolution of certain Laws of Thought, which, as innate in the human mind, are the fixed and constant constituents of the rational nature. Be it so; but these innate laws— the tendency of which is to bring the human mind into conformity with the nature of things in the world around us—these laws are themselves subject, as the history of philosophy shows, to countless and incalculable disturbing influences; and if, as now, we are thinking of the evolution of fixed laws, *and of nothing else*, and if they are crossed and deflected by innumerable influences coming in upon them from all sides, then, and on that supposition, the probability of the coming up of a TRUE ASTRONOMY, in the course of myriads of ages, is very little, if at all, better than it is on the preceding supposition of its springing out of pure chance.

But there is no need, it will be said, to have recourse

to any of these extreme suppositions, and which nobody would profess to think admissible. That great scheme of the universe which we designate "the modern astronomy," has become what it is as the result of methods of reasoning—complicated, refined, hypothetic often, as to its starting-point, and nevertheless irresistibly conclusive. It is the noble achievement of the human mind, labouring on the same field—the visible heavens—age after age; often wandering far from the right path, but at length arriving at a harmonious system which we may now safely accept as being conformable to the reality of things.

What this reasoning is—regarded as an intellectual operation—this is not the place to inquire; a strict analysis of it has been propounded by several recent writers. It is enough here to say that it implies, at each step, the following, or the accepting as true, a perceived agreement, or an accordance, whether in relation to quantities or qualities, or some supposed relationship of known causes and effects.

But now, if the aggregate of all human reasonings could be brought under review, it would appear that in a very large—perhaps the larger—number of instances the agreement, or the accordance, which the mind at first accepted as true, was not so in fact—the appearances were fallacious. This probability of error is known to, and it is always kept in view by well-trained minds. Consequent upon this knowledge of the fallaciousness of phenomena, and the uncertainty of even the best methods of hypothetic reasoning, and the necessity of submitting all conclusions to some test, or to many tests— if they can be brought forward—a habit is formed of supervision, and the practice is resorted to of excursive and conjectural advances, in this direction and in that—hunting, as we may say, for indications of error: hypotheses the least likely to be true are invited, and are imagined, and are questioned, so as that we may embrace every chance of detecting any mistaken step.

In explication of this revisional process in philosophic reasoning—this highly-complicated method, which revolves all things known, and all things imaginable—we may, if we please, affirm that some higher "law of thought" comes in to act as the guide of such speculations. And yet this second, or this more recondite law, will itself need another, which shall be still more intimate, and more recondite, and which shall give aid in the revision of its own operations. In a word, at every step of our advance on this path we shall find the need of another power, or of a principle, deeper and further in, and therefore less explicable, than the preceding one. What it is which we need is that which we may as well acknowledge—at the very outset: it is what we would not call "the self-determining power of the mind," because this worn-out phrase has surrounded itself with confusions; but it is that which, in whatever terms it may be spoken of, is the prerogative and the distinction of Mind, in the human species. It is that which, because it is the ultimate fact in human nature, is not susceptible of analysis, and must for ever defy our endeavours to set it forth in explicative propositions.

Apart from a candid and a modest recognition of this ultimate fact in human nature, we find ourselves contending, ever and anew, and to little purpose, with some guise of atheistic or materialistic fatalism. The entire consciousness of the intellectual and moral nature, in every sound mind, repels and resents these monstrous doctrines; nevertheless, so long as we admit, in constructing our systems of abstract Theology, those principles of reasoning on which atheism takes its stand, we shall find no release from this warfare.

It may be demanded that we should adduce some flagrant instances of this pernicious interference of a wordy Logic with the principles of Christian Theology. The name of Jonathan Edwards has been prominent in these pages:—but now will the modern Christian reader of his works wish to repeat the demand for instances of this kind to be thence drawn? In those works—up and down, passages occur at sight of which one stands aghast;—the horror of a great darkness comes upon the soul, and it is not until long after reading them, and closing the book, that any degree of peace of mind is regained. This unfeignedly Christian man, from the peculiar structure of his mind, and from his training, had learned to abandon himself to the tyranny of a wordy, demonstrative method. Come what might—let all principles and all intuitions of piety and moral feeling be outraged, yet if the Logic be right—if each proposition hangs fast by the heels of the proposition which is its precursor,—if all be so, then a belief which is infinitely worse than the worst blasphemies of atheists is, without a doubt, to be taken to ourselves as true!

But has not every residue of this puritanic Theology long ago ceased to be thought of? The day will be bright when any such affirmation may be uttered with truth; for then we shall have learned to think of the Divine Nature—according to Scripture; and Christian Theology shall at length speak peace to our troubled thoughts.

ESSAY II.

THE STATE OF UNITARIANISM IN ENGLAND.

SECTION I.

The fairness of an indirect argument may always be questioned. What we mean by an indirect argument is—the drawing an inference for or against any system of belief, or any polity or scheme of social organization, in a somewhat circuitous manner, from its manifest or its alleged consequences—its progress, its defeats, its *fortunes*, among other and competing doctrines or practices.

In some cases this mode of oblique reasoning may carry with it a conclusive and irresistible force, and may make good its claim as legitimate, in a logical sense, by the incontrovertible validity of the inference in which it terminates.

An indirect or inferential argument *in favour* of any doctrine or system, derived from its rapid spread, and its actual hold of the popular mind, is always very precarious, and should be had recourse to only as accompanied with a careful and a thoroughly honest consideration of all the circumstances of the case.

An indirect argument, *adverse* to the pretensions of a particular system or polity, in like manner demands caution, and freedom from polemical eagerness, on the part of those who urge it; nevertheless circumstances may attach to a particular instance which remove all reasonable hesitation, when we are intending to bring it home to those to whom it may relate, as to the unsoundness of their distinctive principles.

Might we, without offence, take, in illustration of what we are now saying, an instance in referring to which we profess—what indeed we feel—respect and affection for a highly estimable body of persons—the Quakers ? Let all the merits of the " Friends" be fully granted, and let the large amount of their benevolent achievements be put down to their credit, and then we shall be troubled with no misgivings in affirming that Quakerism—such as it has existed in England these hundred years past, is a total mistake—it is not the Christianity of the New Testament. To show why we think so would lead us away from our immediate purpose; nor can an argument of this kind be urgently called for at a time when the rapid decrease of the body—its hastening sublimation—seems to indicate a time near at hand when its last aged representatives shall have been lowered into their graves with obsequies significantly noiseless.

In demur of an unfavourable indirect argument of this sort, such pleas as the following may be urged :—We may say, it is an evil world that we live in; the very purest forms of truth are always the most vehemently rejected : it is, moreover, an *evil time*—a time in which blind prejudice, powerful corporations, secular influences, fashion, fanaticism, are just now in their hour of energy, and are too strong for us; we do not—we cannot prosper in the face of forces so many and so potent. Indulgence should be given to these, and to any other explanations which may be consolatory to the feelings of the chiefs of unprosperous bodies. But after duly listening to them, we come round to our first assumption, that, in certain instances, the damaging inference which we intend to draw is valid, and is irresistibly conclusive.

On the part of those who, after a long trial, have conspicuously failed to bring over to their views any large proportion of the religious community, this plea meets the ear oftener perhaps than any other: "That the times are unfavourable to liberty of thought; that a blind acquiescence in old errors, a reverence for antiquated superstitions, is the predominant feeling with the religious." This plea, we think, is unavailing at this time; and it should long ago have ceased to be used. It is a plea inapplicable to the instance of the present state of Unitarianism in England. It may be alleged that in *no* instance can an inference drawn from what we have called the *fortunes* of a religious community be accepted as of conclusive weight. We grant this; and nevertheless return to our position that, *in certain cases*, a presumption, adverse to the merits of a doctrine or polity, may be so strong as to carry with it an overwhelming force. And we think this to be the case in the instance now before us.

In taking a glance, as we propose to do, at the state of Unitarianism in England, we first step back a twenty years—dated from the present time; and then, in a future essay, propose to bring our report, and its inference, up to this present time, taking account of the changes which may have had place in that interval of years.

The lapse of time, even of so short a space as twenty years, ought not to be left out of the reckoning when we have in view the actual, and the relative position of a community or a party, political or religious. Twenty years—or thirty—carries us over from the era of the fathers, in their maturity of thought and action, to the era of the sons—just at the moment when they are reviewing the opinions of their predecessors, and are forecasting their own course in moving on to an advanced position. The exterior aspect of things may be much the same—or the same, if looked at hastily; but as to the core of thought, as to the inner meaning of conventional phrases, an extensive substitution of one body of notions for another may have taken place.

If then we ask leave to take account of twenty or thirty years as materially affecting the real condition of religious communities, with how much more reason should we take account of the lapse of centuries! But just on this ground we have a cause of complaint. We have listened to mournful denunciations of the "intolerance," the "blindness," the "stolid fanaticism" of this now-passing time, which seemed to carry us back a four hundred years. There *must be* an anachronism in any such wailings as these. *It is not true* that in England, at this time, a fair argument in behalf of great principles has to encounter as much antagonism as it would have encountered in the times of the Tudors.

Let us imagine ourselves to be living in the midst of the "dark ages," when the few enlightened men of that dreary time might bemoan themselves as having been born a thousand years too late, or a thousand years too soon. Let us listen at the closet-door of one of them, and hear him uttering a wail such as this:—"Why toil thus to explore the secrets of nature—the work of God, only to earn the disgrace of holding friendship with the devil? Who and what are thy contemporaries? they are either the victims of its sottish ignorance, or at once its victims and its interested patrons! Where, unless it were in the midst of a wilderness, may reason safely utter her voice? Mankind is leagued against light, and counts every son of knowledge a deadly foe. Demonstration is condemned as the foulest of heresies! The laws of nature are blasphemy! and to set forth the wisdom of the Creator, is to preach the doctrine of fiends! And the people hug the tyranny that holds them down: they love their thraldom, and are prompt to rend, limb from limb, the man who would disabuse their understandings! Luckless man that I am! born too soon or too late: either hide thyself in the grave, or hasten to join the multitude in paying homage to the sovereign folly that sits on high, mistress of the nations!"

But from a dream such as this we awake. It is Sunday morning, and, in compliance with wholesome usages, we direct our steps towards a place of worship, and enter the first that presents itself. The sombre exterior of the structure seems to ally itself to the glooms of the times from which we had just emerged; nor was the interior out of harmony with the face of the edifice. Deep galleries protrude their bulk far upon the central space. The lower area is penfolded by pews, secretive in their intention, and such as seemed to typify that sectarism of the Christian community which has so long made the Church universal look so much more like a penitentiary than a royal banqueting-house.

The congregation has assembled, but the service has not commenced. Dimness and comfortless solemnity reign within the sacred precincts; and we might easily imagine that we had not indeed effected our return from the twelfth century.—The congregation has assembled. So we must say, while we look from side to side of the desolation, and descry here, and there again, a well-toiletted head, or tuft of feathers! Such is this "holy convocation!" Yet we should not omit to mention a half-dozen aged pensioners, and a score or two of liveried children, who claimed the ample spaces of the galleries as their undisputed domain.

The minister ascends to his place;—a spare, keen-eyed man, sedate in deportment, and sarcastic in look, and yet manifestly sad at heart;—sad as a man of sense and feeling must be, whose lot it is to stand, year after year, in front of the perpetual sleet and frost of ill-success. He gazes for a moment upon the unvaried scene—for each of his wealthy patrons is in his place— and he looks as if in disgust of himself, of his vocation, of his congregation, of his times, and of all the world, and then announces the psalm. The prompter of psalmody, aided by a voice or two from the furthest corners of the place, performs the joyous anthem! Again the leader of worship rises, and reads, and prays; while his hearers, like so many columns erect amid the ruins of Palmyra, indicate by their position that they are not altogether unmindful of the specific service in which their minister is engaged. How might any one sigh for the unaffected fervour of a Turkish mosque!

The preacher takes his text, which, as it was not referred to in the body of the discourse, has slipped from our recollection. The querulous, sardonic, discouraging harangue of half an hour, inspires the belief that the minister is preparing his hearers for the announcement that the chapel doors would, from that day forward, be closed, and that no more fruitless attempts would be made to dissipate the obstinate darkness of the age. Not so: but, instead of any such seemingly discreet resolution, the sanguine man, hoping against hope, concludes his discourse by declaring his conviction that some thousand years—perhaps fifteen hundred years hence—mankind, escaping at length from the infatuations of enthusiasm and fanaticism, will yield to the sway of right reason, and acknowledge the excellence of "primitive Christianity;" that is to say, on this proviso, that Christianity itself, which, perhaps, ought always to have been regarded as only a temporary dispensation, should, at that remote date, be deemed the fittest expression, or in any way a necessary conveyance of Eternal Truths!

But before the preacher has attained this heart-warming climax, he complains heavily, and with a swell of indignant eloquence—slightly indicative, perhaps, of wounded pride—of the inveteracy of vulgar prejudices —the obdurate impenetrability of notions once held to be sacred—the crushing despotism of religious establishments, which, as he affirms, leave no chance of success to truth and reason among the great body of the people; while the sects that disclaim all such corrupting influences are maddened by fanaticism. Things being in this woeful plight, what wonder is it that the few places in which the pure light of "primitive Christianity" still shines are scarcely at all frequented? "Such," said the preacher, willing to condole with his saddened flock, "such is the infelicity of being thrown upon a dark age! an age, the glooms of which are rendered only the more sensibly dense by the flickering (and I fear expiring) taper of true knowledge, which we, my brethren, still hold out to our times. But let us remember that we are not alone upon the roll of those worthies whose lot it has been to contend vainly against obstinate and triumphant ignorance. We are placed, in our times, just as Roger Bacon was placed in his. Or, if you want illustrious examples of this sort, think of the great Albert—think of Copernicus—think of Galileo! Heroic men! they, as we, maintained in that, their dark day, sublime truths, which the world, besotted then as now, would not receive, though demonstrably certain."

Nor does the preacher, whatever bright hopes he may entertain of a millennium of truth at the end of another millennium of error, promise to his hearers any speedy change for the better. "The zealous efforts of the friends of *primitive* Christianity," said he, " to disseminate their opinions on an extended scale, had proved almost an entire failure. At home the congregations of apostolic Christians had, in ninety-eight instances out of every hundred, dwindled down to a state of deplorable desolation; and as to its progress abroad, the spirit of the primitive doctrine had shown itself to be *not expansive:* it was not a *missionary spirit;* it won no way among the mass of the people; and every attempt to give it circulation, after struggling into existence, did but struggle to exist."

We caught, from the tones of this comfortless harangue, an infection of despondency. The gloom of the building, its desolation echoing the plaints of the preacher, oppressed the imagination; and we expected that, on issuing from this dungeon of despair, we should behold the heavens overcast with blackness—that the midsummer's noon would be stained, as by sympathy, with the moral and intellectual " darkness of the age." We expected to meet, at the first turning, some procession of monks, or a band of heretics on their way to the fire. In a word, we thought of nothing, as we passed the untrod threshold of this Unitarian Apostolic meeting-house, but to see the blood-stained banner of superstition floating far and wide upon the murky sky!

But how cheering is the reality that wakens us from this dismal dream as we gain the street! At the very moment, twenty churches and chapels of the neighbourhood are disgorging their crowds. Sunday dresses and Sunday faces, illuminated by a Sunday summer sky, give to the scene the liveliness and grace that so well befit Christianity where Christianity is free, intelligent, and sincere. Most of the faces we encounter bear that expression of independence which is peculiarly *English;* very few display that sort of timid, crabbed, cruel dejection which characterizes an age of fanaticism or of superstition. And as the crowd is thinning we meet several of the ministers of the congregations that have just dispersed, and they are men whom we recognize as standing in the front of whatever is free, beneficent, outspoken: they are men, some of them erudite, most of them laborious in their spheres; and of whom, scarcely two, are highly paid for their services.

Surely we may infer that our preacher of "primitive apostolic Christianity" has calumniated his times, and is himself, if not a cynic, a disappointed man: forsooth, just because neither the irreligious of this time nor the religious can be brought to listen to his doctrine—just because he, being himself in the wrong, must give some colour of reason to his comfortless condition, he misrepresents the age in which he lives, and dares to attribute to the ignorance, the obstinate fanaticism, and the interested superstition of the people of England in the nineteenth century, a failure which, in simple fact, is nothing but the natural and the inevitable consequence of a fond attempt to uphold a long ago refuted argument. The complaint of the thoughtful, but persecuted man of the twelfth century awakened the sympathy which is due to greatness unblessed. The moans of this deserted preacher kindle the pity which is all that can be bestowed upon sincere but luckless infatuation.

It is not easy to imagine an occasion that more signally tries the qualities of a man, or an occasion on which he may better establish his claim to the character of a philosopher (taking the term in its very highest and best sense) than when, as an advocate of unpopular opinions, he is called upon to give a reason for the failure of his zealous endeavours to propagate them. A man who can explain his own discomfiture without egotism or petulance, and without misstatement of facts, and without supercilious vituperations of the "vulgar," may fairly challenge an elevation of soul which perhaps distinguishes scarcely three individuals in a century. Placed in a position such as we are here supposing, an inferior mind betrays, in one manner or in another, its ignoble quality; nor will it rest until it has revenged its defeats by slanders; nor be satisfied even then.

But how admirable were that greatness of mind which should lead one who has conspicuously failed in his endeavours to propagate certain opinions, to confess that the circumstances and the reasons of his disappointment have been such as to imply, almost demonstrably, the unsoundness of his argument—yes—that he has been mistaken!

Would that the state of Christianity in England were brighter and better than it is! that the great mass of the people were habitual frequenters of churches and chapels!

that in all churches and chapels the principal doctrines of the Reformation were plainly and zealously preached! Heartily may we wish that " all bishops and curates, and all congregations committed to their charge," exhibited, in their lives and conversation, unquestionable proofs of their receiving largely " the healthful spirit of grace." But if things are not altogether as we would have them be, dare we attribute the irreligion of the times to the presence of any *argumentative* obstructions or disadvantages which crush the spirit of free inquiry, or deprive truth of a fair hearing ? Who is it that dares to say, or to insinuate, that priestly power so sways and so enthrals the popular mind that the advocates of reason are cowed, browbeaten, and intimidated ? Dare we affirm that genuine Christianity does not spread through the land, because its preachers are driven from the field by the hootings of endowed error ? Such things must not be said, for they are contrary to plain and conspicuous facts. There has never been a fifty years in which—there has never been a people among whom—a sound argument has had a better chance of making head against old errors than during the last fifty years, and among the people of England within that time. Nay, during the last fifty years, at several moments, the popular feeling in England has broken with so stormy a force against all ancient and prescriptive opinions, that whoever came forward to impugn them found, in every market-place, a people prepared to applaud and to devour his most daring sophistries. It is indeed true that earthly passions and worldly interests now, as ever, indispose the mass of mankind to entertain religious truths, and so to render the religious, as compared with the irreligious, a small minority; but it is not true that the temper of the times

—specifically, or that political institutions, stand in the way of any one theological system, as compared with others. Piety is indeed overpowered by worldliness of spirit and sensuality; but neither Unitarianism nor any other peculiar doctrine is specially disadvantaged in its struggle to hold a place among the crowd of religious opinions.

On the contrary, Unitarianism has had its auspicious moments—it has had its sunny days. Once and again it has seemed to be just spreading its canvas to the gale, upon a flood-tide of opportunity. If there had been in Unitarianism the vigour of prosperous life, it might, nay, it *must* have lived and prospered at some time during the last half century.* And if, once and again, it has lapsed and has slunk away from the high road of success, no other intelligible account of the fact can be given than this—that intrinsically it is a doctrine of desolation and decay.

What is it, then, that must be confessed concerning the "primitive apostolic Christianity" which is now preached in Unitarian meeting-houses? Alas! this doctrine, which, if indeed it be the Christianity of the Apostles, had then power to conquer all the gods, and to set foot upon the throne of universal empire; now, when it is learnedly and zealously propounded to the most intelligent, the most free, and the most religious people in the world, proves itself to be—what none will listen to—a theory which the poor turn from in contempt!—a doctrine that inspires its converts with no zeal!—a system that can neither walk, nor run, nor stand among competitors!—a belief that scatters, not gathers; that desolates, not blesses!—a phantom of

* From 1780 to 1830.

silence, gloom, emptiness, coldness, despondency! This is the primitive apostolical Christianity of Unitarianism; and it is so by the confession of its advocates.*

SECTION II.

The entire number of places of worship (endowed and licensed) in England, might be classified in some such manner as the following:—that is to say, we might take, as the ground of a distinction, the degree in which they are *ordinarily* filled. The purpose of our argument will be sufficiently answered by a fourfold division. Following, then, this rule, the *first* class comprehends the crowded; the *second*, the fairly filled; the *third*, the moderately filled; and the *fourth*, those that, from Sunday to Sunday, round the year, challenge to themselves, in a pre-eminent degree, the solemnity which waits upon desolation; or, in other words, such as are occupied by the parson, the clerk, the pew-opener, and five, seven, fourteen, or twenty resolute folks, who have vowed that nothing, while life and limb are spared, shall drive them from the venerable walls.

As to places of the first class—the crowded—we might exclude them from consideration on the present occasion, as anomalous instances, it being fairly presumable, and it is found to be so in fact, that such cases of extraordinary repletion result from special causes, such as the peculiar attractions of the preacher, his genius, his fervour, or perhaps his fertile talent in devising paradoxes. Here and there also, local circumstances, fine music, or

* Passages confirmatory of what is affirmed in this Essay have been drawn from authentic Unitarian publications

mere fashion, crams a place of worship. Be it as it may, it would not be safe to draw general inferences from such instances. The *second* class, or the well-filled, may (with a few exceptions easily accounted for) be considered as so distinguished because the religious instruction which is obtained in them is of a sort that approves itself to the consciences of men as sound, efficient, and salutary. To this order belong most of those churches of the Establishment wherein the doctrines of its founders are preached in an able and acceptable manner. It includes also a fair proportion (perhaps a majority) of all Dissenting meeting-houses and chapels in populous neighbourhoods, in which the same doctrines (the doctrines of the Reformation) are maintained by men of good education, good character, and respectable pulpit talents. We come then to the third, and perhaps the most numerous class, namely, the moderately, or half-filled; they are neither desolated nor flourishing. More seats are claimed or let in them than are occupied. Of this sort are, first, a proportion of parish churches throughout the land, in rural districts, whereunto resort, every Sunday (bad weather excepted) the sober folk of the parish, who would do what they do, though the parson would preach Islamism, and perhaps be little the wiser, and not much the worse if he did. Secondly, under this general head are to be reckoned some number, we fear, of orthodox dissenting places, in towns and out of them, and which contain a very similar *genus* of "good sort of folks," better taught, perhaps, in Christianity than some of their neighbours of the Establishment, and decided foes of all " rites and forms of worship which are of man's devising," but not much more vivacious either in their intellectual or their moral life than other people. Where such half-filled dissenting places are surrounded with a dense population, we would undertake to assign, instantly, the conspicuous and unquestionable cause of so lamentable a waste of pew room.

Last come the empty. It is no *bull* to call a thing *empty*, whether it be box, vase, house, purse, church, or chapel, which is not found to contain what one reasonably expects to see within it, even though there be not an absolute vacuum. In this sense, an *empty* place of worship is one in which, though there is some dozen of men, women and children, there is *no congregation.* Instances of very dissimilar sorts come under this head; as first, a few parish churches, the officiating minister in which, either by his bad reputation, or his inefficiency as a teacher, secures for his own voice and his clerks all the advantages of solemn echo from bare walls. But to whom among the sectarists belong these deserted chapels? We are prepared to affirm, that an exceedingly small number can be claimed by the orthodox dissenters of any denomination. Here and there, indeed, some pitiable drone, barricadoed in his pulpit by "the endowment," and protected from public opinion by his utter obscurity, "keeps the doors" of an ancient meeting-house "open" (to use a technical, and a very significant phrase) by his somnific inanities; and, perhaps, on some crowded highway, where a multitude of souls might have been saved, he holds up, weekly, the glorious gospel on a stage, for the scoff of each Sunday straggler! Instances of this sort among the orthodox dissenters are, we say, extremely rare. Who then claims the remainder? It is Unitarianism. And in what proportion? In the proportion of ninety out of every hundred of all its places of worship.

We must dilate a while upon this fact, and again recur to our classification. If we err in particulars we shall willingly receive correction, and yet even in that case we need acknowledge no detriment to our argument. We believe, then, that English Unitarianism has scarcely a place that is ordinarily *crowded*, or over-filled. Assuredly it has not five such places; and we do not hesitate to say, that nothing can be more improbable than that a preacher of this class should excite that sort of intense feeling which could attract a throng. A very clever man, or a learned one, or a man of eminent perspicacity, or of fine taste, may adopt the Unitarian creed; but how rarely shall we find among its advocates a powerful and well-proportioned intellect, vivified by glowing sensibilities, and rife with the soul of eloquence? Unitarianism, by its repressive property, is forbidden to become attractive to a promiscuous multitude.

Three or four (we doubt if there be five) Unitarian chapels in England are well filled, although not crowded. But in these few instances *all the Unitarianism* of one side of the metropolis, or of a populous manufacturing town, is brought together, and makes indeed a fair show, if only it be thought of apart from the space whence it has been gathered.

It is a remarkable fact, that the system of doctrine of which we are speaking seems not to be susceptible of any middle state of prosperity. Unitarian places of worship are either the three or four, or possibly the five, well-filled chapels in London, Birmingham, Liverpool; or they are the three or four hundred dungeons of desolation which are found elsewhere. Where, in towns of the second and third-rate size, are the edifices that bring together, on a Sunday, a fair proportion of the several orders, namely, the opulent, the trading, and the poor, to listen to Unitarian doctrine? Hardly will any such instances be met with. Unitarianism exists either by collecting scattered individuals from large circles; or purely by aid of endowments, where a *congregation* has long ceased to be thought of. So much for our third class.

Nothing can be more significant than the facts that present themselves in turning to the fourth class, or the empty. No sect at all approximates to the proportion which the empty chapels of the Unitarians bear to the entire number. To say that, of a thousand parish churches taken indiscriminately in town and country, one hundred and twenty-five, or one-eighth, are graced with the chilly grandeur of vacuity, is, we think, allowing a too large number. We doubt if the Methodists, either Wesleyan or Calvinistic, have three empty chapels in a hundred; the Baptists may perhaps claim five or ten in the same number; the Independents three or four; the Quakers fifty, or more. But by their own statements, ninety-eight Unitarian chapels in every hundred are desolate. Yet, as our argument is of a general kind, and is quite independent of nice calculations, we are willing to suppose that ten in a hundred own a congregation; nay, let it be twenty; let it be said that not more than four-fifths of the Unitarian pew-ground is a desert. Here then we might stop. We should be content to leave the inference to every man's common sense. Most assuredly, were we Unitarians, we should accept the fact, under the circumstances which belong to it, as a sufficient proof of the badness, or, if not so, at least of the hopelessness of the cause. If Unitarian chapels are empty, it is not because "this is an age of darkness and fanaticism," it is not because Unitarians are liable to imprisonments, confiscations, fines; but it is for the simple and the satisfactory reason that, with the Bible on the pulpit cushion, it fails to make good its pretensions—the mass of the people being judges.

It is useless to flinch from so conspicuous an inference. Christianity has, indeed, often been crushed, or been beaten out of a country by force of arms, and cruel persecutions; or it has expired amid the general decay of learning, or in the absence of political security, or in the decline of national life. We mourn in such cases this extinction of the living power, yet we cannot marvel. But what ought we to think, and what are the appalling surmises which must come in upon the heart, if it should appear that Christianity, in its pure and its primitive form—Christianity, which was announced as a blessing to the poor, and to the multitude—yet, when it is proclaimed among an enlightened people, in an age of freedom and of intellectual activity, can gain no hearing? What if we see that this "Apostolic doctrine," entering upon a congregation which had been fairly taken from all ranks, presently scatters it—retaining nothing of the good things upon which it laid its hand, excepting the endowments, and the desolated walls? And what if these things take place again, and again, and yet again? Is there no significance in facts such as these?

But now, in proof and illustration of our allegations, we must bring together a number of admissions which we find scattered through several numbers of a work that is the recognized organ of this Denomination.*

" Our chapels are but thinly attended, and our interest

* The Monthly Repository for the time to which this Essay relates

but slow in progress. Perhaps, if we advert to the increase of population in these kingdoms, we must not speak of progress, but of retrogradation."

"From the efforts of missionaries," says the writer, "let us turn to the actual condition of our congregations. These we may divide into two classes, the ancient and the modern: those we have received from our predecessors, and those created by the present generation. Of many of both classes the tale is brief and mournful. There are a few of the old chapels, situated in large and flourishing towns, in which congregations worship, respectable both as to numbers and character. From the narrow sphere of the Unitarian view, however, *these are greatly overrated.* Everything is small or great by comparison. To a child, a house of six rooms is a mansion; to Unitarians, a Bristol or a Manchester audience is magnificent! But let these half dozen flourishing congregations be deemed of as highly as we will, still *six* prosperous societies out of some three hundred is a small proportion. We do not mean to intimate that *all* the rest are dying or dead—far from it. There is a large middle class which supports a healthy appearance; but many of the old chapels among us are in a pitiable state. Of our own knowledge, we can speak of *some scores* that scarcely show signs of life. The number of hearers in them will not average more than *thirty*, the salary of the minister not more than seventy pounds per annum. Few beings are more to be pitied than a Unitarian minister, placed in one of these societies. A man of education, with the miserable pittance of some seventy pounds per year, which, with much toil and solicitude, he *may* perhaps, but not in all cases, raise to a bare hundred. With this he has a wife and children to support, and a decent appearance to maintain. Nor is this insignificant sum to be obtained without sundry and constant vexations from trustee influence and trustee domination. If animated by a laudable wish to extend the boundaries of his pasture, the minister is encountered by coldness and opposition. The poor who attend his services would gladly lend their countenance and aid; but the great man, who is also the keeper of the purse, frowns the intention down. On other occasions, the minister is checked in his purposes for want of pecuniary assistance, or by the engagements and vexations of a school. There are many, very many of our ministers in this condition. Men of talent, education, and lofty moral feeling, are suffering for the cause of truth, and, by reason of others' unfaithfulness, in remote villages and declining towns, suffering in a way and to an extent that nothing but moral strength and the force of principle could enable them to sustain. Imagine these men placed in situations fitting to call out their powers, to fan the flame of their piety and zeal, to reward with a competency their labours, and how different would be their condition and their characters! In the actual case, however, how much of moral power is thrown away! how much of intellectual excellence is lost! and for what! To re-enact the story told in Mr. WRIGHT's narrative of his missionary life and labours—to conduct in decency a few sexagenarians to the grave, and then to close the doors! Let us not be supposed to jest with the subject; it is too serious, and too true, to admit of a smile. If this is not the probable end of no few of the old Presbyterian chapels, we are yet to learn what other fate they can in all probability undergo. The question, then, is easily solved, whether or not it is worth while to sacrifice some of the excellent of the earth to such an object? Can such a consummation be avoided? Not in the actual state of things. But if the Unitarian body would rise to a sense of its duties, and to a manly advocacy of the cause of truth, the most desirable change might be effected: but of this more anon

"Equally grieved are we when we contemplate the condition of the congregations which have been raised within the last fifteen years. Many chapels have been built; how few are adequately attended! If it were not an invidious task, we could establish this assertion by the mention of actual instances. Doubtless there are *some* of our young societies that promise to survive, a few that flourish, but many of them are struggling hard for existence. In nearly all of them the minister is in a condition little better than those are who are attached to the former class. From what has been said, it is evident that the cause of Unitarianism in these kingdoms, as far as its condition may be estimated by the numbers who constitute its congregations, is by no means in a satisfactory state.

"We dare not hope that the kingdom of Christ is advancing under our auspices. The world around us is lying in wickedness. The home of the majority of our readers is surrounded by many who are in the gall of bitterness, being enslaved by sin; and what healing stream have we recently set to flow, what light have we kindled to cleanse and illume our suffering fellow-men? Our neighbourhoods are incessantly increasing; the young swarm around us on every side; those of riper years arise in crowds. Where is there, on our part, an increase of exertion, an augmentation of moral energy, to meet the growing demand? Alas! the general effect of the thickening of the population is to hide from public view the temples devoted to our worship, to hide our candle under a bushel, and to restrict the moral influence which we exert. How long will these things be? Have we arrived at the lowest point of depression? May a change for the better be expected? All things, we iterate, are in our possession, requisite to exert a most healing and efficient influence on our fellow-men, all but the great mover, the life and soul of action—the will."

Not a word of comment needs be subjoined to these quotations; we leave the inference to every man's good sense, and pursue our intention a page or two further.

SECTION III.

Far should we be from intending to insult the unhappy! Nevertheless, we must say something of a case which appears to be singularly undesirable, whether it be regarded in a secular or in a spiritual light—we mean that of more than four-fifths of all the preachers of Unitarianism in England at the present time.

In spite of pride, in spite of reason, in spite either of abstract principles or of internal satisfactions, every man (or all but madmen and enthusiasts) esteems his own position in society very much as he perceives it to be esteemed by those around him. To some extent, a man is happy who is thought to be so, and wretched if he knows that the world pities or condemns him. If this be not a universal truth, it is a general one. Now it is granted that a faithful Christian minister, the servant of God in an evil world, is called, at times, and in peculiar situations, to bear up against the general contumely of mankind, and is compelled to recollect the real dignity, and the high importance, and the future honours of his office, in order to support himself under the scorn of a licentious or of a gainsaying world. Something of this sort may happen even in our own enlightened and religionized country. Much more does it happen to the Christian missionary, as he urges his discouraged steps daily through the crowded ways of an idolatrous city! But in such instances a wise and good man, although, as a man, he feels oppressively the weight of the circumambient scorn of his fellows, nevertheless readily turns to considerations which sustain his courage. He recollects, for example, the immense and conspicuous superiority of the religion he bears with him over that which he impugns. Then his thoughts fly homeward, and he remembers that the doctrine which is scorned by the men of India is honoured by the men of England; or his meditations carry him back to the ages of the primitive triumphs of the Gospel, or forward to the millennium of its universal ascendancy. Thus he rebuts contempt by aid of reason and of faith.

We are willing to grant that, unless he can bring home to his heart, often, and without question, a large measure of such meditative comfort, a Christian minister who stands, from youth to age, in the centre of a circle of desolation, is one whom we should deem especially miserable. In how great a degree the deserted Unitarian preacher (and such are, as it appears, eighty, or more, in every hundred) may sustain his fortitude by abstract meditations, or by distant hopes, is a question we shall not attempt to solve; but, instead of this, we shall examine a little more closely his actual position. And first, for its most palpable item—his pecuniary remuneration.* That his income is small, and that it is incapable of much augmentation, he does not complain of, for this is a disadvantage which he saw distinctly before him when he devoted himself to the ministerial calling, and which he shares with too many of the clergy of all denominations, of whom, perhaps, a majority are very inadequately recompensed for their services; but there are peculiar circumstances attaching to *his* salary which must make him who receives it feel himself humiliated in existing on such terms. Not like the poor curate, or the incumbent, who receives a sum which the law gives him, and who, so long as he discharges certain duties, is as well and truly entitled to his tithe or his stipend as the squire is to his rents; nor like the poor Dissenting minister among the orthodox sects, who subsists, though hardly, indeed, upon the free-will offerings of a needy flock, cheerfully rendered to the man of their hearts; not so; for the pittance on which the children of the Unitarian minister so barely live has been obtained for him—must we not say it, wrongfully?—his income, or three-fourths of it, is derived from the perversion of a testamentary grant. Fifteen shillings in every twenty must burn his palm as he takes them, if he be a man of keen sensibility. The thirty, sixty, hundred pounds *per annum*, which, if it be not the whole of his salary, is that on which his continuance in his place absolutely depends, had been destined, by the puritanic donor, for the maintenance of a doctrine which the man who receives it is always labouring to impugn. Sad position! hard service! The minister who stands in a pulpit under such conditions might well, as he glances at the tablet dedicated to the memory of the munificent

* Written in 1830

dead, imagine that he hears the "stone out of the wall" uttering the reproachful taunt, "He who eateth of my bread hath lifted up his heel against me!"

But we will suppose only (and it is far below the average of instances) that not more than one-third of the Unitarian minister's salary proceeds from a perverted endowment: whence come the two-thirds? Not, as we have said, from the collected pence or shillings of four or five hundred hearers, who, in sparing so much, spare their utmost, but from seven or eight, or a dozen, deep and grudging purses, upon the brims of which a covetousness is written that utterly condemns the Christianity of the holders. Six or eight handsome equipages convey weekly the supporters of the chapel to its doors, but each sets down a grudging contributor to their minister's income. Unhappy man, who pines upon a hundred pounds, in part wrested from the insulted dead, in part wrung from the reluctant living!

We hardly need adduce specific evidence in support of these assertions. Nevertheless, the instances being universally known, we do no wrong in bringing forward a passage or two from authentic sources, which bear upon this point. A Unitarian writer, after affirming that "Unitarians are, for their numbers, the richest body of religionists in the kingdom, and contribute least to religious objects," goes on to say that—

"The full evidence of this assertion is not adduced till it be stated, that perhaps *one-half* of the insignificant stipends paid to their ministers proceeds *from the charity of preceding ages*. We do not, we think, overestimate the amount of endowments in possession of Unitarian trustees. In many instances the *whole* of the salary proceeds from endowments; and though the minister is obliged to unite two arduous professions in order to find the means of a humble subsistence, or, where a school is not attainable, is obliged to live on the very edge of poverty, and, though there is one or more persons in his flock of ample and superfluous means, yet the utmost that is done by voluntary contributions is the raising enough to defray the expenses of opening and cleaning the chapel; and we have known instances in which any extraordinary outlay, arising from repairs or the delivery of lectures, has been subtracted, either wholly or in part, from the minister's pittance. In other cases not the whole, but a part—*generally the chief part* of the tiny sum received by the minister—proceeds from endowments. A *few* instances there are in which no endowment is possessed; and we declare it as our conviction, that the societies where this is the case are in general the most flourishing. And now then, we freely and heartily say, that we wish that all the endowments possessed by our body were irretrievably sunk to the bottom of the ocean. Other denominations, poorer than we a hundred-fold, have them not, and flourish : we have them, and we languish. They have been, they are an *incubus* to our cause, and the orthodox could not do us a greater service than to wrest them from our hands."

SECTION IV.

But we turn to the other side of the Unitarian minister's position. Amid his pecuniary humiliations, can he solace himself in contemplating the success of his spiritual labours? Can he derive, from the manifest efficiency of his ministrations, a consolation which reconciles him to his melancholy lot? He, and he alone, upon the supposition of the truth of the Unitarian system, holds in his hand that potent engine which, a while ago, overthrew temples and ascended thrones, and vanquished the nations. What does it achieve in *his* hands? We put this question to his candour. These are not the days of mystification—these are not the days in which a man may hide facts from himself and from others by vague and unmeaning declamation. We ask, then, the Unitarian minister to tell us, and let him tell us as if he were giving evidence before a dozen plain men, what does he see, within his particular sphere, of the power of the Gospel? Let him answer, first, in reference to the numbers whom he statedly addresses, and then as to the apparent benefit which is derived from his instructions by those that hear him.

Or, if an inference from single instances be disliked, let us look at Unitarianism (this only genuine Christianity) as it stands in the country at large, and viewed as an instrument of national virtue. We ask aloud, Is Unitarianism, with all its chapels, worth, to the people of England, as an actual means of effecting a general reformation of manners—is it worth the revenues of the poorest of our bishoprics? Is it worth the salaries of a score of excisemen? Nay, tell us plainly, is it worth anything? If all the Unitarian chapels in England were let to-morrow for penitentiaries or for warehouses, would the aggregate virtue of the English people exhibit, in the following year, any appreciable deterioration? Indeed, we think not.

How cheerless, then, and how comfortless, are the endeavours of each single labourer, when the worth of the aggregate labour of all is too diminutive a thing to be measured or reckoned! How deplorable is the lot of a man who not only is unsuccessful in his particular sphere, but who, on looking round among his colleagues, far and near, sees ninety of them, out of every hundred, in the same dismal predicament—hopelessly unsuccessful! How shall he defend his bosom against the inroad of the most heart-sickening of all convictions that can smite the human breast—the conviction of toiling through life fruitlessly?

This thriftless labourer meets in society those with whom he set out on the course of life; each is alert (if not all successful) in the pursuit of interests the promotion of which, though private, is the promotion of the commonwealth and general prosperity; but he, although not less well-educated than they—more so, probably— not less intelligent, not less capable of achieving success by energy and talent—he, although perhaps possessing an advantage over his fellows in some of these respects, yet floats for ever upon a stagnant pool, in the waters of which nothing moves—over the surface of which not a living thing will flit! They—the companions of his boyhood, are ploughing, sowing, and reaping; *he* is ever sowing—sowing sterile sands, that are watered only with briny tears of despair! Once in the round of seven days he bends his steps, heartfallen and sick of the profitless usages of devotion, to his chapel. No glistening eyes of the poor and afflicted, whose hearts he is to cheer, watch his approach; no joyous sounds of cordial universal worship are to greet his ear. The few are in their wonted places. Would he were left to indulge his melancholy musings in solitude! He delivers the appointed couplets of "adoration;" of the few worshippers, a few only respond. He reads the Scriptures; but of these one verse in every five shocks his fastidious taste, or asks a crooked criticism, to turn aside the edge of its obvious meaning. He prays: yes, *he* prays; but who is it that joins him? Do not the more knowing of his flock inwardly disallow the solemn impertinence which assumes that there is any efficacy in prayer? None but the simple believe in it. He preaches: he utters—so he says—the soul-wakening doctrine of immortality, stripped of every corruption, and therefore, by necessary consequence, potent to reform the profligate, and to spiritualize the earthly-minded! Preacher! show to the world the roll of your actual triumphs! The week's work is done, the *congregation* is dismissed, and the functionary returns to his home; and, as a *public person*, he feels himself an insulated being. Laden with care, he is a sinecurist, unconnected with the multitude of men either by relationship of secular utility, or by the bond of spiritual sympathy, or by the part he takes in any efficient labours of Christian beneficence.

"The Unitarian"—we quote an authority—"is an insulated being. He stands apart from the rest of his fellow Christians. If he has society out of his own connection, he must seek it with those who believe less, not more than himself: if he wishes to be friendly with the orthodox, he is looked upon with distance: if to join in their benevolent plans, with avoidance: if to rectify their errors, with horror. He can find his way neither to their head nor their heart. The public services of his temple they avoid, as they would a lazar-house. He is cabined, cribbed, and confined on all sides: his days are spent in inaction, and his charities are narrowed by reason of restraint. He is a stranger in a strange land, having a peculiar language, a peculiar spirit, a peculiar creed. . . . . What wonder their compositions and addresses are cold, when the audience is small and lukewarm? What wonder their affections are dull, when the atmosphere in which they live is heavy and sluggish?"

But we are compelled to say a word more of the infelicity of the lot of a Unitarian minister. We suppose him to be, as many of them unquestionably are, a man of benevolence, and a man of intelligence; and he is one who is accustomed to look at the progress and prospects of society in a broad and philosophical light. We ask such a one then in what way he thinks the missionary labours of the present age will be regarded by posterity? Say, that these endeavours to convert the pagan world shall for the present fail, and be abandoned; or say that they shall prosper, and shall actually usher in a glorious universality of the heavenly doctrine; we care not now which of these suppositions is assumed. Take the former; and, if it should be so, will not the men who are now carrying their lives in their hands into the depths of barbarism be reckoned among the most courageous of philanthropists? Will small praise be theirs in the lips of the Christians of distant times? Who dares think otherwise than that, even although their immediate labours should be almost fruitless, the *men* shall be honoured as heroes of mercy? They have done what they could.

But let us take the second, and brighter supposition; and does it seem an extravagant one, that the costly effort which is now in progress for evangelizing the heathen world shall prosper and spread itself, and shall go on conquering, as truth conquers delusion, until all nations have come to bow the knee to Christ? At the moment of the climax of such a success as this, we ask, whether the lot of those who stood foremost in the enterprise, and who sustained the sorrow of initial discomfitures, will not seem to have been enviable ? We ask, whether the men who, on this supposition, may claim to have been the promulgators of a new dispensation of mercy to mankind, will not be named, and be thought of, as among the most illustrious, and the most favoured of the human race?

Fully we believe that, to the eye of future times, the scenes, the actions, the personages of the present evangelical warfare shall stand forward as those scenes, and actions, and personages of the age which are the most worthy to fix the gaze of the men of after ages. And who is it would wish to be altogether severed from the glories and the labours of the missionary work? Not for sceptres, not if the material universe and its flaming suns were the bribe, should a man choose to stand off from the missionary enterprise. Not for an immortality of earthly satisfactions should any one be content, either to confess the guilt of an inward indifference to the missionary work, or, feeling himself alive to its successes, be fettered and held in inaction by the indifference of the party to which he belongs.

But is not this fanaticism? Let him who calls it so come forward and make good his allegation. The hope and the zeal of the evangelical community is not the less built upon substantial reasoning, even if it has become loud and eager.

What part then has Unitarianism in the blessedness of the missionary work? By the missionary work we mean—not the proselytizing at home from other persuasions, but the veritable evangelizing of heathen or Mohammedan nations. A work eminently becoming a great and Christian country; a work from which no *Christian* man, now that it is actually in progress, can be content to stand, either excused or excluded.

"There never was a system," says a Unitarian writer, "which was so general in its regards, which bore so invasive a character, as Christianity in its earliest days. . . . . Every preacher was a missionary, going about doing good, sent, and glorying in his office, to proclaim the acceptable year of the Lord. We are sure, therefore, that the spirit of missions is the spirit of Christ and of Christianity." Or, to use the language of the same writer in another place: "All must acknowledge that Christianity is fitted for proselytizing, for in this way it gained its first and its fairest triumphs. If, then, Unitarianism be, *as supposed*, unfit for this work, it is not the truth as it is in Jesus, and the sooner we are rid of it the better."

So indeed we say. But with this implied inference, significant as it is, we have nothing now to do: we leave it to those whom it concerns. First, for the facts of the case, which are soon enumerated. The Unitarians, by their own showing, are the only holders of "primitive apostolic Christianity;"—of Christianity "uncorrupt, rational, vital." Whatever, therefore, of intrinsic power or expansiveness belongs to the Gospel, must belong, by eminence, to the Gospel when it is thus disengaged from all human additions. Of all forms of the doctrine of Christ, Unitarianism must be the most energetic, inasmuch as it is the most pure; nay, as it is the *only* pure. Moreover, Unitarians possess all the requisites for giving effect and expression to that apostolic zeal which burns in their bosoms. "Latent power," we are told, "they have in abundance; moral character, intellectual worth, and worldly affluence,—none of these things are wanting." In truth, we are assured, with a solemn iteration of the unquestionable fact, that the Unitarians are, for their numbers, the richest body of religionists in the kingdom. And we must say, that if they are not, in fact, the most *numerous*, as well as the most wealthy body of religionists, they have had a fair chance of becoming so, if indeed this had been possible. Why should not "primitive apostolic Christianity" have spread itself in England, during the same years, as widely as Wesleyan Methodism? We cannot tell why: unless we are permitted to say, that Unitarianism is an impotent doctrine.

And now for the result, which we may give, first in general terms, and then in specific details. And in doing so, we shall confine ourselves to authentic Unitarian documents.

Referring to the modern missionary zeal, which, in its substance, our authority applauds, he confesses that "Unitarians have not moved forward with the general mass." "There is a deadness in many of our most useful institutions, a flatness and apathy in regard to religious matters, too frequently prevailing among our lay brethren." Or, to come nearer to the matter in hand:—

"The missionary labours of the Unitarian Association during the last year, must be pronounced an almost entire failure. Three missionaries" (that is to say, *itinerants at home*) "have been employed, and they have been employed nearly in vain. . . . . The missions" (*itinerancies*) "conducted by the young men at York College, have been from time to time diminished, till now they have, with the exception of that to Welburn, little more than a name to live."

Again:

"Throughout the kingdom, the result of the missionary labours undertaken by Unitarians of late, has been a disappointing one. How happens this? Chiefly, we doubt not, because the spirit of Unitarians in this kingdom, is not the missionary spirit. Very many are hostile to missionary exertions, and especially the more rich and influential. The societies that have been and are, have struggled into being, and struggle to exist. They have in some instances been formed by a few, in opposition to the will of the many; while the many looked on in apathy or scorn. The propriety of their existence has been gravely questioned; the overture for aid to maintain them, met with a smile of astonishment; while almost in every instance, those who affect to give the tone to others, and who unfortunately have had but too much influence, have not only kept aloof from, but spoken warmly against them. In a word, the current of fashion has been, and still is, of an anti-missionary hue. Missionary exertions have been denounced as vulgar, as interfering with the harmony and polish of refined and miscellaneous society."

With a singular *naïveté*, after making these ominous confessions, the writer goes on:—

"There may be some who think that the cause of the failure of our missionary labours is to be found in the unfitness for proselytism of the tenets which we hold. If this opinion was well founded, a stronger presumption of the falsity of Unitarianism could not be imagined!"

This may be evidence enough, in relation to our present purpose, but we add a sentence or two, drawn from the same source.

"The institutions that exist among us for the promotion of the great purposes of religion, are few in number, and languishing for the most part in operation. Even the British and Foreign Unitarian Association itself, though so catholic in its objects, so judicious in its exertions, and inheriting from its predecessors—the Fund, so honourable and well merited a reputation, has by no means met with the general and hearty co-operation that it deserves."

"The Gospel, they" (the orthodox) "argue is of infinite value. The Unitarians are sufficiently indifferent about it: little do they to put others in possession of its blessings. How can they duly estimate its value, or have the spirit of Christ? Nay, may they not even disbelieve that which they are by no means anxious to further?"

"In consequence of the want of co-operation, our institutions and our cause want spirit, activity, and energy; and the orthodox look on, and beholding how much we are at ease, how quiescent we each are, how little alive to the success of any object, and especially how lukewarm about the salvation of our fellow-creatures, judge that there must be something radically wrong in our system; a cooling and chilling influence, which breathes not from the pages of the Gospel."

So much for the general statement of the anti-missionary temper of Unitarianism. What are the specific facts which have compelled Unitarian writers to make confessions such as these?

"But the most painful case of failure yet remains to be noticed. India, the first field of our missionary exertions in foreign lands,—India, whose spiritual welfare awakened an interest in the breasts of many of the most enlightened and pious men of America, as well as England,—an interest which exhibited the Unitarian body in the most pleasing attitude that it ever assumed; India, which with the name of its wise, learned, and benevolent Brahmin, gave the fairest promise of an eventual, though perhaps a tardy harvest; this country, which had excited our own hope more, perhaps, than any other spot, America excepted, is now without a Unitarian missionary and the means of Unitarian worship! But we correct ourselves; we do wrong, in so saying, to that excellent and persevering man, William Roberts. We were thinking, in writing the above, of Mr. Adam."

It would be altogether irrelevant to our purpose to adduce the pretty well-known histories of the individuals above alluded to. Let the labours of William Roberts at Madras, or elsewhere, and the defunct efforts of Mr. Adam at Calcutta, carry all the importance that can possibly attach to them, and let them be held available for the desirable purpose of convicting any man of misrepresentation, who shall be so hasty as to affirm that Unitarians have attempted, or are attempting, *nothing* for the diffusion of Christianity among the heathen! Far be it from us to advance any such calumnious predication! By no means; the Unitarians *have* William Roberts at Madras, and they *had* Mr. Adam at Calcutta!

But we turn to an account of an annual meeting of the "British and *Foreign* Unitarian Association," the object of which is the diffusion, at home and abroad, of the unsullied light of rational, liberal, primitive, and apostolic Christianity. From the statement of the treasurer, it appears, that (notwithstanding a "falling off of donations and collections") the "most opulent body of

Christians in England" raised during the year, the sum of "one thousand and odd pounds," for the furtherance of their pious intentions! The expenditure has consisted of—1. The charge for purchasing and printing books, namely, £454 15s. 11d. 2. Upwards of £300 expended on congregational and missionary objects at home; and 3. (let Christendom hear it!) *two hundred and fifty pounds*, on account of the Foreign Fund!

Yet even this large adventure for converting the people of India—rather for diffusing Unitarianism among the *English* of Calcutta, such is the fact—did not escape animadversion as an improper diversion of the funds of the Association from the field where they were more needed. And though the objector allowed, that, the Calcutta mission, having been commenced, they were "bound to endeavour to make the best of it," he was far from admitting, and none of the speakers affirmed, that Unitarians should think of entering boldly as competitors with the orthodox on the high course of foreign evangelization. And yet, why should they not do so? What obstacle stands between Unitarians and the great pagan world? What, unless it be Unitarian indifference? Why would it be imprudent to originate some eight or ten missions to Africa, India, and the islands of the Southern Sea, but because it is utterly absurd to suppose that any such act of religious charity would be supported or approved by the Unitarian body? It is a missionary age, and the missionary spirit is allowed by Unitarians to be eminently proper to Christianity; and yet Unitarians neither go forth to preach the Gospel themselves, nor do they send others!

We are bound, however, to view this matter of foreign missions as it is viewed by Unitarians; and we learn from the highest authority, that Unitarians, while calmly sitting at home in their empty chapels, are wont, with a benevolent easiness of feeling, to congratulate themselves and their party on the successes of orthodox missions! How comfortable a thing it is, if, while others are doing our work for us, we may snore away in seed-time, sure as we are that our friends will give us the jog when the harvest is all ready to be housed! Now this, we learn, is precisely the position of Unitarians at the present moment. The orthodox, in the intemperance of their fanatical zeal, are labouring to convert the world. Yes, but the Unitarians, when the world shall be everywhere converted, are to fill their garners with the sheaves! Hear one of them:—" I see multitudes *doing our work*, whilst they imagine they are acting against us. They are preparing the way for that simple system of Christianity which we profess." In the same enviable temper of undaunted hope, the speaker goes on to comfort himself and his colleagues as follows:—" When I see numbers of churches building throughout the country, my first impression is, how error is supported! But when I look further, I consider that they are all building for us!" By the way, would it not be more seemly for Unitarians to talk of filling their own chapels *now*, than of filling orthodox churches a hundred years hence? Meantime, and while compelled to confess that by far the larger number of their places of assembly are fallen into a condition of " deplorable desolation," the announcement that " all the new churches" are building for Unitarians, is likely to awaken grim suspicions in the minds of shrewd Unitarian laymen—men of the world.

On another occasion the same intelligent and estimable man tells us that " those who have examined the work of Mr. ELLIS on the South Sea Islands, the *Polynesian Researches*, may perceive that in them the principles of Unitarianism are essentially taught!" Let us listen to and digest this assertion. As we must not think of it as an instance of sheer effrontery, it must stand as an example of enormous infatuation. What do we mean when we speak of a man's being driven to a miserable shift? Something surely like this:—A leader of Unitarianism is called upon to make an animating speech at a public dinner; it comes in his way to allude to the missions of the present day: but those around him well know that Unitarians have nothing to do with these Christian enterprises: what remains then for him to say about them? Why this: that the preachers of the doctrine of the Trinity are "essentially teaching the simple principles of Unitarianism?"

Such are the facts. Let them for a moment be viewed in that light in which they will appear to posterity, on the supposition that Unitarianism is Christianity. In that case it will stand on the page of Church history, for the astonishment and scandal of all thoughtful minds—*first*, that the fanatical and deluded professors of a corrupt and idolatrous creed were the men to originate, and perseveringly to carry on, the truly Christian enterprise of turning the nations from their superstitions; and that in this enterprise they were conspicuously recognized and prospered by Heaven. And *secondly*, it will appear, that the only Christians (such in a genuine sense) of this missionary age, were also the *only men* who took no part in the work; that of these "true Christians," the majority openly opposed the undertaking, "looking upon it with apathy or scorn," and "meeting an application for aid with a smile of astonishment;" in such sort that the confession was wrung from the chiefs of the party, that "the spirit of Unitarians" (the only Christians) "is *not a missionary spirit*," and that they are "sufficiently indifferent whether other men and nations partake of the blessings of the Gospel or not!"· These are the facts which are even now going down to posterity. Upon the unalterable page of history it is even now being written, that the attempt to propagate Christianity has been scorned and denounced by the only men of the times who, according to their own account, possess the doctrine of Him that said, "Go ye out into all the world, and preach the Gospel!"

SECTION V.

To insist at length upon the inference bearing against the pretensions of Unitarianism, as furnished by this state of things, is not our immediate purpose. But we say, that the man upon whom the edge of that inference falls, is, if conscious of its force, one of the most unhappy of his species; or, if not, he is one of the most infatuated. We will take up the only two suppositions that the case admits of: either the Unitarian minister is himself indifferent to the propagation of the Gospel; or being zealous for it, he finds himself one of a party that by none of his eloquence can be roused to give him any aid. Take the first of these supposed cases. It is true, that a layman, who has nothing to do with religion but to sit his hour once a week in his pew, may be very tranquil, and very well satisfied with himself, even in the consciousness of an utter destitution of Christian zeal; but it can never be so with a public functionary; nothing can render the weekly performance of religious services before a small and lifeless congregation, by one who is himself devoid of zeal, otherwise than insufferably burdensome;—nothing, or we ought to say, nothing but large or *secure* secular advantages. For the sake, or, to use a phrase proper to a mercantile transaction, for the *consideration* of a *thousand per annum*, or of even two hundred pounds absolutely unalienable, a man may courageously bear himself through the irksome formalities of public worship. Not so the needy man, who, if he displease his employers, may be discharged from his pulpit, and lose his morsel of bread. To such a one, disheartened and anxious, the conscious want of religious zeal in himself, and the sight of the conspicuous inefficiency of his performance, will be enough to afflict him with an unutterable disgust. And a tenfold force will belong to this inward misgiving, in times like the present. We are not misunderstanding the invariable principles of human nature, when we say, that the zeal, and the disinterested activity, and the self-denying diligence, and the gladsome excitement, which are now stirring among the better part of the clergy of all denominations (Unitarians excepted) must press as an adverse power upon the self-condemned heart of the man who feels himself alive to no kindred emotions, and who can take no part in all that is around him. We repeat it, that a minister of religion, consciously destitute of zeal, who might have been contented, or at least tranquil, fifty years ago, can now do nothing but abhor the profession to which he finds himself tied.

But let us look at the other supposition—the case of a Unitarian minister, who, like the writer from whom we have made frequent quotations, feels, in all its force, the unquestionable truth, that Christianity is essentially an invasive, expansive doctrine; he confesses that something, nay, much, must be wrong in its professors, if their spirit be not a missionary spirit; he admits, that those (whatever errors they may fall into) who are actually going forth to preach the Gospel to the heathen, are most happily, most consistently, most nobly employed; he cannot but grant that, though scoffed at by the scoffers of their times, posterity will do them justice, and will call them the most heroic of philanthropists; nay, that Heaven will confess them as its servants; he would fain, spite of the corruptions to which they adhere, take part with them in their labours: he steps forward, but his companionship is avoided; (and it must be so.) Those who are zealously propagating the Gospel of God, their Saviour, will shrink with fear from contact with the impugner of its capital doctrines; (they must so draw back.) Rejected, he turns towards the men of his party. He sees them affluent and well-informed; but, alas! utterly destitute of any motive powerful enough to command labours, sufferings, or contributions in the cause of the Gospel; or worse than this, they are sarcastically hostile to the "visionary and useless crusade of the times." Scarcely one lay Unitarian in a hundred confesses to be animated by a zeal like his own; and nothing could be more preposterous than to hope that the party at large should be moved to bring forward their twenty or fifty thousand pounds yearly, for the support of a religious undertaking. What but an utter despondency, what but an anguish of sorrow, can belong then, in this age of religious zeal, to the zealous Unitarian minister? What can be added to the discomfort of his lot, unless it be the dark surmise which naturally springs from the perplexity of his position, and the faintness which that perplexity forces on his heart? After all, must he be tempted to say, is this Christianity, which proves itself to be potent only when it is corrupted, and which invariably becomes effete when it is pure; is it worth the spending of life, fortune, family welfare, talents, reputation, in its service? Why occupy a life in attempting to purge the feculence of a system, which, whenever it is thoroughly purged, lies motionless as a corpse? Does Heaven indeed demand so large a sacrifice to so little purpose—to *no* purpose? Racking and interminable questions! wretched condition of inextricable doubt! Rather than endure it, it were better to plunge into the oblivious flood of universal scepticism. Pursue but a few steps further the path of disbelief; reject altogether this cumbrous, supernatural scheme, and then, although perplexities enough may still hang in the way, they are no longer the peculiar burden of *individuals*. They darken, indeed, the path of humanity, but they do not rest as a reproach, and a snare, and a curse, upon a single head; they are no longer the scandal of him who, with luckless presumption, has assumed office among men as the interpreter of God.

We have now only to repeat what we have ventured to affirm, that, viewed on every side, secular, professional, and spiritual, the lot of an English Unitarian minister is at this time pre-eminently undesirable; and we affirm it so to be on this ground, that he stands in a false position, and is devoting life, intelligence, acquirements, and many estimable and serviceable qualities, to the hopeless task of upholding a scheme of religious doctrine which makes no way, and which, while it is too incoherent, as related to the Scriptures, to win th

UNITARIANISM IN ENGLAND.

approval of the people at large, is too much entangled with the supernatural to gain any favour with philosophical unbelievers.

In this essay we have spoken of the state of Unitarianism in England—such as it was thirty years ago. In another essay we propose to inquire what changes itself has undergone in this lapse of time, and what has now become its relative position as compared with other religious communities, and with the national progress.

ESSAY III.

NILUS:—THE CHRISTIAN COURTIER IN THE DESERT.

Treasures, convertible to the purposes of Christian edification, as well as of entertainment, are yet entombed in the folios of the patristic literature. But if it be so, why have not these riches been made more generally available for the benefit of the Christian community of these times? This is a question which it is natural and reasonable to ask, and for an answer to which we need not go far. The reader of this Essay, for one, and the writer of it for another, may each of us find it in or among his own prepossessions, his preoccupations— whether theological or ecclesiastical: or let now the reader and the writer be quite candid and confidential— for no one is listening at the door; it is in your prejudice, kind reader, perhaps, and in mine, that we must look for the obstruction which shuts us out from the enjoyment of an inheritance whereupon otherwise we might forthwith enter—an inheritance left to us by our predecessors in the Christian life.

If, in opening the voluminous records and remains of the Christian life of the early ages, I seek to enhearten myself for a labour so arduous as is implied in the perusal of this mass, by help of some new-born zeal in behalf of this or that religious whim, or superstition, or sectarian belief—if I do this, I shall gather, as I go, the chaff—I shall leave untouched the precious grain. Assuredly there *has been* a genuine Christian life in each successive age; but it was not at all the life which I am pleased to think of, and which I am looking for, and which I am resolved to find in my folios, whether it be there or not. It has been a life which was new to each age that has developed it for itself, but antiquated in relation to the following ages, each of which develops its own: it has been a life which we should not presume to call LIFE, if we did not believe it to contain those spiritual rudiments that are unchanging and eternal—that are the same yesterday, and to-day, and for ever;—a life wherewith we may well hold communion now, and into the heart of which we may safely make our way; yet on this one condition, that we put off, for a time, our polemical eagernesses—that we lay aside our weapons and our jackets of iron, and enter, in a subdued mood of mind, as if we were standing and trembling—one foot on the threshold of that general assembly and universal concourse of the faithful of all times which is gathered in presence of the Judge of all.

Let then the reader give me his hand, in a kindly manner, for half an hour or so, and I will do my best to lead him right away into the midst of Christian life—such as it was in the fifth century.

It is true that the materials before us, in this particular instance, are not very ample; but yet they are more so than in many analogous instances; and what is better, they are more *specific* than are most others, and (apparently) they are more genuine and trustworthy than most. In opening them we are not offended by exaggerations and childish absurdities; we are not invited to gaze at a puppet-show of wonders; we have to do with sheer human nature—with its keen sensibilities, with its vividness of feeling, as displayed in times of hope and of fear, and all, powerfully moulded under the energies of a firm Christian belief.

What we gather from his own extant writings, and from the brief notices of contemporary or later writers concerning the personal history of NILUS, is soon reported; it does not need to be condensed.

This good man, to whom we would not choose to apply his conventional designation, "the holy Father and Abbot, NILUS," is reported to have been of noble birth in Constantinople, and to have occupied, as due to his position in society, a high place, opening to him the honours and wealth of public life and official dignity in the metropolis of the Eastern Empire. And this position might be irrespective of his personal qualifications for the discharge of its duties, or even of his individual wishes or ambition. For a time he filled the place of Prefect of Constantinople, but whether this was for years, or only for months, is not known; yet it was a time long enough to confirm him in the long-cherished purpose to release himself from every secular distraction (if such a release might indeed at any price be obtained) and to follow the yearning of his soul toward the peace-giving enjoyments of the anchoretic life, far—far from the haunts of men. It was thus that amidst the pomps and din of the metropolis of the Eastern world, and the barbaric glitter of its court, and the revelries of its effeminate and voluptuous nobles and, moreover, as surrounded by the revolting debaucheries and the hypocrisies of the religious order of those times—it was as thus placed that he pictured to himself the heaven-like delights of the contemplative life—life in the desert—LIFE properly so called ;—the day spent in the shadow of a great rock; by night, a sufficient shelter from the dews of heaven found in a cleft or cavern of the same, or in the cool recesses of an abandoned sepulchre! Holy Scripture his only book and his constant study; the companionship of some like-minded with himself his solace; his few bodily wants, how easily should they be provided for! herbs, and a morsel of the coarsest bread, how content should he be with such fare! and how well pleased thus to dine, and thus to bring himself quite near to the incorporeal liberty of angelic existences! Who, or who that is wise, would not choose, nay, would not earnestly covet, the lot of those who thus pass the appointed days of their sojourning on earth, and thus breathe an untainted atmosphere, and thus make the clear vault of heaven their roofing by day and by night? How much better were this, than to sit long hours, nauseating the sumptuous dainties of royal banquets, in the imprisonment of imperial halls and of hollow ceremonies—a guest in those halls, enchained by the false and irksome usages of rank and office; loving no one; justly suspicious of every one; loved by none; envied by all—might not a wise and Christianly-minded man think the tranquil lot of the life-long captive in the imperial dungeon beneath his feet a happier lot? True it is that the perishing and despicable body of the prisoner is enchained; but then the spirit, how free may it be! The heart is at ease, or may be so ; the tongue also is enchained, entombed in that pit; prayer and praise may arise, where none are at hand to rebuke these utterances of the soul sent heavenward with a force that penetrates the massive vault!

Yes! the prisoner in the dungeon, far down beneath the marbled pavements of the palace, may be envied by him who paces it, laden with the baubles of that false existence to which he is bound. But in truth there is no necessity for making a choice in an alternative so extreme as this; conditions far less severe, are they not at my option? Liberty and life, and the near neighbourhood of the unseen world, may they not be found and enjoyed in the desert? Shall I not then hasten thither? Why postpone this felicity a day? At some spot in the depths of those holy solitudes where the Eternal Majesty awhile ago held converse with His chosen servants, there will I seek, and there shall I find that peace which the world denies, and which, indeed, it has no power to bestow—and does not bestow, even for an hour. So it came about that the courtier, the magistrate, resolved to spend his residue of days—in the wilderness.

Nevertheless, in the way of this resolve there stood opposed obligations which he dared not abruptly violate. He must disengage himself from them by aid of that sort of slow and pain-giving process which we inflict upon ourselves when it happens that the gratification of some wish or taste which, abstractedly considered, we believe to be lawful, or even commendable, is forbidden us by homely reasons of duty and of Christian virtue. The wish, the whim, the taste, crouches, on such occasions, within the soul, silent and motionless, assured as it is that it shall not in the end be thwarted; sure as is the beast of prey of its victim, seen to be now trembling at the cave's mouth. But there must first take place, and with a fair semblance of hones reality, an outside parley with the unwelcome remonstr nces of duty—with the outcry of nature, and with the plain meaning of the Divine law,—so it was with this Christian man at this crisis of his life.

Nilus had a home, as well as a seat among princes; he was a husband and a father. A wife, a son, and a daughter* are not to be thrown off as easily, or with as little compunction, as what he would feel in laying aside his robes of office. Himself and his wife were at this time still in mid-age—so we must infer from the terms which he employs in excusing to himself the resolution he had formed. The separation, he says, was *now* meritorious—it was an act worthy of the Christian athlete; but if it were much longer delayed, what praise could it then deserve? The resolve was therefore formed; and how to carry it out with the least possible expenditure of fruitless feeling was the only question. For this purpose he assumes an aspect of immovable fixedness; his words are few; his tones are those with which he might have been used to pronounce sentence of death upon one from whom he would, mercifully, cut off all hope of pardon. He takes his children by the hand (the son a youth just rising from boyhood), he commends the daughter to her mother's care, and then announces his purpose to depart with the youth for the Arabian wilderness:—a stern purpose, resolutely accomplished. How far it was wisely done it is not now in these pages our business to inquire. Yet it was not done in apathy on the side of the husband, for he was a man of keen sensibility, as appears from the narrative; much less was it submitted to on the part of the wronged wife and mother with indifference. In this instance we hear of

* A *daughter* we must so read the text, and not two *sons* The narrative demands this version

no plea of "incompatibility of temper," which might serve to gloze an immoral act, and to render the parties more than acquiescent in the separation. If the husband felt what a man feels who undergoes amputation, the wife yields to the iron resolve of the husband, and gives him, in floods of tears, her *formal* acquiescence, without which the Church of those times would not have sanctioned the act; and she smothers her fruitless sorrows, and hides her enforced widowhood, with her daughter, in an Egyptian convent.

But now we remind ourselves of our intention in this essay—which is not that of holding up to warrantable reprehension the mistaken notions, the fallacious reasonings, the dangerous, though specious practices of an age gone by. This we do not mean to do; we take the things which we find, whether they be altogether approvable or not so, and we look at them in kindly mood, much as we are accustomed now to think and to speak of the whims and the strange notions of some estimable Christian friend of whom we are wont to say, "I quite disallow my friend's notions, and I smile at his peculiarities; but when I have said this, and I *must* say it, then I will acknowledge that I often admire, and would gladly imitate, his lofty and yet lowly Christian temper, his elevation of spirit, his self-denial, his singleness of purpose, his labours of charity."

Thus it is, then, that we now make acquaintance with our anchoret—once a magistrate and prince. To revert, for a moment, to the initial act of his ascetic course—this separation from his wife. It should first be mentioned that, according to the notions and the usages of the Church of those times, this was the inevitable condition of entering upon the "religious life," either in the anchoretic, or the conventual mode—a final cessation of conjugal intercourse, a renunciation of the domestic existence must be made, or there could be no upper class Christian existence. This being understood, then let us turn aside for a moment, and make search, in our own hearts, for those motives which might, in that age, or indeed in any other, but especially in that age, prompt a purpose of separation. Our hypothesis in this instance is this—that it is *not* a case of apathy, or of mutual weariness, or of "incompatibility of temper," but of vivid sensibility and sincere affection, tender and warm on both sides. This is our *hypothesis ;* and then our *principle* is an uncompromising disapproval of any such dissolution or abrogation of the conjugal union; those reasons—if there be any, by which it might be made to appear in any case warrantable, must be peculiar indeed ; and the exceptive instances must be so rare as to excuse our taking account of them.

The one bright spot on the broad surface of the human system—that illuminated area outside of which, in all directions, things are only in different degrees sombre—is that home circle within which reign love and duty—conjugal, parental, filial ;—and these, blessed, as they may be, by the influence of a vivid and genuine Christian faith. Thus blessed and thus ruled also, the domestic life yields a clearer and more convincing evidence of the Divine benignity than could elsewhere be found, though we were to search the upper heavens for a better instance.

But now let another, and yet not a contrary, deep truth be admitted—for it could avail us nothing to "cloke or dissemble" what cannot be denied: our other truth is this—that the life seen and temporal, and the life eternal are at a jar, and that this jar—this misfitting, makes itself felt most sensibly just when each is at its highest pitch of perfection in its own sense. Abate each of these intensities a little—bring down each to a mean level—a degree or two below the "settled fine" to which each aspires to rise—and *then* the jar is scarcely felt; there is then little or no consciousness of it in those concerned. What we should mean in saying this might otherwise be worded. Take the instance of a husband and wife, each of them affectionate, amiable, wise in temper, and discreet in behaviour; but of a rate of sensibility less than the highest, a devotedness of the heart less than the most absolute, a depth of soul that is less deep than an abyss. Take, at the same time, a rate of religious feeling which, in about the same proportion, is abated or tempered; and *then*, when the life of the present life is ruled and sanctified by the motives and the beliefs of the life eternal, the product is an equal measure of love and harmony; earth and heaven are seemingly all at one; human affections are raised and purified; and the divine life is exhibited in a form that is approvable, and attractive, and edifying.

Why then should we desire anything more than this? Why should we not stop short where the substance of a tranquil happiness may be found? This is not a question that need ever be answered, for it is one that will never be pointedly advanced, except in those instances that, in truth, admit of no answer applicable to the case. Let the sensibilities be as acute and as profound as sometimes they are; and let the conjugal love embrace the entire existence of each, and let it be such as touches the springs of the moral life; and then add to our supposition this countervailing element, namely, an equal intensity of the religious affections—even such an intensity as is daily urging the soul onward toward a fruition of the Divine favour; the powers of the life eternal are so striving within the soul, as at times would seem to render the most costly sacrifice of earthly felicity —yes, the choicest felicity—not merely tolerable, but, may we not say so, a sacrifice, an anguish, to be wished for!

Now, then, we have in view an intelligible solution of what might appear to be a moral paradox. That the selfish, the crabbed in temper, should easily reconcile themselves to the pain of a parting, and that such also should do so who have been trained under a religious system which attributes a false merit to the act, or that such also should do so who live under some modern dispensation of contempt for the law of God—these cases are not perplexing. But can we understand those other instances in which the most intense and genuine affections have been voluntarily rent in two by forces that show themselves to be still more intimate? We seem to catch a glimpse of a state of feeling at the impulse of which a rending like this might actually take place, as a voluntary act.

The apostolic rule, with its implied reasons and its limitations (1 Cor. vii. 5) clearly recognizes, and it allows as warrantable, a feeling which, if we only suppose it to become much enhanced, might bring us to a state of mind such as we have now imagined. That it actually existed in force, and that it did issue in the final separation of loving husbands and wives, is a fact of which the evidences are many, occurring upon the pages of the ascetic biographies, as well ancient as modern. It is more than I would venture to affirm that our NILUS was a loving husband *of this order;* but we should gather surely, from the language of his narrative, the belief that his injured wife was indeed a loving wife, whose keen affections ought to have been respected.

Fully to understand cases of this sort, of which so many present themselves in the patristic and in the Romish devotional writings, we must carry ourselves back to the same times, and endeavour to realize the moral and religious views and motives of that dim transition period. The healthful, the practicable Christian morality of the apostolic writings had, at an early time —as early, certainly, as the end of the second century— blended itself with the spurious oriental doctrine, with its unnatural refinements and its lurid theory of the world, and with its distorted notions of every reality of human existence. This mixture, poisonous in its qualities, and fatal as it was to the spiritual health of those who received it, affected most directly the upper and the educated orders within the Christian community. It was the Christian gentleman, such as our NILUS, and the Christian lady, such as were many " noble women" of the same age, that had wandered beneath the shadow of the Oriental Philosophy, and that, while pleasing themselves in that dimness, lost the ruddy health of better times, and had become pallid, and the prey of whims.

Feelings, and refinements of feeling, which even we— the better taught Christian men and women of these times, may at least recognize and understand, how vivid might they become when they were favoured by the opinions, the feelings, and the usages that were on every side prevalent in the fourth and the fifth centuries! Moreover, there is a peculiarity of those ages which should be well kept in view, and it is this—that the companionable equality of the sexes, which is the proper fruit of the Christian morality, and which is a principal element of our modern European civilization, had little or no place in the ancient and the Greek civilization. No doubt it would have followed in the track of Christianity, had not the course of things been turned aside by the incoming of the ascetic doctrine, and by its pernicious usages. This purifying Christian influence was in fact counteracted at a very early time, and consequently (if very rare instances have been allowed for) the Christian husband did not think of finding a Christian friend, and an adviser, and a help in his wife. The believing wife, on her part, expected no corresponding aid from her husband; but instead of any such healing and sanctifying mutuality in the religious life, the two, although both of them believers, were taught to regard each other, not indeed as *enemies*, but as hinderers of each other's progress on the arduous path of Christian perfection. The next step, where feelings of this kind existed, it was not so difficult to take, as, to us of this time, it may seem. Such husbands and such wives might soon come to persuade themselves that they were acting meritoriously when they said, "It is true that, according to the Divine institution, we are one; but this institution itself is such that it needs apology, and, in fact, do we not feel ourselves to be—in a lofty and spiritual sense—antagonists rather than helpers? Let us then separate, and each, singly and unencumbered, henceforth tread that rugged path which leads heavenward. Farewell! till we meet where all shall be as the angels of God."

If the injured wife and mother, in the instance before us, had desired revenge, which her silent tears forbid us to suppose, she might speedily have found it; or found it, if indeed the story of the sufferings of her husband and son in the wilderness had reached her in the cloister where she hid her life-long grief. Nilus, as it seemed, had too easily persuaded himself that the contemplative life, which he found to be impracticable in the imperial city, might at once and certainly be enjoyed in or among the recesses of Sinai. He should have informed himself better of the state of things in the peninsula; he should have consulted, if not a "Handbook of the Desert," yet some of those lay persons, merchants, or military men, whose views of things were uncoloured and truthful. It was not so, as we must suppose; on the contrary, he had conversed—enraptured, with holy monks lately returned from the Holy Places, and who described to him "life in the desert" in all its purity, simplicity, and cerulean tranquillity; a life how blessed, how nearly neighbouring upon heaven, how ardently to be desired, and how cheaply purchased, although it should be at the price of wealth, honours, and every tie of earthly relationship! so he thought; and thus accordingly he acted.

The holy men of the wilderness, especially those frequenting the Sinaitic Peninsula, congregated themselves so far as this, that they constructed their huts—each one for himself, within the distance of a few paces from those next adjoining. Their time through the week they spent in solitude, but they were wont to assemble on the Sunday within the walls of a church—a building sufficient in its garniture for the celebration of divine service. Having selected a spot where a spring secured for them a sufficient supply of water round the year, they, or some of them, constructed huts of such materials as might be collected in the desert—fragments of rock, and the long grass or reeds found at spots in the wadys. Others betook themselves—and perhaps they made the wiser choice, to the natural caverns of the mountains, within which a better defence against winds and rains might be found, and a more safe retreat when the enemy was abroad. Some of these clefts of the Sinaitic region offered a more even temperature, summer and winter, day and night, than could be found in the most substantial buildings, and which, perhaps, are such as might even now tempt a traveller to make an experiment of—life in the wilderness—for a few days, at least.

There is much uniformity in those descriptions of the anchoretic life which meet us in the patristic records. Yet there are differences. The hermits of the Upper Nile—the emaciated tenants of the sepulchres which honeycomb its rocky banks—had many of them become scarcely human in their style and behaviour; and albeit they were christianized, professedly, yet were they the genuine successors and representatives of a fakir race that might boast a very high antiquity. Some, perhaps many, of the anchorets of Upper Egypt were pitiable beings, who, at moments when persecution raged in cities, conscious of their inability to stand the fiery trial, had fled, and had sought safety where alone, at that time, it might be found. Some, and more than a few of them, were in this plight;—they had lost or broken every social tie; they were outcasts, perhaps outlaws, and they were glad to hide their miseries in a sepulchre.

But if, turning hence, we choose to roam along the shores of the Euxine, and if we stop where a wooded amphitheatre, with its watered slopes—gay and fragrant with flowers, might tempt princes from their palaces—if in such a natural paradise we make search for the holy anchoret—the tasteful and luxurious intellectualist—the Basil of the fourth century—and if there we find him, we shall come to question the propriety of applying one term, or one set of terms, to modes of existence that, in almost every sense, are the contraries, the one of the other.

The anchoretic life assumed a middle aspect throughout those countries which in fact lie midway between the regions we have named. Monasticism, such as we may gather an idea of it from the pages of Ephrem Syrus, or from the personal references to it occurring in the writings of the great theologue of Bethlehem, Jerome, was comparatively a reasonable scheme of religious, or of literary retirement—more regardful of the ends of a secluded and abstemious course, than ambitious of repute on behalf of incredible austerities.

Men who sought something more extreme, more satisfying to a romantic turn than they could find in the monasteries or the hermitages of Syria and Palestine, moved further on toward the Arabian desert, or they boldly struck into the heart of it. So did our Constantinopolitan courtier. The terrific grandeur of the scenery, surpassed by no Alpine area in the world, together with its sacred historic associations, were of that kind which well combine themselves with emotions of religious awe and wonder, and especially with that powerful—that all-powerful impulse of the human mind, to draw itself up toward any point supposed to be near to the world eternal and invisible. Palestine must yield to Sinai in the esteem of those who thus yearn to live, as near as may be possible while in the flesh, to the splendours and to the terrors of the world upon which we are to enter, at the moment when the flesh returns to its earth.

There were anchoretic communities located upon the narrow areas, and within the wadys of the Sinaitic region; but there were also some of the solitaries who, either for the sake of a more entire seclusion, or perhaps of greater security as toward the Bedouin freebooters, lodged themselves in caves or crevices of the holy mountain. It seems that Nilus and his son Theodulus had taken this course, and had become tenants of a nook, high up on the side of the hill. We may be allowed to conjecture that, in removing himself from the resources and amenities of civilization, he had reserved to himself funds or stores sufficient for at least some months of the experiment in this new existence. The tender paternal feeling, of which the narrative gives evidence, would impel the father to provide against the death of this delicate youth, as well as of himself, by absolute starvation.

As to those who constituted the monastic community below, their mode of life or manner of existence was nearly the same as that of which we meet descriptions everywhere in the patristic writings. A few of these recluses—and it was a few only, did not think themselves bound to eschew the use of bread (or of wheaten cakes unleavened); these, therefore, furnished with a rude hoe, and appropriating to themselves a few square yards of the arid surface, found it possible to raise a crop sufficient, each, for his consumption through the winter months: during the summer the spontaneous products of the desert were available and sufficient.

As to the more sternly purposed of the brethren, they condemned, as to themselves at least, the grain upon which cooks and confectioners expend their skill for the pampering of gluttonous appetites. Men of this class—or, as they were called, the athletic aspirants to the "angelic" style of existence—these roamed through the wadys, gathering berries, or searching for esculent roots; subsisting each day upon such as were perishable, and collecting a store of such as might be dried and preserved. So it was, as always it is, that those who aim at extravagances for conscience sake, are, by sheer force of nature, driven into shifts of inconsistency. It is certain that to collect and to dry, and to make a store of acrid berries, is nothing else than a violation of the caution, "Lay not up for yourselves treasures upon earth;" or it is so if, indeed, the storing of wheat in a barn is a violation of that precept. Yet we are now intending to look at the eremitic life not critically, but in a kindly temper. It should be added that (so we are assured) some of these solitaries took food only on Sunday; others, twice or three times in the week; the more feeble, once in the twenty-four hours.

Thus thought of, we may easily believe, as to life in the desert—free and cheaply purchased, and enacted under an Arabian sky, that it might eagerly be taken to, even by multitudes from among our dense populations (if only it were near at hand) as most desirable, when the alternative is the squalor, and the hideous conditions, and the crushing cares of an attic or a cellar in London or Glasgow. Add to the attractions of desert life—to its liberty and its exhilarating atmosphere, a vivid belief of the life eternal—its nearness, its certainty, its splendours, its rewards, its triumphs over cruel persecutors and over Satan and his hosts; and give also to the eremite that which *most* of them possessed in the fourth and fifth centuries—portions of holy Scripture either in hand or in memory—give him these good things, and these solaces, these indulgences—and must we not admit that his lot is such as many of ourselves might think enviable?

The Arabian desert, then as now, and as at all times within the historic period, was claimed as their own by the lawless tribes whose hands are against every man, and who subsist by the sword, and not either by the plough or the bow. In the narrative before us we find the Bedouin of the fifth century depicted, in outline and in colouring, the same being as ever; the difference between the ancient and the modern marauder being that which has resulted from his abandonment of his primeval and sanguinary idolatry, and his acceptance of the faith and the usages of Mahomet's institute. These tribes, at times anterior to their conversion, and to the consequent superinduction of a loftier fanaticism than that known to their fathers, were no doubt more ferocious—probably much more so, than they are at present.

Yet even in those earlier times the Arabian tribes yielded themselves to the control of constituted powers, and their sheiks were able, on their behalf, to enter into treaties of peace with the bordering authorities of the Eastern Empire. Unconquered and unconquerable, they nevertheless recognized the neighbouring states, which, within their proper region, they set at defiance. It appears, moreover, that the monastic establishments existing within the bounds of the desert, such as those in the peninsula of Sinai, had come to act in some mode of useful intervention or mediation between the European and the Arabian populations. On the ground of this mediation, the chiefs pledged themselves to the monks for their secure abode in the wilderness. These treaties were however violated at times, especially when a tribe or gang, pressed by want, surmised that the monks had accumulated a larger amount of winter stores than usual.

Such seems to have been the state of things at the moment when NILUS introduces us to the incidents of his life in the desert. This moment was soon after (we do not know how soon after) the time of his entering upon it with his son.

NILUS, with his son in hand, had descended from his retreat on the lofty flanks of the mountain, intending to pass some time, according to his custom, among the brethren, whose settlement occupied a watered gorge beneath. Suddenly, like a thunderstorm, and without warning, down came rushing upon them a band of these lawless Arabs. It was at the early dawn, and the holy brethren had just concluded the morning service;—the last notes of the hymn of praise had died away. Like famishing savage animals, these barbarians sought for, found, and seized, the whole of the stores of food which the brethren had laid up for the approaching winter. This treasure secured, the ruffians dragged the fathers forth from the church, stripped, and driven like sheep to the slaughter. The senior of the fraternity only, or two or three others, then met their death, giving to the others an example of meek resignation in the endurance of the most savage treatment from these barbarians.

Those of the monks who escaped death hid themselves among the rocks: some were led off prisoners; and among these was THEODULUS, the young son of NILUS. He himself, as he candidly tells us, made his escape. A presentiment of calamity or death had come upon the senior presbyter, who, the evening before this fatal day, when inviting his brethren to their repast, had, with

more than his usual suavity, addressed them in this way:
—"How do we know that this may not be the last time of our all thus assembling around the same table?"

NILUS, we say, had contrived to escape from this slaughter. A rugged path, unused, and which was held sacred, led up from this lower ground to the heights of the holy mountain. By this way some of the monks, and he among them, had sought safety. But how was it that he could thus abandon his son, whom he saw bound and led away, and destined to he knew not what terrible fate—a fate worse than death? The father's explanation of the conflict between his personal fears, the instinctive love of life, and the impulses of parental affection, does not serve to bring him into view as a hero. We must understand him as meaning that his too hasty feet ran away with the reluctant body and the better mind, carrying the entire man in the direction of safety! Those who break themselves away from the ordinary trials of life at the impulse of their personal tastes, and for realizing some romantic conception of unearthly felicity, are very likely to fail on the first occasion that makes a sudden demand upon their manly courage, and their willingness to suffer for the rescue of others. It was no want of sensibility or of affection, in this good man; but there had been a miscalculation of his own moral forces, which had led him into a position in which he failed to do his part. In pursuit of the dream of a hermit's tranquil life, he had rent the ties of natural affection towards a wife and a daughter; but here, in the hour of danger, he runs for his life—he scrambles up a precipitous ascent, while at each turn of the path he looks back, and thence catches a last glance of his son, who is led off by savages!

When at length these bandits had retired with their booty and their captives, and all was again silent and safe in the gloomy wady, the surviving brethren descended from the craggy heights, and hastened—it was before dawn of the next morning—to perform the last offices to the slain. All but one—the senior of the fraternity, had been a long while dead; but he was still conscious, and, it is said, he was able to address to his brethren the quantity of a paragraph, or more, of scriptural consolation. Let us not imagine, said he, that some strange thing had happened to himself and to them. It was the way with Satan thus to ask of God that the faithful should be given into his hand for undergoing an extremity of trial. Think of Job; and think of the exceeding great reward which God has in store for recompensing the virtue of his faithful servants. Thus having spoken, the old man kissed his brethren, and breathed out his spirit. While it was still dark, he and the others were committed to the earth.

The brethren were still on the spot, conferring one with another, when a youth, running breathless, and in extreme agitation, came up. He had been carried away with the son of Nilus, and with him had been doomed to die that very morning. Both were to be slaughtered as victims offered, by the barbarians, to their obscene divinity: he had got the knowledge of their intention—he had seen the horrid preparations which they had already completed—the altar and the fagots. "Unless," said he to his companion, "unless we can effect our escape instantly, we neither of us shall see the light of another day." For himself, he had resolved to attempt it; not so his fellow-prisoner, Theodulus, who, more overcome with bodily fear, and better sustained, perhaps, by religious motives, determined to await his fate, let it be what it might. The other, seeing that the savages were now lost in sleep, after their drunken revels, slipt away, crawling out beyond the bounds of the encampment, and then starting up—his heels winged with terrors, he had reached the place where now they met. How often have a man's pair of heels—so thought this youth—done him a better service in an extremity than a legion of guards could have rendered!

The narrative which follows, and the description of the truculent doings of the barbarians of the desert, and the patience in suffering, and the joy in death of hermits, old and young—these adventures are beside our present purpose. But whether these narrations may be taken as authentically given or not, the descriptions which occur in them of the desert scenery are quite true to fact, and the incidents also are highly characteristic, as well of the region itself, as of the marauding Bedouin manners; only that the wild Arab of that age was no doubt a more savage and sanguinary creature than are his descendants of the present time. For not only has the prophet of Mecca humanized, to a great extent, the rude men of the wilderness, but their relations with surrounding governments have become more intimate, and have had the same tendency.

The instances are not of infrequent occurrence in the ascetic biographies, of those who, in meeting a violent death, suddenly, and at an early age, drew comfort and courage too from this source, namely, that *thus* dying, and *then* dying, the athletic experiment was with them broken off at an auspicious moment. "Death," says a young martyr, "finds me with my vows unbroken, and my virtue safe, and my title to a heavenly inheritance not forfeited. That eternal reward for the sake of which, and to earn which, I have endured years of hardship, and have inflicted upon myself so much suffering, shall all be mine! yes, *it is* mine; and now I go to claim it." A feeling like this is indicated in an instance which here occurs, and elsewhere we find it more fully expressed. Let us say that our modern and our Protestant theology is offended by this language; but let us admit, also, that a life of self-denial and an early death, welcomed on the ground of a full faith in things "unseen and eternal," even though it may involve some doctrinal misapprehensions, should be tenderly rebuked by those whose own dispositions, and whose style of discourse, and whose modes of life give a very ambiguous evidence as to the firmness or the sincerity of their belief of a heaven to come.

The distracted father, informed, to this extent—but not fully instructed as to the fate of his Theodulus, who was in the hands, and at the mercy of savage men, if not already—which, indeed, was the better supposition—slaughtered, gave utterance to the tortures of his heart in loud wailings. He allowed himself to imagine all kinds of horrors that might have attended the last hours of the youth; or in thinking of him—a tenderly trained boy as he was, as now vainly striving to obey the unreasonable commands of a ruthless master;—he is buffeted, he is torn with the lash, he is cut and maimed; at this very moment how might he be uttering fruitless cries, and pleading for mercy with those who knew of none!

In the midst of these lamentations—tearless, for he could not weep—NILUS was at once silenced, and was put to shame, by the more masculine, and, as he thought, the more Christian-like behaviour and language of a woman! The incident, even although we should strip the narrative of its theatrical and rhetorical decorations, is quite characteristic of the times with which just now we are conversant; and in truth, even in its tone of exaggeration, it brings before us a very significant point of difference between the Christian feeling of the fifth century and that of the nineteenth. With us, of this time, the vivid belief of "an inheritance incorruptible, undefiled, and unfading—reserved in heaven," has become commingled in all possible modes of indefinite speculation, and of iterated formalism, and of unmeaning sentimentality, with that utter non-belief in any such futurity which we find around us. Who shall say, even as to his own habitual states of mind, when he looks beyond the last hours of his earthly course— who shall say how far the atheistic indifference of those with whom, through life, he has been conversing daily, has availed to thicken that cloud which the eye of faith would penetrate?

It was not so—it was far otherwise with our Christian predecessors of the early ages. With them—or with those of them who were sincere, simple-hearted, and devout—with such persons, the hope of the Gospel—the hope of a blissful resurrection of the body— the well-defined immortality that had so lately been brought to light by Christ (or had been brought to the light) held its entireness—its clear and palpable integrity, free from all abatements, from all admixtures with contrary doctrines or beliefs. That which the believers of those early times saw ranged in opposition to the Christian idea and hope of the life eternal—that which the believing men, and women, and children of those ages looked at as confronting them—the host that mantled the mount Ebal of that age—was the foul and the foolish paganism of the bygone ages of ignorance. It was therefore, as aided by a contrast so forcible as this, and so unambiguous, that the Christian confessors of the martyr times met so well a fiery death: and it was the same divine faith, perpetuated and sent forward through a century or two, that served to give vitality to the ascetic community, or to those of this class whom we may think of as worthy of our sympathies. But we return to the narrative before us:—another aspect of the same subject will present itself in the course of the following Essay.

The widowed mother of the youth whom we have just referred to, and who had met his death joyfully, though inflicted with tortures, was near at hand where these surviving hermits were assembled. When she heard—and heard in all its details—of the martyr-death of her young son, she uttered no lamentation, but, retiring awhile, she put on her jewels and her gayest attire, and, returning, stood forth as if joyous, prepared to take her part in some festal ceremony. Lifting her hands to the heavens, she addressed her Saviour God in language of thanksgiving—language which, if it were more brief than it is, and also less rhetorical, would inspire a greater confidence than it does in its authenticity. But whether it be strictly authentic, or too much enlarged and decorated, it may be taken as characteristic of the style and feelings of the times. This Christian mother had dedicated the youth—her only son, to the Lord; and now she received with exultation the evidence that the trust had been accepted, and that the obligation was fully satisfied. The youth—all entire as he was in his vows—his continence—his athletic virtues, had fought the good fight of faith; he had met the enemy, and he had conquered; and now she, his mother, might think herself a sharer in his triumphs. With his pure and faultless soul he has gone up to the fruition of joy. " His death is also my reward—his wounds are my crown. My son, if thy body had found room for more stripes than were inflicted upon thee, so much the more would have been thy recompenses; grant me then, give me back a portion of thy reward, in payment for the pains I endured at thy birth!" She claims to share his glories and his rewards; she had suffered on her part, he on his; he had endured extreme, but brief tortures; she, in thus vanquishing the maternal instincts, and in thus compelling herself to hear unmoved, as a mother, the recital of his death, had endured a worse pain; and hers must be a lasting anguish. " I am inwardly rent, I am torn, I am tormented, and must endure these pains so long as I live. Not such a mother am I as are the multitude of women, who, in losing their offspring, are wont to make the air ring with their lamentations; they—weeping at the death of a child as if they were the mothers of the bodies only—the limbs, the flesh, the blood! all *their* thoughts are centred upon earth, and its cares, its pains, its hopes; no wonder, therefore, that in this their ignorance of a better life, they thus bewail their loss—for it is the loss of all. It is not so with me; am I not the mother of the soul? I do not rend my garments; I do not tear my naked bosom and my face with my nails; I do not pull out my hair by handfuls! Thou livest, my son—livest with God, to die no more; and with thee shall I also live, soon as this frail body falls to earth. Happiest of mothers am I, who have borne so noble an agonist, and have thus returned him—whole and triumphant—to God!"

We thus briefly render the purport of this Spartan mother's long apostrophe to her martyred son;—to give it more at length would not be serviceable. There is, however, one suggestion which we should not omit to gather from it. If, indeed, it were a solitary or a rare instance, the inference we have in view would not be warrantable; but, in fact, this episode in the narrative of NILUS is one of a kind of which the instances frequently occur in the records of the early ages. By this time, and, in truth, at a time much anterior to this, Christianity had wrought its effect with great power upon the mind and character of woman, and it had effectively and for ever lifted her from her abasement, and had placed her in her due position of spiritual equality with man—if not of companionship. The first requisite in that renovation of the social system which the Gospel was to bring about for the world, is—the moral equality, and the rightful influence of woman;—an equality and an individual development of mind, and an energy of the purest affections, which forbid the degradation of the sex, either in the oriental manner, or in that of ancient Greece, and which, irrespectively of prohibitions or of decrees of Councils, renders polygamy impossible wherever Christianity prevails. In the next following Essay the same subject will again come into view, and we now pass it; only saying this, that, little as we may relish the declamatory style or the vaunting tone of this Christian widow on this occasion, and open as her harangue may be to criticism, on the score alike of good taste and of sound theology, this is certain, that a bright and firm belief of the immortality which is set before us in the Gospel had so become a fixed habitude of the female mind within the Christian community, as to give to the weaker sex that one counterbalancing element of power, in relation to the stronger sex, which is compatible with its gentleness, with its style, with its characteristic qualities, as feminine. Emboldened, and yet not made bold —strengthened, but not rendered masculine—by the vivid consciousness of her individual relationship to Christ her Saviour, and by the bright assurance of immortality—woman—the Christian wife, mother, sister, daughter—now surrounds herself with a nimbus of the light of heaven, without any compromise of those graces which are her own, as the grace of this world; and so long as she understands her place, and is worthy to fill it, the truth has a threefold weight of meaning when applied to the Christian woman—that godliness is to her indeed " a great gain."

The remaining adventures of NILUS in the desert are soon told, if we note only such facts as seem to be characteristic of the time. We have said (p. 115) that this narrative is free from those offensive admixtures of miracle which so much disparage most of the patristic writings of the fourth and following centuries. Greatly has NILUS the advantage in this respect, when he is put in comparison with Jerome, and even with Augustine. We need not specify, as an exception to this praise, what he affirms concerning the bodies of some of the monks who had been slaughtered by the barbarians. As to some of them, he says, that five days had elapsed since their death, and yet that no sensible corruption had taken place; there was no effluvium, no discoloration, nor had the bodies become a prey to beast or bird. He says that one of those who were mortally wounded still survived; if so, then others might only recently have expired, and the survivors might have been able to keep at bay the vulture and the jackal. Be this as it might, this is certain, that some of Nilus's contemporaries, the writers of ascetic memoirs, would not have been content with affirming the *mere fact* of the integrity of these sacred corpses, but would, moreover, have assured us that exquisite perfumes floated on the breeze far and near around them, and that a hovering effulgence had guarded the dead from the beast and the bird. The absence of any such decorations in this instance affords us a reasonable ground of confidence as to the general truthfulness of the narrative.

It was contrary to existing treaties, as between the Christian recluses and the Bedouin sheikhs, that the brethren had been thus ill-treated; the marauders were in fact lawless bandits; and their violences, when made known to the chief who claimed authority over them and over the district, called forth an utterance of his wrath and his grief. In the end, reparation, so far as might be possible, was made to the survivors, who were kindly received by the chief. In reaching his quarters, an eight days' journey, often reckoned at twelve, across the desert, was to be undertaken, in the course of which the usual suffering from thirst was to be endured. At length, when all were near to perishing—men and beasts, the nearness of water is announced; there is a rush forward toward it; there would be a scramble when it was reached. Nilus, not less eager than his companions to slake his thirst, yet would not compromise the gravity and dignity of his deportment, by quickening his pace so far as to derange his costume. Not too old to run with others, if he had pleased to do so, he was too regardful of sacred decorums to attempt it. Nevertheless, and notwithstanding his well-measured paces, he was the first to catch a sight of the pool or well. In ascending a hill he beheld the object of desire, but saw, with dismay, a party of wild Arabs crouching around it. The travelling party soon came up, and then the question was, which company should run for their lives? A few moments of hesitation, and these barbarians, measuring the array of the party, snatched up their arms, left their provisions, and made off. What rejoicing, what libations, what feasting now ensued!

Thus refreshed, the journey's end was soon attained; and after a brief suspense and an eager quest—this way and that, in the crowd, the father and the son met each other's glance, and were locked in each other's arms. The youth had been spared and redeemed, and had now found the kindest treatment, and position too, among Christian men.

But in the midst of his joys, did not the father reproach himself for all that his son had endured? He did so. Why had he brought this boy away from the security and the good things of the city, the place of his birth, where no thought of danger, or of disturbance, or of want ever troubled him, to take up his comfortless, precarious abode in a howling wilderness, the haunt of lawless and savage men? Why indeed, we may well ask, had a tender father done this? and why, though he does not put this other question to his conscience, why had he forsaken his public duties, and rent his domestic ties? We can only say, in answer, that when religious motives come in to lend their force to personal whims or to romantic fancies, there is no extravagance in conduct which we may not look for as the consequence of such a combination.

It is soon demanded of the youth, Theodulus, that he should recount his adventures from the dark hour of the barbarian onslaught to the present moment. This narrative may be reported in substance, shorn of its embellishments, as follows: The young man excuses himself from repeating what the companion of his captivity had already related, or how it was that the two were awaiting their fate, all things ready for a foul immolation to be effected before sunrise; the altar, the knife, the libation, the incense, the cup—all was ready; nor was a rescue from their fate to be expected unless God should come in to the help of the helpless. Escape by flight might be possible, but how uncertain, with these savage men around them on every side, and in the depth of an unknown wilderness, which was outstretched between them and any place of safety. One who should attempt to find his path over the hard, pathless rocks, needed, not so much human skill, as a power of divination. Yet the one of these youths, venturous and active, made his choice for flight; the other, as he says, broken in spirit, threw himself upon the earth, and there looked for a ray of hope, if it might be found, in thought and prayer.

"While we are in security, and address ourselves to prayer, how does our foolish mind take its circuit among the things of life! What images court the idle fancy! Ideas of trade, and voyages; we are building houses; we are planting groves; we are contracting marriages; we are actually married; we set out on expeditions; we think of gains, of judgments, markets, courts, thrones, officers; we avenge ourselves upon our enemies; we meet our friends; we join in festivities; we exercise public functions, and we manage our home affairs; ay, and we fancy ourselves seated upon the throne of imperial power! Yes; but it is otherwise in the dark hour of danger and dismay. In such an hour the stern aspect and pressure of some extreme calamity drives the soul in upon itself;—thought is digested—it runs no more astray. In submissive tones we address our prayers to God, even to the Almighty, who in the midst of the most desperate sorrows is able, as with a nod, and in the twinkling of an eye, to bring in deliverance for us! To Him did I then make my humble supplication." This prayer, as we find it reported or manufactured, has its eloquence; but the one characteristic which we note, just now, is the readiness, the copiousness, and the pertinence of the scriptural references which make up the body of it. A well-taught youth, in these days of the Bible, would not, in this respect, excel this Theodulus of the fifth century. Wander as they might, our Christian predecessors of that time were thoroughly conversant with holy Scripture; and they paid it all respect, and they appealed to it, and to no other authorities.

The companion of Theodulus had trusted his life to his bodily powers. "He has put his trust in his heels: I put my trust in the Almighty: let it not seem, in the event, as if his confidence were better than mine!" The youth was thus praying, with tears and cries, when the barbarians suddenly awoke, and, to their dismay, beheld the sun already risen! They had overslept themselves; the canonical hour for the intended sacrifice was gone by; and besides, there must be two victims, but one had escaped, and where was he? None could say. Then did the spirit of the youth return to him; God had come down for his deliverance, at least for the present moment, and he might behold the light and breathe the air of another day. To no further violence was he then subjected, but was carried to a neighbouring town, and there offered for sale. "No one would give my price; none thought me worth more than two gold pieces!" The Arabs threatened to cut off his head at the next moment, unless some of the bystanders would give them their price. At length a kind-hearted somebody risked the bargain, and thus Theodulus is saved. He is rescued from death, and from slavery too, and is cherished with Christian kindness.

The father, during the days of his anguish and uncertainty as to his son's fate, had "opened his lips to the Lord"—if only he might be restored to him, promising, on his own behalf and his son's, that thenceforward he should be the Lord's. The son, on his part, cheerfully assents to and seconds the purpose of his father, even, in like manner, as the virgin daughter of Jephtha had submitted herself to his rash vow. But now this obligation might be fulfilled in a mode less appalling, and more accordant with the spirit of the Christian system. The ascetic vow would fully satisfy the conditions of *this* dedication.

Then follows what is curious in itself, and is indicative of those unwarranted refinements which had come in along with the ascetic philosophy:—there here occurs a generous parley between father and son, the purport of the altercation being, to make an equitable assignment of the merits and the recompenses that had been severally earned by the two, in passing through the sufferings and the trials of this season of affliction, and in doing what remained to fulfil the conditions of the vow.

In the first of these Essays we have protested against the undue intrusion of logic in theology; and here we might find fair occasion for protesting against the intrusion of what may be called arithmetic in the same. So are the notions and religious usages of successive ages seen to sway from one extreme point to the opposite! If there be fruit to be gathered from an acquaintance with the revolutions of opinion in past times, it will greatly consist in what we learn when we collate the swervings of the human mind in one age, with its swervings in another age.

At length NILUS and the young Theodulus found the means of squaring their accounts with each other, and with heaven. The good bishop into whose hands it had been their happiness to fall, besides his immediate hospitalities, offered them aid in their journey, if they should decline his invitation to abide with them. Moreover, he overcame the diffidence and the scruples of NILUS, who at length consented to receive priest's orders at his hands.

In one of the many religious houses which had lately been founded in the desert, westward of the Nile, and around or near the Natron Lakes, the father and the son sought and found what they now knew could not be secured in the peninsula of Sinai, overrun as it was by lawless hordes. In taking this more reasonable course there was, indeed, a compromise to be submitted to; the romance of the eremitic life must be abandoned as impracticable; and instead of it there was to be quietly accepted the non-romantic monotonies, the personal restraints, the imposed rules and forms of a monastery, as well as the annoyances of a life-long imprisonment with a company of persons collected from various quarters, and themselves of various moral quality, whose waywardness, and humours, and infirmities, and even—incurable vices, must be borne with; and all this must be endured within the narrow and gloomy limits of a religious fortress, in the heart of a scorching wilderness.

Nevertheless it was here, and as abbot, and as writer, that Nilus found, or made for himself, as an energetic spirit will not fail to do, the highest and the choicest earthly good:—it was not meditative quietude—it was not that spiritual luxuriousness which at first he had aimed at;—but it was a field, and a large field, of useful Christian labour.

Of what sort chiefly these labours were, the extant writings of Nilus give us sufficient evidence; or perhaps, without indulging too far in unproved conjectures, we might say that, just now, we have evidences of another kind under our eyes. Within these few years past the stores of the British Museum have been enriched by inestimably valuable manuscripts, recovered from the forgotten heaps of the monasteries of the Natron Lakes. A precious sample of these treasures—just given to the world, and consisting of fragments of the Gospels, of high antiquity, may fairly be looked at in the light of its probable connection with the subject of this Essay. Nilus, himself intimately conversant with holy Scripture, and holding it in profoundest veneration—himself also a man of learning—a disciple of Chrysostom—such a man, when he found himself at the head of a Nitrian monastery, and looked up to as the adviser of the monks of the monasteries of the district, would he not promote, with his utmost zeal, those labours of transcription which already were carried on in these religious houses? We can believe nothing less than that it must have been his delight—his recreation, to visit the rooms where the copyists were at work, and to cheer and superintend their labours. Be it that, in saying this, and in believing this, we advance more than we can make good by positive evidence. From the ground of these surmises we turn to the extant writings of our NILUS—abbot of one of these monasteries.

At the moment when, as we have said, the Prefect turned himself away from the turmoils and the pomps of the imperial city, his only thought was that of entering upon the delights, so pure and so tranquil, of a stony paradise in the solitudes of Sinai. But from this dream he was rudely awakened, as we have seen, at an early time, by an onslaught of real perils, real sufferings and privations, and of real griefs and cares. Yet this schooling yielded to him, in due time, much of "the peaceable fruits of righteousness." NILUS, as is manifest from his writings, had become familiarly conversant with holy Scripture; he had also listened to Chrysostom; he had deliberately made his choice as between this world and the next; and now, having at length learned what he had needed to learn in a course of suffering, and having convinced himself that his first project was impracticable, he betook himself to that mode of the ascetic life which he found to be best suited to his habits and his strength, and also more likely to allow of his making himself useful to others.

In his position as abbot he became known, far and near, as an experienced, and a wise, and faithful guide in the exercises of the religious life. Many had recourse to him in this capacity—some by personal intercourse, and many by letter. To these he replied in a brief, pointed, and pertinent style; and a sample of these "answers to correspondents" fills a folio volume. More than a thousand of these epistles, addressed to more than seven hundred individuals, persons of all orders—monks, deacons, presbyters, bishops, abbots, and secular persons—are in our hands: we are assuming this collection to be genuine.

This good man found leisure, moreover, for composing various tracts and treatises, longer and shorter, most of them, as to their immediate intention, relating to the motives and the practices of the ascetic life. These also are of quantity sufficient to fill—version and notes inclusive, a bulky folio. These various compositions give evidence of the writer's deep-felt and unfeigned piety, his keen good sense, and his correct judgment in questions of conduct and temper; of his independence also, and his plain-spoken faithfulness, and of his knowledge of holy Scripture, and also of the world, and of human nature. As to his asceticism, we hold it to be a mistake, but it was the fashion of the times, and just now we take no account of it. What we do take account of is that which is no fashion, or whim, of any one age, and which is wholly irrespective of the rise and fall of religious parties, and of those fortunes and misfortunes of the Christian commonwealth wherewith the passions and the ambition of the foremost men of the age were concerned, and which fill out the bulk of what is called church history.

The extant epistles of Nilus were (as we have said) addressed to more than seven hundred individuals, and these persons, or most of them, were either the inmates of the neighbouring religious houses, or they were men in secular offices, or they were the clergy of the churches of the surrounding districts or provinces. To some of these he administers rebukes with the utmost freedom, and even sharpness, and yet with discrimination; to the nugatory questions of some he returns a few lines of pertinent reply. Some of the epistles are of little or no value in any sense; but after setting these off, there remains a large number, perhaps the greater number of the whole, that administer spiritual advice to religious persons who had sought it from him in humility and sincerity.

What is it, then, that we ought to infer from these letters of advice? It is this: that in an age of widespread disorder, an age of theological contention, of shameless ambition among churchmen, and of growing superstition, there were *many*—there were more than here and there a one or two—who, in the obscurity and silence of monasteries, and also of private life, were cherishing that life of the soul which is the true beginning on earth of a blissful immortality, and who, with conscientious carefulness, were striving to bring their dispositions and their conduct into conformity with the mind of the Saviour Christ. And now let us ask what it is among the interests and the occupations of this brief and troubled life that ought to be thought of as real, and substantial, and good; what is it that, after a long experience of the things of life, and an enjoyment, too, of many of its delights, what is it which we come to think and to speak of, to those who will listen, as indeed worthy to be sought after and desired—what, but those dispositions, those affections, those tempers, and those courses of behaviour which, under the Divine discipline and guidance, are the fruit of daily assiduity in the religious life?

Dark ages, or bright ages, and through times of sluggish movement, and through times of progress and energy, and while the visible course of the world's affairs is prosperous, and while it is tempestuous, and let church historians make a good report, or let them make an ill report of " a century," still it is always true that a host of souls, unreported of in any chronicle or census, even a " great multitude" of human spirits, is in training for their places in a kingdom that is not of this world.

ESSAY IV.

PAULA:—HIGH QUALITY AND ASCETICISM IN THE FOURTH CENTURY.

As a test of the quality of the Christianity of any age or people, or of any small community, we might take this indication of it—namely, the bearing it is seen to take upon the relative position of the sexes. We are told that "in Christ," that is to say, under the Christian dispensation, and when this is in its genuine condition, there is "neither male nor female;" and inasmuch as the sacred proprieties of the domestic relationships, and the duties and offices of husband and wife, parents and children, masters and servants, are very carefully insisted upon throughout the apostolic writings, this must mean —not that duties and decorums are forgotten, but that there is a higher and a spiritual sense in which all those differences and all those inequalities which attach to the present state are merged and cease to be appreciable, as related to those unchanging realities which belong to the life eternal.

If this be the meaning of the apostolic rule, then we may conclude it to be certain that, whenever and wherever the Christianity of a people so takes effect upon the male and the female halves of society as to divorce and disjoin them religiously, or in respect of their highest and their spiritual welfare, such a system, or the so-called Christianity of a people, has got out of course; as, for instance, if the so-called Christianity of a people is such that it secures the attachment of few except the women, the children, the infirm, and the aged; and if it is almost exclusively, as towards these, that the ministers of religion are required to exercise their functions, while adult males, with rare exceptions, stand aloof from it, either in indifference or in contempt; if things be so, there can be no room to doubt that the substance having long ago been lost from the people's "form of godliness," a specious exterior is all, or nearly all, that now remains to them. Or if, to take up a very different, or an opposite supposition, Christian belief, in its power, so takes effect upon the male and the female mind as to sunder that which "God has joined together," then, and in such a case, a deep-going error, whatever it may be, has commingled itself with principal truths, and consequently that much confusion has been let in upon the social economy, and upon the domestic relationships. Thus it was in the times which just now are under our notice: to what extent it was so we may best see in taking up single instances, or such instances as are reported to us authentically, and with sufficient amplitude.

Yet let the reader understand what is my purpose in this Essay, which, as in the last, is this, that while we note errors *incidentally* as we go, we aim to bring out to view whatever is true, and true alike in every age, and which is, or may be fruitful of instruction, to those who will think so, in all times.

What has been advanced in the preceding Essay concerning the simple-hearted NILUS has been gathered from his own narrations, and from his extant letters, and from his other writings; but now we have no choice but to sift a laudatory memoir, in dealing with which we must discharge a mass of magniloquence and affectation. It is the learned and the facund Jerome who is our authority. While at Rome he had become known to more than a few Christian ladies of quality, toward whom he acted as their spiritual adviser. With some of these ladies he maintained correspondence after his retirement to Bethlehem; and some of them followed him to Palestine, and established themselves in religious houses not remote from his monastery. Among these was the high-born and illustrious lady, the " PAULA, saint, and widow, and abbess," as we find her named in the Romish and Eastern calendars.

Picked from out of some half-dozen of Jerome's epistles, the biography of this lady-ascetic is briefly this:— By parentage and by marriage also she stood related to the ancient aristocracy of Rome; the great historic names of the republican times shed a splendour upon her house: so we are told. Ample revenues, moreover, were hers: —Nobilis genere, sed multo nobilior sanctitate: potens quondam divitiis, sed nunc Christi paupertate insignior. And we must infer that the family estates or revenues, or a large portion of them, instead of having been surrendered or alienated when she retired from the world, continued to be at her disposal, for to the last she was a builder of churches and a founder of monasteries.

PAULA, rich and noble, had married early. Her husband, as rich and noble as herself, had died, leaving a son and four daughters to the care of their mother, herself still young. Of these daughters one, named Eustochium, has taken a place in the saint-list of the Churches, and is known especially as the disciple and the favoured correspondent of Jerome. She was a lady so learned, that this great writer did not hesitate to address to her some of the most important of his critical and ethical writings. At the time when she lost her husband, PAULA was, in mind and habit, in and of the world: her widowhood dated from her thirty-second year. This sharp affliction threw her into the society of a "holy widow" and a severe ascetic, then highly reputed in the Christian circles of Rome. Yielding herself to the guidance of this friend, she sought and found an assuagement of those griefs that are earthly only, in an absolute dedication of herself, body and soul, to God—a vow, made in conformity with the fashion of the times. This dedication implied, first, a vow not to contract a second marriage; and then the adoption of those austerities to which so much merit and importance had come to be attached in the opinion of the ancient Church.

Rome was, at that time, as always it has been, a centre, visited by holy bishops from far and near; and so it happened that the wealthy PAULA (such things do not belong exclusively to one age, but meet us in every age) thought herself only too much honoured, and the most happy of women, when these reverend persons condescended to be her guests. In converse with some of these (among them was the noted Epiphanius of Cyprus) she had listened, with intensity of feeling, to glowing descriptions of the holy places of Palestine, and the neighbouring Bible countries. Her enthusiasm had become inflamed; and her longing desire to set foot upon the sacred soil, and to kneel at altars, and to kiss footprints, had risen to a pitch of irresistible impatience. The passion for pilgrimage had become so strong that no obligations, no natural ties, no maternal instincts, could restrain it: it had possessed itself of her soul.

Some of the holy bishops with whom she had conversed, and who had been her guests, were now returning to their sees in the East. The zealous polemic, Epiphanius of Cyprus, was about to do so. PAULA took her passage in the vessel in which these bishops were about to embark. Her near relatives, and her surviving children, attended her to the water's edge: her son, still quite young, and conscious of his need of a mother's care at Rome, clung to her, and, with floods of tears and loud entreaties, besought her not to desert him; or at least to delay a little while the rending of this tie. But the Roman lady—the descendant of heroic patricians, is of firmer mould of mind than to be thus turned from her purpose; a young mother's eyes are moistened by no tears while she looks heavenward, and, stifling nature, obeys, as she thinks, the call of heaven—illa siccos tendebat ad cœlum oculos, pietatem in filios pietate in Deum superans. But why should she not read the will of heaven where it is written in THE BOOK—written plainly enough? Yet just now we keep another purpose in view, and are not intending to find fault, but to find Christian energies. Auspicious winds filled the sails, and the heights of Cyprus soon came into view. PAULA and her daughter, Eustochium—and she, with her new vows upon her, and both of them dead to the world, as they thought (in intention they were so) and cut off from its gentle affections, set foot on the island where churches and monasteries had everywhere supplanted temples.

After a short stay with the holy bishop, the mother and the daughter—or, as we should now say—the two "sisters," the elder and the younger—embarked anew, soon to set an impatient foot upon the sacred shore of Palestine. We should gain little of entertainment, and little of edification, in following these ladies, as they passed from spot to spot throughout Palestine—Jerome their guide, or at least the learned expositor, and the journalist of the tour. At Bethlehem, near to him, she at length fixed her abode. For three years it was in a roadside public-house—angusto per triennium mansit hospiteolo—but afterwards she established herself in a commodious monastery, which she had caused to be constructed near at hand, and into which many devoted women were in course of time admitted.

In her journeys throughout Palestine, and in her frequent visitations of the religious houses and the hermitages, far and near, in Egypt and in the Arabian desert, this Roman lady, who heretofore had been wont to travel in a luxurious palanquin, borne on the shoulders of eunuchs, was content to ride upon an ass; and she did this under the fervours of the sun of Syria and of Egypt. Before her departure from Italy she had adopted, and had learned to endure, those austerities which were the conditions and the characteristics of the "ascetic philosophy." We are assured that from the moment of her vow she never sat at table with a man— no, not even a holy bishop—nor ever spoke with any man otherwise than in public. She eat no meat; she abstained from fish, eggs, honey, and wine: oil she used only on holidays: she lay upon a stone floor, with a sackcloth mat. Her time was spent in prayer, in almsgiving, in visitations of the sick; and at length in the government of the religious societies which she had established. In these houses the strictest discipline was observed; the seven times of devotion were punctually regarded; the Psalter, entire, was daily recited: the dietary was of the very simplest kind, and the fasts were severe and frequent. All the nuns wore the same sombre habit, and all took their turn in performing the menial offices of the house. In a word, the ascetic regimen, which in all times has been very much the same in its visible aspect, and in its severities, was, in this instance, if we may take the extant records of it as our trustworthy authority, fully realized.

We have already said that this Roman lady retained her patrimonial wealth: it must have been so; for in addition to extensive almsgiving, practised in and around her establishments, she built churches and monasteries, very many; and in doing so she gave evidence of her consistency and her good sense, for she excluded all costly decorations from them. The church, or the monastery, was so constructed, and was so furnished, and so embellished, as that it should best subserve its professed purposes, namely, the promotion of piety, and the welfare of the indigent. Thus occupied, and thus living in earnest, according to the light of her times, she passed about twenty years in her seclusion at Bethlehem, and there she died, a pattern of Christian assiduity and of *unity of purpose*—living a life on earth which in all things was intended to secure the life eternal.

With what belongs exclusively to the religious fashions of the times we have nothing now to do; but we have this to say, that although it was not in the intention or the thoughts of the Christian men and women of the ascetic ages, a moral process was then in course, to trace which, from its commencements, we must look back from the fifth century, five hundred years. This was a process which, even now, has not quite reached its completion; for it shall then only be complete when Christian principles and Christian moralities shall thoroughly have taken effect upon the social system—that system being moulded chiefly by the influence of Christian women—women in their sphere—not out of it.

A page or two may suffice for setting forth what we here intend.

If five hundred years be reckoned back from the times now in our view, they bring us into the scenes of that critical time when a right-hearted few among the Jewish people were nobly contending for Great Truths with the ferocious Antiochus. It was then, and it was then *first*, that these great truths—even the main matters of the "law and the prophets," came to be sealed in blood upon the national mind; and it was then also that a glimmer, and more than a glimmer, of a bright immortality, had come to shine upon that mind. But it was then also that another consequence of the struggle—most deeply touching the well-being of the nations that ages afterwards were to become Christian—rises to view on the stage of religious history. It was in the course of that same cruel conflict that Woman first made good her title to be regarded as man's companion, and as quite his equal in moral greatness, in courage, in constancy, and in consistency: it was then that "out of the weakness" of her sexual disparity she not only became "strong," but she very often proved herself to be, as in all martyr times she has been—the stronger of the two; and this, not in the instance of here and there a heroine, but, in very frequent instances, even though of the feeblest bodily framework. It was then, and then first, perhaps, that the mind of woman—quickened by the definite conception of a resurrection to life, even to "a *better* resurrection," thenceforward took her place as the teacher and exemplar of a pure, a firm, a lofty morality; she did so as wife, as mother, as sister.

The moral results and the religious traditions of those times of suffering had held themselves entire, in many Jewish homes, throughout the years of the following century; and so it was that they came up, and we recognize them afresh in the Gospel narratives. If there be anything in the wide compass of ancient history that —out of all question, is genuine, is true—it is—woman's part in the Gospel history. Who could then have imagined, and who should have invented these incidents, and these brief utterances of pure, deep, feminine feeling? The Jewish women of that time had not been moulded by Christianity; for they had already been created, and had received their training, in preparation for its arrival. The doctrine which was to give moral greatness, along with meekness and purity, to those who should receive it, lodged itself at once in the mature hearts of Jewish women who, in a true sense, were the daughters of the noble women of the Maccabean age.

The preparation for the Gospel, in every city of the Roman world, was the Judaism it found there—with its Holy Scripture—Moses, and the Prophets, and the Psalms, read every Sabbath in the synagogues. But this was not all; for an order of feeling and a mode of conduct which neither the Grecian nor the Roman civilization could at all supply, or could imitate, were everywhere in readiness among those women—whether Jewish or Grecian, who had long been the stated frequenters of the Sabbath services in the synagogue. Thus it was that the principal element of our modern social well-being—that one element which is the source and the reason of whatever is pure, and loving, and right in the domestic relationships, was provided for, and was immediately realized, in the apostolic societies. Women, acting *in their independent moral individuality*, took their place as members of the Church; and they became also—for services suited to them—its ministers.

At how early a time this genuine and most auspicious evangelic position of woman in the Church came to be interfered with and lost, none can now tell us. At the earliest time at which our materials are more than mere fragments, the mischief had made great progress. Inasmuch as the ascetic philosophy had taken up the sensuous and oriental idea of purity, and thus had actually sensualized, by unwisely attempting to refine, those feelings which are specially feminine, the tendency of it was again to degrade woman, and so to nullify the claim she had long before made valid, as able to take her place of companionship, and of absolute moral equality, by the side of man.

And thus it was that another course of severe and long-continued suffering had become the necessary means of arresting the downward progress of things. The Antiochus of the Maccabean times found philosophic emperors and prefects—even some of the choicest men of imperial Rome, who were well inclined to take up his unfinished work. So it was that once again, in the unmoved endurance of "cruel mockings and scourgings" and of fiery tortures, woman—Christian woman, challenged anew her equality with man; and nobly did she then win the praise of possessing " a like precious faith," and a like courage, and, if not the same bodily nerve, yet a strength of soul which stood proof against the far keener anguish which she felt, as of feebler frame. So it was at a very early time, as we are authentically told, not only by Christian memorialists, but also by a Roman gentleman and pedant, who coldly says that he, and his ruffian tormenters had been quite baffled by the firmness of two young women of servile condition, whose constancy he had put to the test—all to no purpose, for he could wring no criminating confession from them.

The martyr times—a two hundred years, or more, of intermittent suffering—reckoning from Trajan to Diocletian, had not only served to give to Christianity its proper attestation, but, in doing so, it had again made sure of this—its vitalizing principle, namely—the moral position of woman as man's equal in the sight of God. But the martyr age had now passed by, and even before it had reached its end, the constant tendency of the social system to fall out of its due equilibrium had again shown itself in the prevalence of those spurious notions of purity which never fail deeply to disturb the relationship of the sexes. Nevertheless, this disturbance (to make a new experiment upon which, in this age, would be an extreme folly) had found some compensations: and, in respect of those long ages of European barbarism which were to succeed, it subserved purposes which were highly important; but these have often been specified.

We return, for a moment, to the lady abbess, who, like our friend NILUS, soon came into a position of authority and of extensive influence; for she not only governed the religious houses which she had founded, but she made periodic circuits, or, as we may call them, visitations, professedly, perhaps, for her own edification, in converse with the recluses; but, no doubt, she was welcomed among them as an adviser, and as one who was vested with a virtual authority, and who spoke as the superior of a large community, scattered over the lower Egypt, the Arabian desert, and Southern Palestine.

Nilus, as abbot, had turned to good account the magisterial habits of his early life; and his style and deportment, and his knowledge of the world gave him an advantage which would soon be recognized and submitted to. Paula, as abbess, might believe that she had laid aside, for ever, and had forgotten, the demeanour, the tones of voice, the graceful gestures, the instincts of birth, of rank, and of wealth; but should we have thought so, if it had chanced to us to see her, followed by her bevy of nuns, as she glided forwards to her place in church on an Easter Sunday morning? If we wish to imagine this high-born personage of the fourth century, we might be aided in doing so by looking at the portrait of her counterpart of the seventeenth century— the Mother Angelica Arnauld, abbess titular of Port Royal; both of them lofty-minded women; but in both of them there "dwelt richly" that "word of Christ," which, while it ennobles the meanest souls, brings low the loftiest; that word which, in its bearing upon the mind, and the conduct, and the affections of woman inspires her with a courage not at all inferior to that of man, and which, while it does so, abates nothing of her gentleness, or of that devotedness to the welfare of others which is especially her characteristic.

We should not quite forget Paula's spiritual directo through life, and her eloquent panegyrist. Jerome' powerful intellect, his extraordinary accomplishments and his knowledge of the world; and perhaps, also, th blandishments of his personal manners, when he foun himself among persons of rank, had made him the object of many flattering attentions from women of this class. Such were PAULA and her daughter EUSTOCHIUM. Everything, in this species of intercourse, was right and safe, and was far remote from scandal; it was sanctioned by the religious notions of the times—by the prominent position of the parties, and by those austere decorums which were everywhere regarded by leading persons in the Church. But there was then (and the same ingredients in human nature will, in every age, show their presence)—there was then prevalent much of that sort of unctious adulatory interchange of spiritual courtesies which has place between favoured clerical persons, and high-born religious women. This style is rendered peculiar by the speciality of the conditions under which it arises; for, just in proportion as it stands far removed from a touch or breath of scandal, it becomes so much the more intense in its own quality, and, whatever that quality may be, the reaction upon those concerned is so much the more real, as it is exempted from the suspicions of both by the conscious rectitude of each. If now it were asked on which side this peculiar influence produces its most marked results, we should incline to say that it is on the side of the clerical recipients of this purely-meant feminine devotion;—in these instances the idol suffers more injury than the worshipper. It might not be very difficult to trace its presence in the rosy colour it sheds upon certain phases of doctrine, or in the smooth rhythm of our religious conventionalisms; or, in the tone and style of pulpit, and still more, of platform oratory. But how has this perfumed and zephyr-like adulation been accepted, in different times, by clerical persons?

Might we here indulge in sketching a picture or two which may offer some curious contrasts? Let us think, then, in the first place, of the group of which Jerome's brief notices furnish the outlines. On a rugged, pathless ascent of the rocky region, which is within a day's journey of the Holy City, we see a company advancing: —there is that accomplished theologue—the terror of Vigilantius, and of all such-like heretics, but the courteous companion of orthodox ascetic ladies; it is Jerome who leads the way. Under the blaze of a Syrian summer's noon, he rides an ass; he has drawn his monk's hood far enough over his face to throw his sharp, prominent features into a half shade, which Rembrandt would have caught at. At a little distance in the rear—and she also riding an ass—follows the graceful descendant of the heroes of Livy's fabulous books: it is the lady PAULA. She defies the scorching beams, and she welcomes her sufferings as a sort of martyrdom: by her side, or lagging a little in the rear, and she also seated on an ass, is the fair nun, the pupil of Jerome in Greek and Hebrew. She stoops and languishes, but she will not be girl enough to utter a petulant murmur. Yet it was not thus that Eustochium was used to pass along the broad ways of Rome: yet all now is right in her mind, and she enjoys inward peace: then follow the attendants, with a wild Arab or two, hired as guides and guards; these, wrapped in their mantles, and poising their long lances on the shoulder, muse as they go; or muse not at all; but if they do muse, it is upon the whim—so unintelligible—which prompts such persons to endure such a journey only to gaze at stones!

If we turn from this scene, and look toward the western world, we may see the humble—the haughty, St. Martin lounging on a divan in the palace of a Cæsar, his low-bred presbyters and deacons, reclining on velvet, to the right and left of him. Kneeling at his feet, and not daring to raise her eyes so as stedfastly to gaze upon the saintly visage—kneeling at the feet of this monk, there is an empress—and this empress all but spurned!

Now, for the sake of a needed refreshment, shall we descend the stream of ages, and, brunting the chilling fogs of a winter's afternoon, in England, take our place by the roadside? Here comes the Bedfordshire tinker and the roughly-used Baptist preacher; he is mounted on a raw-boned mare; he is on his way to "Meeting" at a five-mile-act barn, and he has consented to allow the farmer's wife (the farmer is his good deacon, and the sharer of his past persecutions, and she is a buxom person) to take her place behind him on the pillion. The way is long, the ruts are deep, the evening is cheerless; but John Bunyan, though of social temperament, is a shrewd man and wise; and he is a great master of human nature, and so he jogs on in bluff silence. He hears no woman's flatteries; probably they would not have been offered to him; he invites no conversation; he will listen to none: he is intent upon getting a better hold of his "ninth head of discourse." John Bunyan has determined to keep himself always on the safe side of things. Has he not given us lively portraits of Madame Wanton, and of Mrs. Inconsiderate, and of Mrs. Lightmind, and of others? As a minister he has one rule of conduct; it is not the ascetic rule, but it is not the less efficacious; it is far more so:—it is puritanic; and if we will follow him to "Meeting," and will there listen to the hour-and-half sermon, we shall find that a consistent and high-toned morality is the preacher's interpretation of that Gospel, which he proclaims, even as glad tidings for the "chief of sinners."

Shall we come down another hundred years? It may be a November evening, or it may be a May morning— no matter, for the gentle and true-hearted George Whitefield is snugly seated by the side of that noble-hearted lady, the Countess of Huntingdon; she, as pure as purity itself; and her clerical friend blameless, if ever man has been blameless; or we may find him in her ladyship's drawing-room; he is the man of the splendid company, although there be present the chief wits of the time—Chesterfield, Garrick, Littleton. What now is there in all this which should call for criticism or serious reprehension? Nothing; and yet it may be permitted us to say that when the ministers of religion allow themselves to accept freely those warm testimonies of regard which their female hearers and followers are so prompt to render to them, they are likely to pass into an ambiguous mental condition, which intercepts the free exchange of thought between themselves and the men—the laymen—of their social and pastoral circles. Thus it comes about that sermons are composed and delivered which women eagerly applaud, but which men listen to with far less than thorough satisfaction: they too may applaud, for the preacher is eloquent, and they believe him to be sincere; yet these educated laymen come out of church convinced on no one questionable point; and they feel that while the slender and soft experiences of female religious life are understood, and are duly treated by the preacher, the hard, the arduous, the perplexing, the titan realities of *man's* course through this difficult world—these strong things, are either not grappled with at all, or they are always misunderstood, as a man misunderstands things which he has never seen otherwise than at a distance, and through a mist.

ESSAY V.

THEODOSIUS:—PAGAN USAGES, AND THE CHRISTIAN MAGISTRATE.

SITUATIONS which, at a glance, may attract our attention and invite comparison by their apparent similarity, will often, on nearer view, instead of being identical, scarcely present an element of analogy. At this moment the British Rule is, year by year, extending itself, as if it were never to reach its limit, and it embraces all races of men and all their religions. All beliefs, and every variety of usage are thus coming continually into more intimate, and therefore into more difficult, relationship with modes of feeling which can have no sympathy therewith, and with creeds towards which the European mind can barely conceal its contempt, and—as a climax of perplexity—with institutions that are abominable—that are insufferable, and that are wholly incompatible with even the most lax rule for the maintenance of public order.

The British domination in India is that of a professedly Christian Power over subjugated heathens;—a difficult position: but shall we not find some kind of guidance, cautionary guidance, at least, in looking back to those times when Christian magistrates extended, as we do now, the sceptre and the sword widely over pagan populations? There was a time when the magistrate, absolute and irresponsible as he was, and himself undoubtedly Christian as to his personal beliefs, issued edicts, and enforced them too, over all countries around the Mediterranean: and he did so while a many-coloured polytheism was still the profession, and gave law to the habits, of the great mass of the people, high and low. Individual emperors, from Constantine to Justinian, differed much in ability, and in personal merits, and in position also; nevertheless they, or the later emperors, pursued a course toward the paganism of their times, toward the heathen populace, and toward the priests of the antiquated idolatries, which might be represented as uniform and coherent, and which was such as might be spoken of as "a policy."

Might not, then, that policy be spread forth to view, and be made use of as an exemplar which we should do well to imitate, even now, when we are called upon anew, by the recent course of events, to consider and to reconsider those principles under the guidance of which we intend henceforward to govern countries containing a fifth part of the human family? Most of these people are polytheists, or those of them that are monotheists are still more difficult to be dealt with, for they are fanatics for their one truth.

No doubt there are those among us who, accepting the commendations that are bestowed by the Church writers of the fourth and fifth centuries upon the pious and zealous emperors of those times, would, with little hesitation, take pattern by these Christian magistrates, and would even outdo them in the fervour of their endeavours to trample out the smouldering fires of every false worship. But if a caution were needed for arresting the course of any such zeal as this, it might soon be found in looking to the facts of the alleged case; for in doing so, we may presently become convinced that, in almost every instance of an apparent analogy between the two situations, the resemblance is apparent only; while the difference, or the contrariety, is real and extreme.

These points of difference, or these contrarieties, are obvious, and they may be soon enumerated: they are such as these, and our comparison is that which presents itself in bringing under the eye the Roman Imperial government, from the time of Constantine's declaration in favour of Christianity, to a late time, when paganism had everywhere gone down, as a feculent sediment, resting at the very bottom of the social mass: or it would be enough if we should take as our limit the latter years of the reign of Justinian.

After some small exceptive instances, belonging to the outskirts of the empire, have been allowed for, then it may be said that the master of the Roman world, for the time being, or its masters—east and west, ruled *their own:* the οἰκουμένη was their patrimony: its centre was the head and the heart of a living body which, throughout long periods, had throbbed with one pulse, and had moved with one intention. The wide interpretation given to the right and privilege of Roman citizenship had related all to all, and all to the one source of power. The nations, diverse as they were, had now, through ages, looked up from the east and from the west, from the north and from the south, to the one resplendent orb of imperial wisdom, and had all kept the ear attent to the one voice—whether a thunder or a whisper—of the imperial will. The nations "under the whole heavens" acknowledged the rightfulness as well as the power of the imperial rule, and they gloried in its glories, as well as bowed their necks to its forces.

How can a political condition of nations, such as this, be brought into comparison with a condition so utterly unlike it as is that of the nations and races which have been brought to pay tribute to the Committee assembling in Leadenhall-street? The difference here is such as to imply and to embrace all other imaginable dissimilarities, and it is so great as that it might be held to excuse our declining to institute any comparison at all between the two cases. Can it be rightful, or would it be politic, or shall it be safe, to enact in India, as from London, that which was enacted for the Roman world, from Constantinople? The pagan populace in remote countries, and its priests, might think themselves aggrieved by certain edicts, or harshly-used by some over-zealous Christian Prefect; but the Roman people at large—the hundred nations of the οἰκουμένη, did not feel itself aggrieved; it was their own Cæsar who had spoken. Everything has an opposite aspect in the modern instance. Nations trodden to the earth by a race that is gifted with more nerve and mind, and that has ampler means than their own, are writhing beneath the selfish foot of a detested invader, whose misunderstood beneficences are, in their view, ten times over-paid for by the rigours of his fiscal exactions. Warrantably so, or not, this is, and this must, for long years to come, be the aspect under which British supremacy is regarded by the nations of India. Again the grounds of comparison fail us, if we consider what had been the training of the Roman mind up to the time of the Christianizing of the empire, and what has been that of the people of India, and what their preparation for accepting the religion of their European masters.

The nations, east and west, that were embraced in the circle of the empire, at the time now in view, had all become partakers in the same civilization; they had all drunk at the same fountains of knowledge; there was one mind-world: there was, and there had long been, a communion of thought, and a brotherhood in science, and in philosophy, and in poetry and art, the Greek language being the medium of this intellectual commerce. Even the people of the Syrian stock had taken up and had assimilated the mental and moral aliment that was supplied to them by the poets, the orators, and the sages of Greece. So it was, therefore, that when the Christian argument, such as we find it set forth in the pages of its assailants, and of its apologists, of the third, fourth, and fifth centuries, was brought forward, it was carried on in the hearing of all men of the educated classes, from border to border of the Roman world. All men, or all who chose to give an ear to a controversy of this kind, had become more or less well informed of the grounds and the merits of the cause which was then at issue between the Church and the Polytheistic religions.

Consequently, at the moment when the Imperial edict startled the Roman world, a brief season of surprise was all the shock that men's minds were subjected to in learning that Christianity had at length got the start of its rivals. At a later time, and when measures of a more decisive kind were carried out in its favour, and in discouragement of the waning superstitions, nothing that could be unintelligible to either party took place; nothing was done for which a preparation had not been made in the thought and the feeling of all concerned. Edicts, touching the temples and the usages of heathenism, were only the ostensible acts and the steps in a transition which all men felt had been taking its slow and inevitable course around them, for a long while.

Nothing that resembles, even remotely, this relative position of Christianity and heathenism, attaches to the contact of the former with the latter in India in these times. If the people of India were indeed of another race, and if they spoke languages older than Babel, and if their superstitions had arisen millenniums ago out of the infernal pit—or describe their intellectual and religious state in terms as strong as any we can find, we shall scarcely overstate the fact of the incommunicable divulsion of the two worlds of thought and feeling—the European and the Hindoo-oriental. Athwart the bottomless gulf which divides the one world from the other world, nothing passes to and fro: or nothing—in its genuine form.

It is true that, annually, some scores of Hindoo youths —the frequenters of non-Christian colleges, acquire enough English to read Shakespeare and our Quarterly Reviews, and to make us believe that India has now set foot upon the field of European thought. But we must not trust ourselves to any such films of correspondence as this; we should not so easily persuade ourselves that the nations of India are coming near to us, either morally or intellectually, or that they are able to assent to our historical beliefs with an enlightened consciousness of the grounds of any such assent. Hindoos may indeed accept the Gospel at our hands, and, if they do so, it will bring its blessings with it, to their infinite benefit individually, and there may be hundreds of conversions, and Missionary Societies may be warranted in appealing to their successes;—nevertheless, the nations with their millions that have come under our rule in the East still remain incalculably remote from any condition which should qualify them fairly and knowingly to adjudge the cause at issue between the several religions of their ancestors, and the one religion of their masters—their conquerors. Our inference, therefore, is this: That those measures for the maintenance of Christianity and for the suppression and removal of polytheism, which the Christian emperors of the fourth century might warrantably adopt, cannot, for a moment, be thought of as applicable, under any modifications, for effecting similar purposes, by ourselves, in India.

Throughout that period during which Christianity and Paganism were in conflict and in balance, and while the issue might still seem doubtful, there was, on the one side, not only a doctrine and a system of morality which were allowed to be infinitely superior to anything that could be found on the other side, but along with this superiority, and as its consequence, there was a determinate belief, held by thousands of men and women with a fulness of persuasion and an attachment, immoveably firm. On the other side there was nothing more substantial than popular beliefs, which, long before the time of this conflict, had come to be spurned and ridiculed by sages and their disciples. These relics of paganism, these ceremonies, and these domestic worships, which were sustained by no vital forces, might be likened to the faded costumes and the dingy embroidered trappings that are seen bagging upon the wooden effigies of the kings and knights of the middle ages. The worn out, the tattered and botched heathenism, which Julian fancied he might make to stand again upon its legs, was everywhere, and in every city of the empire, and in almost every home, confronted with the truth, the reason, the living and the stirring energies of the Christian faith.

How, then, can a parallelism be thought to hold when we turn from the doings of the Roman world, in the times of Theodosius II. to the policy and the measures lately pursued, or now intended to be pursued, in India?

Often, during these forty years past, benevolent audiences have been assured from platforms that the superstitions of India were waning—were dying out from the mind of the people, and that Satan's empire was tottering to its fall;—a little while, and it shall afflict our eyes and ears no more! Recent events have subjoined a dire comment to these hasty announcements. The Polytheism of India, with its lurid ferocities and its filth, just because it has never allied itself with any conceptions of beauty or of order—as did that of Greece—and just because it takes no spring from any axioms of reason, has confixed itself upon the Hindoo soul—has grown into it—has gone down in its impurity, and in its cruelty, and in its absurdity: as a girdle of brass it encircles the moral and rational faculties, and forbids even so much expansive movement as might issue in a release from its hold.

Confronted with this inveterate polytheism, which could not be firmer in its grasp than it is, if indeed it were as old as its own chronology declares it to be—confronted with this Hindooism there are, as representative of British Christianity in India, instead of a positive and coherent belief, two irreconcileable, and, in fact, hostile opinions, professed by those with whom the people of India come into contact; for on the one side there is that mode of feeling in matters of religion which has always been characteristic of the governing class there, the men in authority, and the young men especially, who, as administrators of the foreign rule, are spread over the country, and to whom, directly and indirectly, revenue is paid. On the other hand, the Hindoo mind, here and there at least, converses with those whose genuine and fervent Christian feeling has brought them to India. Thus it is that, on the one side, the European, the English influence, is such as is felt to be substantially atheistic: on the other side, the same exterior European and English civilization speaks to the Hindoo mind in tones animated by a profound belief of whatever is emphatically Christian. The mere knowledge and consciousness of so vehement an antagonism having place among those who have come to rule and to teach them, would deeply affect the minds of races even less shrewd and intelligent than are the people of India.

It is not—and we need to be continually cautioned against so great an error as to suppose it—it is not as if all men individually who take their stand on the one side of the above-mentioned antagonism were utterly irreligious, or were purely selfish, and rapacious, and regardless of all things but the amassing of fortunes. It is not so; for many of this very class are men of benevolence, and are honestly desirous (so long as Indian revenue is safe) of governing India for the good of the people. Nor is it as if all men, individually, who take position on the other side were simple-hearted, and self-denying, and ready for martyrdom: this is not so.

But whereas, at home, principles of all kinds, speculative and practical, are intermingled in every imaginable manner—in the promiscuous utterances of social intercourse, in public discussions, and in the literary commerce of a free people, and are thus softened down, and are mitigated, and are stripped of their sharpest characteristics; in India, on the contrary, each of these forms of opinion retires from contact with its antagonist, and it receives an exaggerated expression of its meaning, and it comes to be uttered with a sort of emphatic and polemic vehemence. The two beliefs, or the belief and the non-belief, are severally announced in the presence of a heathenism, such as is that of the Hindoo races, and of a fanaticism such as is that of the growling Mahometan population. Thus uttered, it gathers force in the utterance.

It is the natural and inevitable course of things that the daily sights and sounds of worships so foul and so sanguinary as are those of India, should aggravate, should irritate the feelings of Christian men and (let us not forget it) of Christian women, resident in India. And while this process is going on, the very same sights and sounds take effect upon the irreligion of the irreligious—imparting to it a murky levity, a contemptuous virulence, of which all modes of feeling that relate man to a world unseen are alike the objects. Mingled reasons of a mistaken policy, and of irreligious indifference, have brought high-minded Englishmen in India to submit to the humiliation of touching the hat to the Devil; and in doing so (as is the case in every instance of a wrong concession to what is evil) they have brought upon themselves far more of native contempt, than has been compensated by any gratitude they have thus earned from the besotted worshippers.

Men in authority in India who, in discharge of their functions, are forced into contact with Pagan usages—usages insufferably abominable, are not unlikely to reason with themselves in some such manner as this—" Placed where I am, and cognizant of this filth—this folly, and this murder, there is no alternative for me but this—I must either give utterance to my abhorrence and contempt, and then act accordingly;—or I must so deport myself as if I were supremely indifferent to everything— to everything but revenue, and the making a fortune for myself. If I professed to care for justice and mercy, or if I announced my belief in a righteous Almighty and a future judgment, I should render myself amenable, in the view of the people, to principles of reason, truth, and humanity. My part, therefore, is that of a supercilious indifference; at least it is so until the day comes when I shall be able to speak and act spontaneously—to speak and act as a Christian and as an Englishman."

Those who, rejecting this sort of indifference, might undertake to justify a more coercive course of conduct on the part of a Christian government, toward the Hindoo people and their religious usages, may think that they shall find a warrant for it in the edicts and the demeanour of Constantine and his successors, as related to the expiring polytheism of their times; but the two cases are, as we have already said, essentially unlike. And as to Constantine himself, and the apparent inconsistency of his acts, his ambiguous personal convictions, at least during the ten years immediately succeeding the public profession of his conversion, must be taken into the account, if we are looking for an explanation of his conduct in continuing, as he did, to dispense the customary gratuities among the ministers of worships, which were still adhered to by large masses of the Roman people—by many (or most) of the wealthy and noble, and professedly also, by the leaders of the philosophical sects. Sacrifices on state occasions were still offered, and prayers were enjoined to be made to "them that have ears, but hear not." Coins were struck, which in device and in legend were polytheistic. In the phraseology of public documents ancient forms were retained; for so it is in all parallel instances—reform waits long, and knocks many times at the door of government offices. The imperial conversion, if it amazed the Roman world for a moment, as a thunder-clap, did not blaze out upon it unclouded, as day does in the tropics, but crept up upon the sky as does the summer morning in the misty and showery north.

In the course of a hundred and fifty years, reckoned on from the edict of Milan, the ancient worships were in constant course of fading away:—they slunk out of sight;—every year they were becoming less and less the subjects of serious controversy. Thus there are meteoric conditions of the atmosphere, during which detached clouds are seen to be melting into nothing; and if you watch the borders of the heaviest masses, they are shooting forth limbs, which disappear while you look at them:—all vapours are in a state of rapid absorption, until at length the clear blue prevails on all hands. So it was that the imperial edicts, throughout the years of the fourth century, had been anticipated, in almost each instance, by changes that had taken place in public opinion: and these changes—these reformations, in fact—were so many advances toward a higher moral condition of the Roman world, a progress which must have given another aspect to European history, if it had not, so soon, been arrested.

Christianity knows nothing of imperial edicts, or of acts of Parliament; but whenever the edicts of a government are of a beneficial kind, and when also they are hopeful, because well-timed, it is when and where the moral forces of the Gospel have already taken effect throughout the social mass, and have done so to such an extent as that reformatory laws have been called for, and are welcomed—perhaps they may have been impatiently demanded by the popular feeling. Each of the more flagrant characteristics of the Greek and Roman polytheism—each of those vicious institutions, and of those pernicious usages which a modern Christianized community would resent and repel with abhorrence, had come to be regarded as insufferable—as abominable, long before the moment of its prohibition by the state. If the intrinsic moral forces of the Gospel had not, at so early a time, been first abated by the prevalence of the ascetic doctrine, and then turned aside by the revival of the ancient polytheism, under the guise of the shrine-worship, the incursions of the Gothic hordes would not have prevailed, as they did, to overthrow the civilization of southern Europe.

Well would it repay the labour it might cost, to follow, and to exhibit the progress of the Christian energy—regarded simply as a protest against the established injustices and the ritual impurities, the cruelties and the filthiness of Greek and Roman heathenism! How animated, how firm, how irresistible, was this protest, as we catch the echoes of it, in listening to the early Christian apologists! Truly these witnesses for the new faith spake as the prophets of the Highest when, in its defence, and in asking for justice—they reasoned with the men of their times—with philosophists and potentates, concerning "righteousness, and temperance, and the judgment to come." The sophists were soon silenced, and profligate magnates quailed, and were glad to screen themselves behind their material powers, whenever this scorch of eternal reason was sent in upon their conscience; *they* "trembled" for an hour only, but their successors in the next age, gave way, and acknowledged, in the Christian teacher, the authentic servant of God.

Thus was it until the time when the Christian advocate betrays his consciousness that he and his colleagues, in carrying forward their controversy with the patrons of the ancient superstitions, had abandoned their vantage ground, and had themselves come to take a position near to that of the apologist of the gods, and where they had much to do to defend what was so utterly indefensible. Clear, bold, and consistent in principle, were the early apologists, such as Justin Martyr, Athenagoras, Minucius Felix, Origen, Tertullian, Arnobius, in their maintenance of their own part, and in their assault upon the absurd demon-worships of the Gentiles, and upon its immoralities:—all thus far was right, and well these champions knew that there was no room for gainsaying—there was no flaw in their plea. But not so was it with their successors, the Christian apologists of the following century. Ambrose, Basil, Chrysostom, the Gregories, and, alas! Augustine, had waded knee-deep into the mire of superstition, and they were not unconscious of the moral humiliation to which they had yielded themselves. How poorly, for instance, does Augustine maintain his standing when assailed by a Pagan schoolmaster of his diocese; to what pitiful shifts does he resort! or, to follow the course of things another century further, we may look into the orations of John Damascenus—$\pi\varepsilon\rho\grave{\imath}\ \tau\alpha\tilde{\imath}\varsigma\ \grave{\alpha}\gamma\acute{\imath}\alpha\iota\varsigma\ \varepsilon\grave{\imath}\varkappa\acute{o}\nu\alpha\iota\varsigma$—and then read, if we have patience, the decrees of the second Council of Nice! It was not a Christianity so diluted as was that of the sixth and seventh centuries, that could keep alive the moral energies of the mass of the people, and therefore all were soon to be trampled on by Goths, Vandals, Saracens.

We have just now said that the acts of the Roman emperors, in aiming at the suppression of Paganism, will not furnish precedents for the guidance of a Christian government, at this time, in dealing with the polytheism of the conquered races of India. The instances are not, in any sense, parallel; the nations, the ancient and the modern, are in wholly different conditions, moral and intellectual; and the relation of the government toward the people is essentially different. Nevertheless human nature is ever the same, and therefore there is a lesson to be gathered from each chapter of the history of the human family. The propension of the human mind toward a religion of many divinities, male and female, is one of the most constant of its tendencies; and the instances in which, for any length of time, a higher direction has been given to the religious instinct, and a pure theology has been resolutely maintained, are rare indeed. We may be quite sure that this tendency will ever and again show itself. A people, fully taught in the first and greatest of all truths, holds to its profession of it, shall we say, through three generations, or through five? The Jewish people, from the time of their return to their land, have, in this one sense, been found faithful to their vocation; but it has been under conditions so exceptional as to remove the instance from its place as pertinent in any argument. The Christianized nations of southern Europe had relapsed, very generally, into polytheism before five generations had passed away. At this moment the populace throughout the same areas, East and West, are hopelessly addicted to practices which differ in name only, and in costume, from the paganism of their remotest ancestors.

How, then, shall it be in India? In India, as to the relation of the people to the government, everything is, and must long be, if not for ever—anomalous—out of harmony with all theory—exceptional, as to the entire course of ordinary history. Governed from a remote centre, by a race utterly alien and abhorrent to its own, conquered and held in subjection by nothing but steel, or if by aught else, by films of moral influence; governed, if not with an exclusive, yet with a constant and sovereign regard to the annual fiscal result—India must, under conditions so strange (always supposing the continuance of the British supremacy) and more and more so, it must stand as a PARADOX, in the large volume of human experiences.

Who, then, shall venture to predict the future of India when this paradox is to work out its solution upon a field whereupon is assembled a fifth, or a seventh part, of the human family? But if the India of ten years hence defies all sagacity to foresee it, nevertheless, if we choose to assume the permanence of the British supremacy there, then—and this contingence being the datum of our conjectural hypothesis—then there are some results of the reaction of India upon England which may be foreseen with a degree of certainty. No one will say that ten years hence the Ganges and the Indus shall float red uniforms from their mouths to their sources, but if we grant this fact, then we may predict for England itself a mighty result, deeply affecting whatever, among ourselves, is of the highest importance.

It does not come within the province of the writer of

this Essay to speak of "exports and imports," and "revenue," or the like; but he may speak of those revolutions in the world of thought and action which outweigh revenue, and which are of more enduring consequence than the maintenance of empires.

Reaction, in any case, will, as to its intensity and its extent, be directly as the speed and the frequency of the intercourse between countries, or nations. In all times, known to history, the Eastern world and the Western, have interchanged influences—the West acting upon the East, the East reacting upon the West. In each of these instances while the obvious, and the noisy, and the tangible part of this intercourse has been that of the West upon the East—such, to wit, as the conquests of Alexander, the Crusades, the Portuguese, the French, the British settlements and conquests—the deep, the silent, the enduring part of the same intercourse has been the reaction of the East upon the political constitutions, upon the social equilibriums, of the nations of Europe, and upon their arts and commerce, upon their philosophy, and their habits of thought. So it is likely to be in the instance before us. England acts upon India; and the nations, its European competitors, admire, and wonder, and grudge, at the spectacle of such valour, and of such energy, and of such success! But meantime, as always it has been heretofore, during the lapse of five and twenty centuries—India is reacting upon the dominant race; it is doing so silently, irresistibly, and with a deep-going force, a force of that kind which, while it bespeaks the presence of the Almighty, puts contempt upon the interference of man.

It may be well, for a moment, to bring into view the

instantaneousness and the vital activity of that intercourse which, at this moment, is linking England with India—that umbilical cord through which the circulation, to and fro, is going on. Recent events have thrown India in upon hundreds of English homes with a force and a meaning the intensity of which will not soon be spent. India, its sites and its scenes, its costumes and manners, its material splendours, and its real horrors, have become terribly familiar to the imagination of bereaved parents and sisters in all social circles. So much nearer to us is India, in thought and sympathy! And the same course of events, adding, as it does, a new stimulus to the mechanical marvels of locomotion, is shortening, continually, the intervals of correspondence, so that, instead of months, we are getting to compute the distance by weeks—lately—now by days;—and ere long it will be by hours, perhaps by minutes! There is Calcutta news! how recent is it? 12 at noon, Greenwich time, and this is 12.30.

Our sympathies and moral emotions, not often unreasonable, are unreasoning most often. Why should they be liable to so much abatement from incidental differences of space and time? We cannot well say how or why it is so, but yet it is: a calamity, a horror, an injustice—when and where has it befallen the sufferers?—and are these sufferers our dearest relatives?—was it on the other side of the globe?—was it a year ago? Nay, it was in the next street, and it was yester-night! Nearness in time and place is the condition of intense emotion; and thus it is that the railway and the electric wire are now becoming the nerves of sensation and the nerves of volition throughout the world. It is time, then, that the doers of wrong, and the perpetrators of cruelties, should look to themselves, for, remote as may be the corners where their crimes are done, what they are about will perhaps be known and published in every capital of the civilized world before the sun is hot of the next day!

It is, then, with this sort of instantaneousness that the things of India, henceforward, shall react upon England; and it is at this same speed that the public opinion of England shall make itself known, the next hour, in India. What, then, must ensue? Just this, that India, whether converted to Christianity, or not converted, and whether governed by Christian men or by secularists, shall feel that it must amend its usages, and that it must learn to be ashamed of what it has been during these four thousand years or more.

The Pagan usages of India, beginning with those that are of the deepest atrocity, and going on to those which, in less degrees, are offensive to the English eye and ear, must now give way—not as did those of the Greek and Roman polytheism, which slowly yielded to a vital movement from within the same social body, but by an exterior force, and because of their insufferable proximity to a higher civilization—that of Europe—that of England. The nearness of India to England, by steam navigation, by rail, and by the electric wire, and by the increasing frequency of intercourse, and by the incessant coming and going, and by the lengthy correspondence which is now permeating all domestic circles, these things have the effect of bringing the Hindoo abominations close under our drawing-room windows, as nuisances that are not to be endured: there will be an outcry to sweep them away.

Not the most determined of our non-interference

statesmen would now find it possible to arrest this reformatory process; much less could he dare to license anew the religious murders, and the burnings, and the tortures which already have been interdicted. As things NOW ARE, to revive such doings would set our English homes on fire, would hurl public men from their position, would raise tornadoes in Exeter Hall, and in every provincial hall, from end to end of the country. "Our Indian fellow-subjects" must learn to be as pious as they please, short of murder.

What is it, then, that will be taking place in the course of this arbitrary and externally-wrought reformation? It is well to consider such a question. How bright an anticipation would it be if we might believe that, in thus removing the superficial hideousness of the demon-worships of India, we shall be penetrating the substance, and that we shall thus dislodge the demon! No such hope as this is warranted by the history of those nations that have been habituated to polytheism through long ages. So happy an event may indeed come about, who shall deny it; but another course of things is far more probable. As to the few—those of the natives who are the aspirants to English culture, and to whom, in colleges, we are opening wide the portals of scientific atheism—the case of such demands a separate consideration; but as to the masses of the Hindoo population, they are undergoing a softening, a breaking up of the horrific crust of their ancient superstitions. The Hindoo children of this present time, from the mere privation of inhuman spectacles, and from the non-occurrence in their highways of exhibitions the sight of which is moral perdition, these are in a course of passive training for—what? is it for Christianity? May it please God to bring about such an end! But we should prepare ourselves to expect a far less welcome consequence;—and this, which is the more probable event, and which is likely to show itself in a few years, or when the youth of India reaches early manhood, is—the wide and rapid substitution of a mild and bloodless polytheism, in the place of that of which the people of India will have become ashamed—taught, as we are teaching them, to look at their ancient atrocities with European eyes.

The people of India, weaned from such things, will be looking around in quest of gods and goddesses—kind intercessors, who shall look down upon them from pedestals in their streets, and shall smile, and show in their attitude, and in their tranquil visages, that which lost human nature so earnestly yearns for—propitious supernatural power, quite near at hand, and offered to the eye and touch.

Who is it, then, that shall now come forward at this silent invitation? Who is it that shall bring before the late worshippers of Brahma, Vishnu, and Siva, a smiling Mother with infant in arms, both of them nimbus-crowned, and proclaimed in all thoroughfares as " Queen of Heaven, Queen of angels, and the Fountain of Grace to every suppliant?" Nor would this divinity hold her celestial court unattended, for thousands of gracious and open-handed mediators are ranged around her, to right and left, and each has his or her peculiarity of aid or favour to bestow. Thy ancient gods, O India, were beings of savage mood, they were stubborn in temper and vindictive, and hard to be placated; but *these* are propitious; they are all loving and indulgent; nor are they strict as toward human frailties, yet are they themselves pure as the azure sky, and free from every taint of earth: kneel to these!—address your supplications to these!

It was a transmutation very nearly resembling this, and yet apparently less probable, under the circumstances, which, taking place as it did during the lapse of the fourth and three following centuries, gave to the southern European nations the polytheism which still holds bound all of them whose soil had been thoroughly saturated with the ancient worships—with the Greek and the Roman polytheism. Protestantism has expelled the Roman Catholic polytheism from those countries only in which the classic polytheism had obtained not more than a brief term of occupation.

But as to India, its soil is rank and rich in preparation for sustaining a bright-coloured and gorgeous worship, such as is that which undoubtedly will now be offered to the acceptance of its millions.

How difficult is it to speak and write, and to read too, otherwise than polemically upon subjects which are still warmly controverted among ourselves! But now in these pages the writer and the reader are supposed to be standing aside from the noisy world, and to be quit of their prejudices. Be it so understood, and moreover, let us assume that, while intending no offence to our neighbour, we must hold fast our personal convictions, and especially that we dare not, at the prompting of a factitious courtesy, or of a false-hearted liberalism, despise the requirements, either of common sense, or of religious consistency.

Now then for our point. Take the instance of a devout and well-instructed member of the Roman Catholic Church. We say an instructed member, and not only so, but one who is surrounded also with the Bible atmosphere and the Bible light of a free Protestant country. To such a one, and especially if he or she takes the discreet and the pious Alban Butler as his (or her) guide, it may be practicable, we dare not say it will be easy, to understand, and always to observe, the distinction which excuses him from the imputation of idolatry, or of polytheism, while he catches hold of the alleged difference between—reverential regard, the hyper-reverential regard, and the proper religious worship, which last alone is to be offered to the Supreme Being. We grant you all the benefit you can any way derive from these nice distinctions: hold tight to the difference, if there be any, the next time when you bow the knee in front of an image, or a picture, and, looking upward, you utter your petition. You tell us that you "honour God in His saints," and that your particular and favourite saint hears your prayer "in God," and so forth. We pursue you not on this perilous ground, for in treading this lava-crust we could not keep the eye from peering in between the crevices where we should see the fiery crimson flood, that awful deluge which, long ago vomited up from the nether world, has, through thousands of years, spread itself over the nations, to their ruin.

Let common sense give way as far as is possible to charity, and then utter itself aloud without reserve. Have we ever stood as the lookers-on in those countries where the Roman Catholic worship has always been the religion of the masses of the people, where it has been liable to no rebuke, to no reprehension, and where the people, the higher and the lower, have never been challenged to bethink themselves of their religious usages? Stretch a charitable hypothesis to its extreme limit, and then ask—as to the prostrate crowd of worshippers, encircling the image of a favourite saint, and addressing to it their fervent entreaties for grace and succor—ask what now becomes of the distinction between the dulia, and the hyper-dulia, and the latria? To these besotted devotees it is, as if it were not; nor does the religion of the mass of the people otherwise differ from that of their remotest ancestors—than so far as is implied in the characteristics that are attributed to their divinities severally. If common sense be listened to, and if a fearless regard be had to conspicuous facts, then we must assent to this conclusion—that though the names are not the same, and though rites have undergone a change, the idol-worship and the polytheism are, in every other sense, the same.

That substitution of a mild polytheism for a polytheism that is fierce, vindictive, impure, and horrific, is the revolution which the course of events may speedily bring about in India. It shall startle many among us by the suddenness of its commencement, by the rapidity of its progress, and by the universality of its triumphs.

Are we intending—or should we be able, if intending it—to bolt the door against the now-coming St. Francis Xavier, and his train of devoted ministers? We dare not attempt this. Spite of us he will set his foot upon the India which we have just now conquered for him. He will bear aloft the most attractive symbols;—he will be copious and eloquent in his commendations of the "Queen of Heaven!—Mother of Mercy! Does she not clasp the infant Saviour of the world in her graceful arms, and shall not the Mother prevail with the Son? And WE who now bring to you the glad tidings of a new dispensation, WE are not of the hated Saxon race that has conquered India; WE are not of the same blood as your oppressors: we abhor their deeds of violence, we denounce their impieties; it is we who are to you the messengers of mercy, and of nothing else."

What is now to be done to stay a Christianizing of India in this manner by the ministers of Rome? Shall the English Church take it patiently, and stand aside? Not if Englishmen are what hitherto they have been. But is there not a middle course open before us, which it would be wise to follow? "May we not forfend the successes of our rivals by adopting their principles and using their means of influence, by taking in hand their tools, by putting in practice their maxims for gaining the multitude? May we not denounce Rome aloud, and yet learn of her in secret? We may draw off from her whenever we encounter her on the highway, but yet may call her in to teach us her craft in the closet. Let but the Episcopal Church of England retrace the mistaken steps she has taken these three centuries past, and then, as thus reformed by retrogression, she will renew her strength, and find it an easy task to Christianize India, even as St. Austin, advised by Pope Gregory, Christianized England."

This we may be sure of, that, in taking any such course as this, the Church of England would at once forfeit the support and favour of that class of public men without whose support these very measures must fail of success. The philosophic and the indifferent, the "non-interference" statesmen, who rule India, if they saw the Hindoo people crowding, by fifty thousand at a time, around the modern St. Francis Xavier, and receiving baptism at his hands in uncounted groups, and taking up with a religion which would be spoken of as "well adapted to their moral and intellectual condition," would hail the event with undissembled satisfaction. Thus feeling, they would frown upon the endeavour to split the difference, or to tamper with so desirable a process. Shall it be that, "for the sake of we know not what nice distinctions, be they metaphysical, or theological, or ecclesiastical—we care not what they are—you are wishing to arrest the course of a reform which will be brought about by your rivals in a far better manner, and more speedily, than it can be by yourselves; in a word, you need not doubt that WE shall lend ourselves to *their* endeavours, and not to *yours*." Thus, consistently with their indifference towards religions of all kinds, will a certain class of statesmen reason.

It must be as animated by another principle, and moved on by another zeal, and inspired by another hope, and governed by another rule, that the Church of England (and other communions with her) shall henceforward perform their destined part in India. The collision and the conflict between Romanism and the Church of England in India, which can scarcely fail to follow in the track of recent events, will throw each anew upon that which is its characteristic principle. The reaction of this new movement in India, upon Romanism at its centre, and upon our Protestant communions in England, may give an unexpected aspect to the Christianity of Europe, and may divorce anew the nations.

Once and again, in modern times, the propagation enterprises of the Romish Church have drawn its ministers onward toward the most dangerous extremes of compromise with Pagan usages. The authorities at Rome have been scandalized and alarmed, and have been compelled to disown these ambiguous doings. But at present the temptation to follow *in the same track*, in India, will be far greater than ever it has been, and will be yielded to. The Romish Church has a rich and vast region in view, over which it may now spread its easy triumphs; and it may do this under the very eye, and by the aid of its rival and enemy: it may spread itself from side to side of the Peninsula, none daring to make it afraid. The government pledges itself for its protection, as a matter of principle, and as a rule of policy too. Who, then, shall stay its course?

This course, if pursued in bringing about the conversion of the nations of Hindustan, must be regarded, not merely as a dangerous and unwarrantable concession to polytheistic notions and practices, but it will be found to demand a deeper and an always deepening falseness, and spuriousness, and hollowness of pretension, and, in a word, a universal UNTRUTHFULNESS, as between the ministers of religion and the masses of the people. But untruthfulness toward man brings with it a searing of the conscience, and then follows the darkest and the most ominous of all crimes—the living a lie in the confronted presence of ALMIGHTY GOD.

In tracing up separately, to its obscure origin, in remote times, each of the characteristic dogmas and practices of the Romish Church (and the same nearly is true of the Eastern Church) no stretch of charity will suffice to ward off the seemingly harsh conclusion that some *fraud*, practised by the ministers of religion upon the people, and intended, perhaps, for their benefit—was its germ. And thus, as we follow the natural development of errors down the turbid stream of time, the same impression becomes stronger and more distinct at every stage—*spuriousness, fabrication, falseness*, as between the ministers of religion and the people; this is the continuous and the growing characteristic of each stage of the process, which at length matures a small fiction into the giant dimensions of an enormous lie. How can the most candid and philosophically-tranquil reader of the original documents of Romish Church history defend himself from this conclusion—that UNTRUTHFULNESS toward the people, and an impious contempt of the awful majesty of God, have ever been the law and the reason of Romanism.

There can be no need to put to Christian men, or to Englishmen, the question—By what means, or on what principle, should Romish superstitions be met on the plains of India, or in China? Do we not fear God? Do we not abhor lying, and scorn fabrications? Do we not hold in utter contempt the quirks and the tricks of the surpliced charlatan? Yes, and we are prepared to take patiently the defeat of our endeavours to spread the Gospel in the East, rather than exult in easy triumphs which we might achieve by impious falsities—by pompous and gorgeous quackeries, or by a prurient practising with a sensual race, in the dark. But if, indeed, there be any among us who are otherwise minded than thus, then an appeal might well be made to them on the supposition that there is an honest ounce of Anglo-Saxon blood yet curdling about their hearts. To such we say— Be honest at least thus far. Enlist yourselves at once as ministers of the Pantheon; there you will stand in no false position, and all the services required of you shall be to your mind: nothing will there be done by halves, and there, if conscience does not upbraid you, no other upbraidings shall trouble your future course.

The work that has henceforward to be done by honest

and Christian-hearted men in India, and in China, is of a new order, and it is incomparably more arduous than hitherto (or at all in modern times) Christian ministers have been called to engage in. It is a work for which no sufficient preparation has been made, either within the enclosures of the English Episcopal Church, or among the communions around it. But it has this one auspicious prognostic:—the work is such that it will create the men who are to do it, and the work, once engaged in, will train them for their duty.

But if it were asked, what is there in the present position, or in the aspect of affairs in India, or in China, which differs much from the now well-understood conditions of the missionary enterprise, all the world over? the reply might be of this sort:—The Christianity of England will henceforward have to maintain itself, and to make progress, as it stands related first—to the ancient paganism—secondly, to the Christianized paganism of Rome, thirdly—to European atheism; and then —as related to these three, in their present peculiar condition of coalescence and of tacit compromise, the issue being a combination of elements that is too intimate and too *natural*, to be broken up otherwise than by the power and mercy of Heaven, specially put forth. But when we say this, the practical inference is the same as it would be if, as in relation to purely secular interests, everything depended upon our skill, industry, sagacity, and forecasting of the probable course of events. The course of events throughout the Eastern world will not fail to be such as shall call up a new class of men—in Europe (may we say it) in Britain—to meet it; and thus, the reaction of the East upon the West will be more remarkable than is the action of the West upon the East.

ESSAY VI.

JULIAN: PROHIBITIVE EDUCATION.

A FOREMOST place in the Greek literature and philosophy of his times would probably have been assigned to Flavius Claudius Julianus, if it had not been his misfortune to become master of the Roman world. As one of the ablest, and the best, and the purest in intention, and the most humane, of the Roman emperors, he would, with equal probability, have been accounted, if nature and industry had not previously made him an accomplished man of letters, and a devoted intellectualist. And yet even so, a sort of "double first" distinction might have been awarded him by posterity if, in combining the two orders of merit—that of a philosopher and that of a ruler, he had not committed that one blunder which the vindictive church writers of his time have miscalled his "apostacy." As a philosopher only, according to the modes of thinking that were prevalent at Athens while he enjoyed the companionship of Gregory Nazianzen, Basil, and other bright-witted and "fast" young men of that babbling place, he would never have troubled himself with the bootless endeavour to restore the superannuated paganism of Greece: or, as statesman only, and with the Roman world at his feet, and himself, at an early time in his course, possessed of a well-earned military reputation, JULIAN would better have understood his situation, and would wisely have left the fierce religionists around him to settle their differences as they could, and to prevail as they might severally against the waning superstitions of the populace. But it was not so; for the philosopher, prompted and moved from his equanimity by the resentments, and by the virtuous disgusts of the man, misadvised the emperor, and thus it was that, in a sullen heat, he threw off his Christian profession, and proclaimed anew the classic fables, as if he thought that the imperial lungs might breathe truth and life into the dead mythologies!

The measures he pursued, in his brief course, for depressing and degrading the Christian community, and for lifting paganism from out of the abyss into which it was fast sinking, were of that order which is likely to recommend itself to public men who, having shone at college, and coming, in early manhood, to mix themselves with the affairs of an empire, bring with them bits and rendings of their academic whims—their theories, their corollaries, and their crotchets. It is your academic men, fresh from Athens, even the brightest and the best of them, that go on blundering and blundering, as statesmen, until the world is fairly sick of their failures.

Nobody, says this philosophic Cæsar, shall have ground of complaint; henceforward all religions are tolerated throughout the empire. This was so far well; but it was not well, nor was it consistent with a truly-intended toleration, that the Christian party should be called upon to defray the costs of restoring the demolished pagan temples, much less that they should have been compelled to "do the repairs" with their own hands, unless, indeed, where "Catholic mobs" had done the mischief. In these measures there was an obvious injustice; but in other means resorted to by

Julian for more covertly achieving his purpose, namely, the ruin of the Christian community, there was as real an injustice, cloaked under a semblance of fair dealing. You Christians, said he, denounce our classic authors— our poets, orators, philosophers, as the promulgators of the most grievous errors;—to *you* they are the teachers of false opinions concerning the gods; by your own showing, therefore, we do you no wrong, we inflict upon you no damage, if we deny you altogether the use and perusal of them. You have your own books, you have your tracts, homilies, and treatises, and what not: be content with these, let these, in future, be your only school-books:—in a word, we prohibit the reading of the poets, the orators, and the dramatists of Greece, in your colleges.

SECTION I.

Thus we have before us the earliest, perhaps, of a series of experiments for realizing what might be called PROHIBITIVE EDUCATION. This first experiment failed, in every sense; and it must have failed, even if its astute originator had lived and reigned till the end of the century. He did not live long enough to be convinced of his mistake in rejecting his brother's advice—to adhere to the religion in which he had been trained. Gallus urged him to listen to the Homeric injunction—βάλλ' ούτως—on the higher grounds of abstract truth; but he might well have followed it, as his safest state policy. There was nothing in the waning paganism which could be substantial enough for sustaining the mighty movements of the empire after once those movements had found their fulcrum in the Christian verities. It is thus that men of the pedantic class misjudge the relative "strength of materials" when they are called up to move forward from universities to council chambers. JULIAN's notions of the classic divinities were, perhaps, an undefined and unexamined compound of elements, among which might be discovered a something from Plato, a something from Plutarch, a something from Lucian, and all attempered as Athenæus would have cooked it—fit for the tastes of the evening party. But he did not understand that, though the sceptre of the Roman world might, even in that late age, have been again firmly held in the grasp of a consistent pagan stoic—an Antoninus—or a religious theorist, of high personal qualities, all things would be put upon the tremble, when it was seen that the sheer nonsense of the classic paganism was to be re-enacted from the imperial throne.

We have just now called it a *semblance*, but in truth there is more than a show of moderation and reason in those epistles wherein JULIAN announces his determination concerning the "Galilæan sect." Much to the advantage of this "apostate" would it be to place these letters by the side of those of Innocent III, in which he moves the king and the magnates of France to exterminate the heretics of Languedoc! or, again, those of St. Bernard, addressed, with a similar intention, to his pupil Eugenius III; or of some fire-and-halter-breathing tracts of much later date, not only Romish, but Protestant also.

The emperor will permit no violences to be perpetrated; there shall be no persecutions on the score of religion; and the exiled bishops shall be recalled. Is it JULIAN, "the apostate," or is it our Oliver Cromwell, who says:—"If men are in error, if they be ignorant and unreasonable, what we should do is to teach, but not to punish them?"—καὶ γάρ, οἶμαι, διδάσκειν, ἀλλ' οὐχὶ κολάζειν χρὴ τοὺς ἀνοήτους. None should be liable to suffer in person, goods, or reputation, on any such account as his religious persuasion, nor be compelled to enter a temple. This premised, then let men be required to act consistently with their own professions. I shall demand this. If our standard authors are, as you say, so many sources of error in relation to the most momentous principles, you teachers of Christianity ought to have nothing to do with them. Why wish to employ them in your schools? How is it? Homer, Hesiod, Demosthenes, Herodotus, Thucydides, Isocrates, Lysias—these great men—held the gods in high esteem, as the sources of true knowledge; is it not, then, intolerable that men, with the same breath, should expound these authors, and rail at the gods whom they worshipped? This shall not be:—I will it otherwise. You must make your choice: abstain from these authors altogether; or if you will have them, teach as they taught. There is your Matthew—there is your Luke—expound these in your schools.

The Christian catechist might go on with his Bible class; but it is not required of him that he should expound Holy Scripture in any other manner than that in which he, and his predecessors had been used to expound them now these two hundred years. And in what mode was this? We have ample means for obtaining a reply to this question. We have before us samples enough of the biblical exegesis of the second century, and of the third, and of the fourth. There is barely a remains of the Christian literature of the centuries preceding the time of Julian's edict which does not show that to allow the Christian teacher of those times to expound his " Matthew and his Luke" in his own manner—in his *accustomed* manner, and then to deny him his Homer, his Hesiod, and the rest, was to take a course as nugatory and as absurd, as it was despotic.

Julian issued his edict in a petulant mood; he might have seen that the attempt to unmind the Christian world at that time was as impracticable as was the endeavour to give life and dignity to the puppet-paganism of the past age. A still more comprehensive—or, as we should now say, a more philosophic—apprehension of the tendency of things around him, was beyond the range of a man like this emperor. He did not understand his age: few men do understand that one page of history upon which their own doings are in course of being recorded. At all times, or in all times of movement and progress, it is inevitable that, among the several forces which are then in action, the greater force draws around itself, and carries with it, in its orbit, the lesser forces that may be near it. The brighter light will outshine and absorb the lesser lights. The more intense energy will take up, and assimilate, the weaker energies. Put the mind-world in strenuous agitation, and then whatsoever has already spent its momentum, must obey the new impulse.

Now when we, of this time, with perhaps our narrow habits of thought, and our stereotype religious tastes, look into the Christian literature of the early ages, we find what it is a weariness to read, what is distasteful, what we disallow; and much also which we think to be very much out of place:—and so it is. But there is another side of the subject. The Christian verities— truths high, and bright, and full of power, had come in upon the exhausted mind—upon the reason, and upon the feeling, of the great commonwealth of the nations, that were then embraced in the Roman empire. To this spent Mind it had imparted a new life; the intellect, long gone astray, had been called back to a path of consecutive thought:—the moral sense had woke up from its trance:—the Paralytic had sprung upon his feet, "leaping, and walking, and praising God;" and he had demonstrated the reality of his recovery by taking up the bed whereupon he had lain for three centuries or more, and carrying it to his home on his shoulders.

What, then, is our interpretation of the seeming pedantry of the early Christian writers? It is just this —the human spirit, awake, alive, and in power, was, in those times, depasturing itself in the fat levels of the Greek literature:—it was taking to itself, with a new assimilative appetite, the aliment it found there. The Mind of that age had listened to the challenge from on high: "Awake thou that sleepest, and arise from the dead, and Christ shall give thee life." So it was: this awakening had fully come; this resurrection had actually taken place; and how should it be otherwise than that nourishment should be sought for on all sides, and assimilated? Too late, by at least a hundred and fifty years—was it for the imperial edict to take effect in any sense whatever: too late to ask the Christian teacher to abjure his mental identity, to throw away his intellectual wealth; or to put off, if he could, his reason, his imagination, his feeling, his tastes!

What are the facts, if we look at them in a more exact manner? The Christian writers and teachers of the third and fourth centuries had, by their industry, their intelligence, and by the vitality of the body to which they belonged, come into the position of residuary legatees of the mental estate of ancient Greece. As to any practical purposes, there were then no surviving claimants of the property; or, if we may use another figure, we might say, as to the intellectual inheritance heretofore in the occupation of polytheists, it was "an encumbered estate," from which the nominal proprietors could obtain no rents, and for the improvement of which they had no funds in hand. The new proprietors came up, and they set foot upon the untilled acres with a free and a bold tread. They were shackled by no obligations to the demons of the departed superstition:— the richness of the soil was theirs:—to the dilapidated temples they rendered neither service nor tribute. This is just the feeling that one has in turning over the pages of the learned Christian writers of those ages, such as—Clemens Alexandrinus, Origen, Irenæus, and pre-eminently so, Eusebius. We need not come down to a later time—to those who were the actual contemporaries of JULIAN.

Let us fix attention, for a moment, upon a single instance—an instance of which JULIAN must, as a literary man, have had some cognizance. The reader may take from his shelves the Προπαρασκευή Εὐαγγελική, of the last named writer, and then tell us how many European writers of this present time he might be able to name— English, German, Italian, French—whom he may believe to be competent to the composition of a work equal to this, as to the vastness and universality of the learning which it exhibits, and as to the writer's command of his boundless materials. Are there, just now, a half-dozen such writers, who might be the modern competitors for a reputation like that which is the due of the author of the Evangelic preparation? This may be doubted.

But the accomplished Bishop of Cæsarea wrote for readers—for Christian, as much as for Pagan readers. The book now in our hands, what is it, then, but a mirror of the Christian intellectuality of the author's times? It is so; and when viewed in this light—its true light—then we are left in mute amazement at the infatuation of a scholar-like man who should think that, by the publication of an edict, he could deprive the Galilæan sect and its teachers of their intellectual existence! These "Galilæans" were already, and they had been so for a hundred and fifty years, the actual lords of the soil in the regions of mind; the Galilæan plough had furrowed —long before this time—it had furrowed—every teeming acre of the land of thought and reason; the Galilæan vine, through many a summer's day of many years past, had ripened its heavy clusters upon every hill-side of the classic poetry; beneath the broad shadow of the terebinth of Palestine the Plato of Greece had found a new home, and new listeners; and the time was soon to come when there would not be a product of the ancient mind which should be left outstanding of the Christian enclosure! What now becomes of the Apostate's bill of limitations?

Every age has its sample of men of JULIAN's type. There is something in them of the sophist, something of the pedant:—they are theorisers where they should concern themselves with the concrete; and they lose themselves often in some specialty of the concrete, where they should be regardful of great principles:— they are men who are quick to see all things—except the sun that is blazing in the high heavens over their heads. JULIAN (we excuse his blindness in recollection of the personal wrongs he had suffered) could not see or understand the miracle of that revolution which the Galilæan Teacher had wrought in the moral and intellectual life of all nations, from the shores of the Atlantic to the banks of the Tigris, and beyond these limits; but his petulance and his error are continually reappearing in the evolutions of human nature; nor are we unlikely at this very time to witness a repetition of the same mistakes, animated by the same virulence.

JULIAN believed that he could stem the tidal wave of his times; and it was no wonder that he failed. Yet it is certain that, although the broad Atlantic may not in any such manner be curbed, any small stream, or even a river, may be dammed up, or turned into a new channel. In this sense, or within certain limits, or, as we might say, within walls, the experiment of PROHIBITIVE EDUCATION may be successfully carried out. This has been done, often, and the instances will occur to the reader's recollection. The bishops assembled at Carthage, toward the close of the fourth century, decreed something of this sort, namely, a superfluous prohibition of those profane studies in which some few of them, perhaps, had indulged, to the scandal of the many. Some of the monastic orders included in their constitutions a rule forbidding the introduction of any but religious books. The Jesuit Society have done the like, where it suited their purpose. The more rigid of our modern Protestant sects have carried out similar restrictive measures in their schemes of general or of ministerial education; and some of them have actually solved the problem of the possibility of giving effect to prohibitions of this kind; so that they might triumphantly appeal to palpable evidences of their success. See, they might say, see how practicable a thing it is, in the training of youth, to forbid their mental growth and expansion.

The principle of Prohibitive Education may be acted upon under conditions which render it not merely practicable, but warrantable; as for instance:—In the establishment of schools for the children of the labouring classes we may confine the course of study to the mere rudiments of learning, for this simple reason, that our funds do not permit of our giving them more; or otherwise, that the brief hours which can be redeemed from the rigorous demands of home necessities will suffice for nothing more. The most liberal and benevolent endeavours to open the path of learning to those who live by the labour of their hands may be hemmed in by hard conditions of this sort. In such instances a scheme of education should be said to be *limited*, rather than *prohibitive*. But such schemes often show their prohibitive side when the insoluble problem presents itself of teaching children the fear of God, in some manner which all " the subscribers and supporters" shall consent to, as not involving a compromise of their " principles," or as invasive of their pet prejudices.

We have nothing now to do either with eleemosynary, or with under-class education, or with the difficulty, real or imaginary, of a combination of secular and religious training. These are indeed matters of the highest importance, but they are not our subject in these pages. PROHIBITIVE EDUCATION is a forced limitation of the studies of those who (professedly) are undergoing an upper-class training; or, in other words, who, with the exception, or the exceptions aimed at in the prohibition, are receiving the full measure of instruction which, in the modern advanced state of literature and science and philosophy, accomplished professors can offer to the youth of colleges and universities. Everything belonging to the culture of the mind is to be taught, everything—except that which indeed is the ground, the means, the Alpha and the Omega, of all culture.

When Prohibitive Education, under conditions of this sort, is carried out in the very midst of a Christianized community, there may be reason to believe, or we may be willing to persuade ourselves, that it is so—that the prohibited discipline, and the prohibited knowledge, are elsewhere effected and imparted, be it at home, or in a private course of study, or some other way, fancied and surmised. It will, however, be found in fact, or in the very large majority of instances, that the vacant room of the prohibited subject has come to be filled up by a positive formation of some sort. Nature (certainly it is so in the world of mind) nature abhors a vacuum; and what is not formally and authentically imparted will be supplied either clandestinely, or spontaneously. The natural complement of a *non-religious* education is—a positive atheism.

Remedies, compensations, re-actions, may come in to balance, or to neutralise, or to abate the mischiefs accruing from a scheme of Prohibitive Education :—or it may be so in a country like England. It is always allowable to think of such curative after-influences, as possible, and perhaps as probable.

The conditions under which prohibitive education may be attempted, or may be carried forward, in India, are altogether of another sort. An upper class, or university education, given to the higher ranks of the Hindoo people, if it be in any sense prohibitive, seals the fate of those who receive it: they are its victims.

The secularism of the present time, as applied to the principles of the course to be pursued in India, congests itself (as to education) into a proposal of this sort.—We will freely spread before you the entire wealth of our European intelligence, in the several departments of literature, and science, and philosophy, taking care—and we pledge our English honour to you in this instance—taking care to say and to teach nothing that touches our religion, or, as it is called at home, "our Christianity."

This offer and this profession, so made to the educationable classes of our Indian subjects, must no doubt be condemned by Christian men, on the ground of reasons which they will regard as absolute and irresistible. Be it so; but the profession itself, with the offer which is made on this ground, includes a great mistake as to the facts thereto relating:—it is a blunder which, like that of JULIAN in his prohibitive edict, must either fail utterly in the execution, or if it succeeds, it will bring with it consequences at the sight of which we shall stand aghast.

SECTION II.

We must not spare homely language, temperately applied, where it fits. There are principles which, although they may be disregarded by public men—driven as these so often are to the employment of miserable shifts in the conduct of affairs, will never be disputed among men of intelligence, how widely soever such men may differ in opinion on controvertible subjects.

There are principles which are at once laws of their craft, and rules of honour, among those who, either by the pen, or from professorial chairs, take rank as teachers of others. If such principles have often been forgotten, or contemned, by men of this class, individually, they are never disputed or denied. Or if, in ages past, they have been little regarded, in these times, it is certain, they must be honoured and acted upon.

The first and foremost of these principles, or axioms, or laws, as we might call them, of the professorial guild, is that which enjoins upon the teacher (not of boys, but of those who are approaching manhood) an absolute truthfulness, a singleness of intention, springing spontaneously, from the combination of clearness in the reason —unclouded intellectuality, and moral integrity:—it is the fruit of uprightness and luminousness. The teacher of men, some of them perhaps a few years only his juniors, must mingle himself with them on such terms of equality as are supposed when all are animated by one and the same intention—when all, with a like feeling, are pushing forward upon the same road—one of them, it may be, a little in advance of the others. Truth is our object, and truthfulness must be our mood and temper, and truthfulness is the pledge we give one to another: —truthfulness—a sin against which is indeed a sin unpardonable.

No such question will ever be put to his conscience by a truthful teacher as this:—How far may I lean over toward the false, without infringing upon the limits of professorial sincerity? A right-minded teacher abhors the trespass, and he holds in utter contempt any approximation toward it; and he scorns therefore to whisper to himself, or to his colleagues, any question of this order.

Falsification must not be thought of: concealment, for a purpose not confessed—is, falsification. It need scarcely be said that, on the ground of an understanding among professors, each may abstain from introducing subjects which, as they are the province of one of them, and are known to be fully taught by him, and which, as they are incidental only to his colleagues, are left by them to his exclusive treatment. Concessions of this kind come not within our scope.

It is a different case if a Senatus—a body of Professors—meet in conclave, and if they collectively pledge themselves to their patrons, not to teach, not to bring forward, not to mention, this or that class of facts, although nearly related to subjects that are professedly taught by them. This is what will not be done by men who respect themselves, and who are regardful of the duties, and the rights, and the dignity of their order.

This independence, this simplicity and integrity, and this absolute liberty of speech—this resplendence of the reason, set upon the pure gold of moral rectitude, is the teacher's qualification, teach where he may; but how indispensable is it if he be sent forth and constituted as the teacher of those whose first fault—the front vice of their ancient race—the turpitude of the ethics they have inherited from thousands of years of falsity and delusion—is this very apathy—this want of consciousness toward truth and truthfulness? If now we might take a fair sample of the European, and pre-eminently of the British mind, and if we were to bring it into contrast with the Oriental, and pre-eminently with the Hindoo mind, the most salient point of that contrast would be—this intellectual and moral coherence and consistency, on the one side, and an almost absolute want of it on the other side.

Such being the fact—and we think it is so—then shall we undertake the teaching and training of the Hindoo—a training and a discipline which is intended to lift him up to our own level—and in doing so shall the initial lesson which we give him be of this kind—that we show ourselves false to our own convictions? We pledge our British honour to the Hindoo to this extent, that, in teaching him, we tell him either that there is no truth in the world, or that we care nothing about it.

It may be asked in what way, or by what chain of inferences, is a falseness of this kind implied in our undertaking to teach our European literature and science and philosophy, while we abstain from teaching our religion? In finding an answer to this question, we must consider it in relation to two probable suppositions, as thus:—The Professor in a College where Hindoos and Mahometans are taught may be an accomplished man who, avowedly, has no religion—who believes nothing; or believes that all religions are alike. In such a case, then, the teacher compromises no conscience of his own, for he has none; but then the imputation of falseness—an imputation which will not fail to be carried forward—passes over the head of the individual teacher, and fixes itself upon the authorities above him. "Here are our superiors, calling themselves Christians, and yet appointing a man to instruct us who is known to hold their Christianity itself in contempt; or, at the best, he is utterly indifferent toward it. They themselves, therefore, either contemn the national religion, or they, like our professor, are indifferent toward it. There must be a falseness somewhere, either in the patrons, or in the professor; or in both."

But let it be supposed that the professor is himself a

religious man;—he is a theist and a Christian. Nevertheless he pledges himself to keep his religion out of sight in the whole of his intercourse, public and private, with the men whom he initiates in the literature or science of Europe. Are Hindoo or Mahometan youths likely to comprehend those attenuated reasons of policy which may seem to justify a course like this—a course in which the centre truths of all philosophy are to be thrust from their place, lest native prejudices should take alarm? This will not be. If such youths might chance to fix an eye upon a page (now before us) of JULIAN's Epistles, undoubtedly they would think that this Pagan's reproaches might fitly be applied to their English teachers—καὶ δραχμῶν ὀλίγων ἕνεκα πάντως ὑπομένειν: for the sake of their stipends they will patiently say, or not say, this, or that, or anything, or nothing.

Along with that defective sensitiveness toward truth and truthfulness, which, as we have said, is the characteristic of the Hindoo mind, there is—and in this respect the Mahometan is little in advance of the Hindoo—a defective conception of the rightful sovereignty of EVIDENCE, or valid proof, on any subject. Through countless periods the people of India have taken to themselves religious beliefs upon no warranty whatever of reason:—prodigious systems of mythology, theogenies, and theories of the universe, in relation to which the question—Is it *true?* would never be put, or, if put, could never be answered. In the Hindoo mental structure it would seem as if the nerves which should connect a belief of any kind with the reasoning faculty have, long ago, quite withered away. It is not so entirely with the Mahometan; but he also needs—and it is the first necessity of his intellectual training—he needs to be made conscious of this principle, that we are bound to seek for, and to obey, *evidence*, and that we must yield ourselves to proof. Thus, if the first lesson in our European training of the Oriental mind be *truthfulness*, integrity, intellectual and moral, the second lesson, which indeed is logical rather than moral, and which might be spoken of as a *discipline* rather than an axiom, is, the bringing these relaxed intellects, these nerveless brains, into a due bearing with processes of reasoning, mathematical, physical, and historical, *considered as forces which are to command us*, and which must carry us along with them.

Our European physical sciences seal the fate of Hindooism; and in like manner it might be said—and it would be so, in fact, if we ourselves could but understand it—that a genuine training and an unrestricted instruction in European history must seal the fate of the Mahometan belief; that is to say, such a course of instruction involves its refutation and its demolition, as a belief which educated men may now retain. As to that *religious* treatment which it is the part and duty of the Christian teacher, the missionary, to undertake, we have nothing to do with it in these pages. What we are speaking of is *college-training*. Now, in a course of college-training, we are bound, or ought to think ourselves bound, so to teach modern history as shall necessarily be destructive of Mahometanism. If we undertake to open the volume of Modern European History to the Mahometan, saving and respecting his faith in the mission of the Prophet, we pledge ourselves to utter a virtual lie at every step of our course. If I am appointed to a Chair of History, anywhere within the arms of the Ganges and the Indus, and if, before entering the hall, I bind myself to respect the prejudices of the Mahometan youth of my class—if I do this, I put myself in a position which is nothing better than that of a suborned witness in a momentous suit.

What sort of European history is it which an honest teacher should unfold in view of Mahometan (and Hindoo) youths who are to receive an unrestricted European education? We may boldly say it is such a history as is not yet anywhere extant in the compass of European literature: it is such a history as must be compiled by men who, at some future time, are to be called up and created for the performance of so signal a service as this, namely—the bringing the Oriental mind into correspondence with the European mind, clear and clean of our European misjudgments, and of whatsoever in our Christianity is national, and political, and temporary.

Mahometan youths should be made to feel that the ground is solid under their feet, at every step in their progress in modern history. The vast extent and the variety of the materials of this history, the inter-relationship of its several elements, and the irresistible evidences upon which it rests, should be placed fully before them. The course of events within the compass of this history is authentically known; it is known in its details: although it may be brought into question at this or that point, yet, as a whole, as a mass, it stands clear of a shadow of doubt. You must take it at our hands, and accept it as not less *sure* than are the physical sciences which you are learning from us in the adjoining halls.

But now how shall it be possible, in any such ample manner as this, and with any such fearless sincerity and simplicity, to teach history, namely, the history of the European nations during the eighteen centuries past, and not touch or teach our Christianity, and not offend Mahometan sensitiveness? Nothing of this sort is possible. No artifice of reserve, no method of concealment, none of the subterfuges of a mistaken delicacy, no rules of a scheme of Prohibitive Education, will avail us in this case. In teaching history we must needs speak the truth, the whole truth, and nothing but the truth; and inasmuch as a bold-minded and simple-hearted teacher has nothing on his own side to conceal, so will he not consent to conceal anything on the supposition, so insulting to those who have put their minds into his hands, that they would not wish to learn it.

SECTION III.

The expressions so often used of late in connection with Indian affairs—"*our* Religion"—" our Christianity"—and " the teaching *our* Religion in India"—convey, and conceal in conveying it, a serious misapprehension of facts which should be better understood. The correlative phrase, " our Religion," has no meaning, unless it implies that there are other religions abreast of our own, and which may claim to be thought of, and cared for, and endowed, along with it, and which, perhaps, may have as good a claim as our own to a respectful treatment.

It is quite true that, when we put ourselves in the position of the subjugated nations of the East (and we ought so to place ourselves sometimes) that, as looked at from this point of view, " our Religion" is only one of several; and it is true, moreover, that, in all matters of fiscal justice, and in all matters concerning the police, and in whatsoever touches the principles and the practices of a perfect religious toleration, these "other religions" possess unimpeachable claims to a careful and even scrupulous regard on the part of a conquering and omnipotent alien Government. All this is out of question, and it can scarcely be necessary formally to say as much.

But what we are concerned with in this Essay stands altogether on another ground. We are not speaking of this or of that religion, looked at from the Hindoo or the Mahometan point of view; nor yet of "our religion" such as it is, and ought to be regarded by the Christian missionary, or by Christian teachers. What we have before us is the proposed impartation of European intelligence—its literature, its physical science, and its abstract philosophy—to the native mind, both Hindoo and Mahometan:—and as to this training and this teaching, we assume that it is to be ample, and genuine, and unreserved, and honest. Furthermore, while an education of this kind is not set on foot for the purpose of teaching Christianity (for *this* teaching should flow in altogether another channel) it cannot be deliberately intended to teach, and to ensure the adoption of, that virulent European atheism which, at this time especially, is the only "other Religion" to which Christianity stands opposed.

In carrying to India the mass and the volume of European intelligence—its specific knowledge, and those modes of thinking that are adopted by the educated classes of Christianized Europe, we must take with us either the material atheism of France or Germany, or else we must take our Christian Theism, and our Christian sentiment and feeling: the one system, or the other must be assumed as the centre of thought, and as the fulcrum and the energy around which all other forces are to revolve, and toward which all things must tend. But then as to this Atheism, we must know what is its name at this moment, and where it is to be found, and who is its high priest, or its Mahomet. For, as to the last of the atheisms that has been much spoken of, it was slain awhile ago, not by Christian hands, but by the ministers of a religion of the same order, which is now, we are told, almost ready to make its triumphant entry upon the stage of the world, and to rule our future destinies. Meantime we may be sure it is Christianity that must stand, where it has so long stood—the centre, the fulcrum, the reason, the law of all movements in the great world of cultured thought, feeling, and action.

We return, for a moment, to JULIAN and his times. He failed to apprehend the fact that, some time before the mid years of the fourth century, Christianity had become the dominant power in the world of thought. Toward it all things in that world tended; around it, as their centre, all things were coming to revolve. Named, or not named, in books; professed, or rejected, this was the sun among the planets, and assuredly there was then no other sun in the heavens. This conspicuous fact this emperor and philosopher did not understand; and therefore he thought that he might shut off the Greek literature from the enclosures of the Galilæan sect!—a great mistake! Nevertheless this attempt, impracticable as it was, must be accounted a less mistake than is the endeavour, at this time made, to shut off Christianity from the range and compass of European science and philosophy.

There are those near us who would vehemently affirm

the contrary of this, and who will tell us that all things, or all things worth the knowing—the encyclopedia of a thorough college education, may be conveyed—Theism apart, and Christianity apart. Grant it that this may be done in a European college; but no such abnegation of the highest truths will be effected without having recourse to an affectation of ignorance, the *animus* of which every youth in the class will perfectly understand, and, understanding it, he is so far protected from its ill influence. But carry out this same *animus*, with its thin coating of affectation, to India. What the result will there be needs hardly to be affirmed.

To the Hindoo, thus instructed in those physical sciences which are fatal to his Hindooism, there can remain nothing but the pantheism which is ever near at hand to the Oriental intellect, and which, when hardened in passing through the fires of the physical sciences, becomes an indurated atheism, for ever impenetrable to every softening influence. The Mahometan, taught to think freely as to his prophet's mission, and if he be taught nothing as to the relative force of the Christian argument, finds, in his rejection of his own faith, reason enough for rejecting that of his teacher; if indeed he can think that his teacher is possessed of any faith at all.

In India, PROHIBITIVE EDUCATION, carried out in colleges, can be nothing else than a training of youth in a species of atheism which shall qualify the upper ranks of the native races for looking on with more than Oriental indifference, while the masses of the people, in some future outburst—not far off—are wreaking now a postponed vengeance, upon their European oppressors.

A *wrongful* policy may be maintained and kept in

vigour long—from generation to generation; for it has no remorses, no scruples, no hesitations, no shame, no reluctances. But a *mistaken* policy, well intentioned, will not fail quickly to get itself set fast in the impracticable:—it was full of incongruities when it started; and these incongruities break out upon the surface as sheer absurdities, after a very little time. So will it be with the endeavour to carry out in India a scheme of Prohibitive Education. Prohibit nothing—or nothing which is not immoral, and then Christianity comes into its due position—not as "our religion," but as the one and the only religion in the world.

ESSAY VII.

"WITHOUT CONTROVERSY."

ΚΑῚ ὁμολογουμένως—" confessedly." A sense must be sought for in which this apostolic phrase* might be applied, either to the "great mystery" which then and there is named, or to any other article of a Christian man's belief; for, in fact, all principles are controverted, and every article of every creed is disputed, and is denied, and is rejected, by some around us; and even by some to whose exceptions a degree of respect is due. So it is now; and so it has been in every age; and so it was at the moment when this pastoral epistle was written, and despatched.

But in this place, as we are not undertaking to expound Scripture, we need not stop to ascertain, with precision, the sense which the inspired writer might have attributed to this phrase, as he here employs it. He might perhaps use the word adverbially, or for emphasis, and in no very strict or definite sense, but merely as a word suited to express his own strong feeling of the certainty of that one great truth, which, surpassing, as it does, the utmost compass of human thought, is nevertheless the truth, most firmly to be held, as it is the foundation of every other article of Christian theology. We may thus think, and pass on; and then ask—In what sense, by aid of an allowable

* 1 Tim. iii 16

accommodation perhaps, we, *at this time*, may apply the same word to any doctrine, or article of belief, which we ourselves embrace with the fullest confidence? How shall *we* bring ourselves to think of any of our elementary convictions, and, always supposing that we are well informed, as to the history of religious opinions, and the present state of controversies throughout Christendom, shall affirm concerning it, that it is received and assented to—ὁμολογουμένως—" without controversy ?" There is no one element of faith to which, *in this sense*, we may apply this phrase. Merely to affirm of a doctrine that *if it be true*, it is confessedly " a great mystery," is little better than to affirm a truism in a frigid manner.

There is, however, a sense in which a Christian man thoroughly informed, may so speak of his own faith, and, severally, of its elements —and it is thus. Let us take the instance of those—and there are many such at this time—who, whether or not they may have passed through a course of theological training, as if preparatory to the exercise of the Christian ministry, are fairly well-informed on all those subjects that are usually included in a clerical education. We suppose such persons to be surrounded also with the necessary aids for prosecuting studies of this order, and for recovering what they may have forgotten: they are, more or less, conversant with religious history, ancient and modern; and as to the controversies of recent times, such persons are, we may suppose, acquainted with them, and they know at what stage or point the always-advancing mass of religious, and of irreligious thought, is just now making a momentary pause. To such persons, therefore, there will not be room to address the supercilious

WITHOUT CONTROVERSY. 225

caution—"You would do well to read Mr. ——'s book, just out; for when you have read it, you will see ground for lowering the tone in which you speak of your cherished, but antiquated, orthodoxy."

Those who stand in a position such as that which we have now indicated, toward the world of religious thought—toward its controversies, and its beliefs, may often be tempted to envy the felicity of some simple-hearted Christian people around them, who, uninformed in such matters, and quite mindless as toward every species of gainsaying, are content to hold fast the "form of sound words" which they have been taught; and thus they live, and breathe, and thrive, walking and resting in the sunny Beulah of untroubled faith. But we are forbidden, by the constitution as well of the intellectual as of the moral world, to recede from a position to which we have spontaneously advanced:—it is not allowable to take up the cup of knowledge, and then to forget that we have tasted it: the taste will remain, as a bitterness on the palate, ever afterwards, unless we go on to sip, and to drink anew. Be ignorant, or, if you would not be ignorant, then learn whatever may be learned. Think not at all; or else think on to the end.

Nevertheless, although it is not permitted to us to fall back upon the immunities of simple ignorance, if once these have been forfeited, there is still a course that may be taken, and in taking which a more solid peace may be secured than the peace of ignorance can be, and where a safer anchorage may be found than is that of the shoal of mindless assentation.

Those who, through life, have acquainted themselves with controversy, and who, perhaps, may have touched it themselves, and who, within their circles, have used and acquired the style and habit of argumentation—those who are often meeting and refuting objections—those who are accustomed to the wearing of armour, and the poising of weapons—such persons well know how difficult it is for them to fix their attention upon great truths, thought of *apart* from all the denials of them—on this side, and on that side. Even into the retirements of the most secluded and abstracted sanctum of religious meditation, the grim spectre of an antagonist makes its way, and, at a glance of the forbidding and pallid visage, a vigilant logic wakes up, and an encounter is threatened!

But there comes a time in a man's course, earlier or later, even of such an one as we are here supposing, when he may well, and safely, and much to his personal comfort, shut the door against argument and contradiction, and when he may bring himself into near communion with the truths of his belief—*apart* from the denial of them, or as if what is true were, in all men's esteem, "confessedly" true. He thus forgets the opinions of others, and he believes himself at liberty to say —Now, at length, and henceforward to the end of life, let me *rest* upon my beliefs, as axioms that are held— ὁμολογουμένως—in their indisputed and azure-like simplicity and certainty.

This faith of a Christian man's meditative evening hour, we may imagine to be enjoyed where he looks around upon the backs of many books which he has read, but which he will not open again; and yet his faith must not be contemned, as if it were a blind faith; for a man is not blind who, having been conversant, long enough, with the stormy things of earth, turns the eye to the region where storms do not arise. The question comes then as to what those beliefs are which, safely, and with advantage, may be brought inside the consecrated enclosure of religious meditation, and which may be privileged as principles that are held—*controversy apart*.

SECTION I.

If there were room for a question, whether I should admit mysteries, and perhaps "great mysteries," into my creed, then this doubt would be removed at the outset; for mysteries that are deep and impenetrable hover around its very first article, which is to set forth what I believe concerning HUMAN NATURE, and the human family, and, consequently, my own place and destiny, as thereto related.

But why, contrary to every systematic rule and custom in creed-making, why begin this with an article of *this* sort? The reason for doing so may be thus exemplified by aid of an analogy. The first step in acquiring a true knowledge of the celestial bodies—their magnitudes, distances, and motions—is the measuring an arc of the earth's surface: this initial and unambitious operation precludes many and grievous errors concerning my own standing-place in the material universe; and, moreover, it puts into my hand the sure means of carrying elaborate calculations outward and upward to vast distances, even as far as to the outskirts of this planetary system, if not beyond that system. If ancient astronomers had been content to take this course, or, if taking it, they had followed it out, what we now call "our modern astronomy," would, by this time, have been an "ancient astronomy," and yet true.

In making a commencement where I now make it, for finding the starting-point of a creed, I escape the danger which has been so fearlessly met by the framers of symbols, namely, the presuming myself to know vastly more than I do, or ever can know. The Divine Nature, so far as it may be apprehended by the human mind, must become known to it in quite another manner than that of abstract speculation, or of logical deduction. And yet systems of theology are made up of propositions concerning the INFINITE BEING, which propositions, if I follow them out in logical order, lead me not into light, but into utter darkness—the darkness either of universal doubt, or of material atheism.

But now, in giving expression to my belief concerning this—its foremost article, touching human nature, and the moral system, I have said that mysteries attach to it:—what are they, or why admit them? Human nature is a *fact*, which is under my eye; and if, with human nature spread out before me, I am willing to abstain from uncertain speculations, and to keep within the range of unquestionable realities—if I refuse to follow any vague inferences; and if I repress, and hold in contempt, mere emotions and sympathies, which are fruitless and idle, then, and on these conditions, may I not preserve my belief concerning the human family, quite exempt from mysteries? Not so; or at the best, in the place of mysteries, which may indeed trouble me, I shall come in front of contradictions and incoherences which must actually stagger and paralyze the reasoning faculty. A physiology of man which excludes all mystery, can be nothing more than an anatomy: it gives the *parts*, the solids, the fluids, the mechanism; but it does not give the functions.

But were not ancient schemes of human nature much less encumbered with mystery, and far more lightsome, and easy of apprehension than are any of those schemes or theories which I might now be willing to accept as expressive of my belief on this subject? It must be granted that they were so; and yet I am not at liberty so to release myself from the burden that has come upon me, for it has come in consequence of a great extension of my range of vision, and in consequence also of a knowledge of facts that were not heretofore known, or, if known, regarded; and the burden of mystery has become as oppressive as it is in consequence also of the quickening of moral sentiments which had slept for ages, even throughout the times of the ancient philosophy. The perplexities which darken my prospect, and sadden my meditative hours, could not in any way be dispelled, unless I might unknow what I have come to know, and then might cease to feel what I could not wish not to feel. If I labour to forget what I know, the mere attempt fixes it the more firmly in my memory; and as to an attempted abatement of feeling, or a factitious quashing of any sensibility, which approves itself as of genial and beneficent quality, this would be—even if I could attempt it, a brutalizing operation; and better were it to become insensible and earthly, in the vulgar method of a life of animal indulgence and sordid selfishness, than to force myself into it by a process of philosophical sophistication.

As member of the community of mind, at this time, and as a partaker of that religious and intellectual training which is therein to be had, I have undergone a discipline which, in its consequences, brings the shadow of the most sombre mysteries to rest upon this—the first article of my creed, concerning human nature, and the state and prospects of the human family. How this comes about may thus be explained.

I may be in company, for a length of time, with some one who is conspicuously eminent above his fellows, and vastly my superior, in wisdom and virtue. I contemplate with involuntary admiration his self-command, his self-denial, his active benevolence, his energy, courage, and assiduity in labouring for the good of others; I observe also his humility and modesty; I admire the translucence of his character, and its strength. But this admiration, and this esteem, which grow in me from day to day, are not mere sentiments of awe, and respect, and affection; for there attends these feelings, or soon follows them, a kindling emotion which is perhaps new to me. I must not call it *ambition*, for it has a high and a pure intention, to which this term does not well apply. This new impulse is an energy, deeply stirring my whole nature; and it utters itself in fervent ejaculations of this sort:—Would that I were such as is this my admirable friend! Shall I not emulate his virtues? Shall I not take him as my pattern, and follow his steps, and become, in some measure, like him?

This emulous and hopeful impulse I feel to be the indication of a law of my moral structure which, although it may long have been latent, and might continue latent, ought to stand as the axiom of any true philosophy of human nature. If now the person whom I thus acknowledge to be so much my superior, were one of a higher order of beings—a member of the celestial hierarchy, the conditions of whose existence are essentially unlike those to which I am subjected, so that *his* virtue, and *my* virtue, can have no convertible value, and so that there could be no room for emulation or imitation on my part—then, and on that supposition, the vivid emotion which just now I have spoken of, must instantly subside, and in the place of it there would come over me a lifeless and powerless awe:— veneration, love, perhaps; but it must be a love that would be ineffective and unavailing.

Or let me take an instance of another kind. The being whom I acknowledge as my superior in wisdom and virtue, may be one who, as to his natural endowments, his intelligence, and power of thought, is not my equal, but far otherwise; nor, as to his early advantages, have they been such as to put him, in the world's esteem, on a level with me, or near it. Nevertheless I yield to him a place of esteem in my inmost thoughts, to which, as if it were due to myself, I dare not pretend: he *is* my superior. In this case the same consciousness of a power in myself, though latent, or very feebly alive, is awakened, and it is pungently stimulated, though in another manner. Here is my humble friend who has got the start of me so far on the upward path, notwithstanding the lower range of his intellect, and the many defects of his early training. What is it that I have been doing these many years? With what trifles have I been occupied? Why have I not become —what he is—yes, and much more than this—advantaged by my stronger reason, and the various culture it has had! Here again I recognize a first principle in human nature—its causative moral power—to think wrongly concerning which, or to allow sophistries of any kind, philosophical or theological, to cloak it with evasions, must be of the most serious ill consequence: it is certain that, whatever may be lost sight of in my creed, this prime article, on which hinges my faith in the reality of the moral system, must not be wanting in it. I must take care to secure a foremost place for this belief.

In these experiences there is a tacit recognition of the principle, that the moral element in human nature is its leading or paramount element, and is that toward which the mental organization tends, as the centre or final cause of the structure. The sight of eminent wisdom and virtue excites an emotion of admiration and esteem which is involuntary and irresistible; and beyond this there comes an emotion taking effect upon my personal consciousness, and inciting me to move forward on the same path. Yet no such impulse takes effect upon me unless there be also a consciousness, feeble or vivid, of a power so to do. I gaze upward as the eagle soars cloudward, and may think his power of wing enviable; but the idle wish to overtake him in the sky has no momentum in it, for nature has denied me wings.

Thus far my experience of human nature does not necessarily throw an inference forward beyond the present economy of mundane life: to gather such an inference I must look at the same human nature on another side.

A purpose of benevolence, perhaps, may have impelled me to visit a den wherein the victims of our "civilization" are enduring all the misery which body and soul may be conscious of; and where they are subject to those worse miseries which they have ceased to be conscious of. Sad exhibition indeed! and yet great principles maintain their supremacy here as elsewhere, but under new modifications. I fix the eye upon some one of the inmates of this den:—flesh and blood like my own, and the rudiments of every sensibility and affection which I cherish in my own nature are there. And yet what would it be to be linked in companionship with this being for a day! What but a martyrdom! For he is as sensual as a swine, as fierce as a wolf; he is knavish, petulant, and wayward, and utterly impatient of remonstrance, entreaty, and rebuke; he will have none of my counsels, and he flings defiance at me if I insult him with my pity. Yet why sketch this rude outline? Better ascend the filthy steps of this cellar, uttering some apothegm of a frigid philosophy—a text from a page of our "sociological science"—and say, as to this brother of mine, he is indeed a pitiable object; but we should think of him as the blameless victim of our faulty institutions, and of the unlucky physical conditions of his place, beneath the wheel of the great machine: it was his misfortune to inherit a depraved animal constitution, and every circumstance of his course in life, from —the cradle!—the babe never slumbered in a cradle!— from his mother's breast!—that breast was destitute alike of milk and of fondness!—every influence from the first hour to this hour, has been the worst possible. How much blame, then, can I think is this victim's due? Boldly say—none!

But again I encounter this same wretched being, and this time it is abroad in the noisy court, or alley, that I find him. There is a brawl:—unprovoked, he is inflicting grievous injuries upon one who is not his match in strength:—it is a wanton and purposeless cruelty, a mere outspend of savageness, to no end. Sad is it to listen to the screams of the sufferer, trampled on and kicked in the gutter. But at this sight my "social science" maxims snap in sunder, and fail me quite; for I feel, and am ready to act too, at the impulse of a contrary belief. What!—this monster of cruelty, is he not *blameworthy?* We shall soon show him that we think him to be so. Away with him: he deserves ten times more punishment than the law is able to inflict upon him.

Now if I am told that I am giving way to an unreasonable impulse of mere feeling, and that instead of aiding the law in its purpose of inflicting punishment upon this wretch, I should be true to my philosophy, and should cease to think of even the worst outrages as *crimes:*—then it comes to this, that in the structure of my mind there is an instinct of justice so powerful, so irresistibly strong, and a forecasting of retribution such, as that, not even the most extreme imaginable instance, in which the desire of vengeance should give way to cold disgust, can avail to quash, or to divert the emotion.

Here, then, is an ungovernable impulse, prompting me to inflict punishment where, if all the circumstances be duly considered, it might seem to be only a new wrong to inflict any. This is a fact in human nature which carries with it several weighty inferences. To find these inferences I must carry home the case I have imagined, and consider it as it may have a bearing upon my own habits of thought, and my personal anticipations of a future, and it may be, a final, retribution.

I find that this brutal wrong-doer, if I converse with him, has become, as one might say, so encrusted with the hideous notions of a perverted morality, as that any appeal I might make to his conscience, or to his sense of justice or humanity, is turned aside: he mocks my ethics;—he has his own code. Such, I may coolly say, such are the infatuations that spring out of misery and vice, rendering any process of cure almost hopeless!

But now may there not be infatuations of a silken sort, which spread themselves around my own egotistic habits of feeling, and which have the effect of rendering me more or less unconscious of what it might greatly concern me to know and think of? this is not improbable; and if so, then it may also be true that—if all the conditions of the two cases were fully understood, and if they were fairly allowed for, the vehemence of the appetite for retribution would loosen its grasp of its one miserable object, and fix its talons on another.

On rare occasions, when enormous crimes are perpetrated, and when the innocent are barbarously wronged, there is a loud outcry for vengeance. Human nature utters itself with passion; but yet it is not a false utterance: it is a true, though an impetuous vaticination. The thunderbolts of Heaven are called for, and Heaven, in its own day, will answer the call. But now if there is to be a future reckoning *in any case*, and if *any* deeds are to be brought into court, that reckoning, undoubtedly, will be universal; it will be impartial; it will be unexceptive:—that inquiry will leave nothing unsought for, nor will it ever be baffled in its search.

It is impossible that I can think otherwise than thus of the future judicial proceedings of a central and a Supreme Authority: the Righteousness of Heaven will be no respecter of persons. No process of reasoning— no labours of the human mind, will avail, or have ever availed hitherto, to disperse the heavy disquietudes that arise from the consciousness of individual blameworthiness, and the forethought of a future reckoning. How idle, for any such purposes, are the dreams of the pantheist! The forebodings of an awakened conscience are not to be assuaged by any devices so flimsy as these.

How then, if not so? In no other way than by finding—
if it may anywhere be found—an authentic and a trustworthy Religion.

SECTION II.

By methods of abstract thought I may frame for myself a Religion which shall be theoretically coherent, and apparently probable; but then it stands contradicted, on the right hand, and on the left hand, by other theories or schemes, each more or less consistent and reasonable, and any one of which might well be accepted in its stead. At least some one of these rival systems, even though it may be of inferior quality, may prevail over my better convictions in a season of intellectual abatement, or of moral infirmity: in an evil hour I may become ensnared by a sophistry which, in a brighter hour, I should reject with contempt. It is at the urgent prompting of the moral instincts, and as driven forward by the forebodings that attend these instincts, that I seek for a religion; and if it is to assuage the anxieties of an enlightened conscience, the religion which I am to accept should not stand contradicted, or be brought into question by any sort of evidence, or any counter-testimony which is *of the same quality* as that which supports itself: as, for instance, abstract reasoning, against abstract reasoning;—or human testimony, apparently good, opposed to other human testimony, apparently good. There is only one religion, hitherto known in the world, which occupies this position, and which I may accept, and may rely upon as uncontradicted and authentic, and trustworthy, after informing myself fully and exactly of its evidences. But how is it that I can acquiesce in the religion of the Bible, and receive it—ὁμολογουμένως—as "confessedly" true, since there are so many who reject it?

It is thus—I am now making no distinction between the Old Testament and the New, as if the latter might be accepted, although the former were rejected. For if the older writings are not the records of a continuous message from God to man, then I decline to trouble myself with any research concerning the merits or pretensions of the later writings. Whatever may be the distinctions which hereafter I may incline to insist upon between the one and the other, *just now* I make no such distinction; but I take the Bible as a whole, and I accept it as the record of a continuous Divine Revelation, and I so take it with a cordial acquiescence, and, after laborious inquiry, I hold it to be true, in its own sense—ὁμολογουμένως—"confessedly" so—notwithstanding the contrary profession of many, and of many educated men like myself; and I do so without hesitation, and without arrogance; and I should do so, even if all were against me, or a thousand to one, or ten thousand to one.

The rejection of the Holy Scriptures as true in their own sense, namely, as being a direct message from God, may at this time be considered as arising from two sources; for, first, there are the contradictions of abstract philosophy; and these, at this time, are resolvable into the pantheistic and the atheistic theories;—the two, merging always the one into the other; for although these paradoxes may seem to be exclusive, the one of the other, the ground of distinction between them sinks away whenever I attempt to set foot upon it. The two schemes are at one on this point, that they both treat the moral sense in human nature as a delusion, and both of them deny the reality of that system of government—present and future, from a belief in which the notions of virtue and vice, of good and evil, and of individual responsibility and religious relationship to the Supreme Being, take their rise. In relation, therefore, to the religion of the Scriptures, pantheism and atheism are not to be considered as two systems, but as one.

Knowing, as I do, that these theories of the universe have beset the regions of Abstract Thought in all times, and, in fact, that they haunt the human intellect, and that, at this present moment, they avail to paralyze the religious convictions of many, it would not be safe on my part to dismiss them, as if in ignorance of their actual presence, and of the influence they exert; for it might be said to me—If you had only acquainted yourself with the *modern form* of these ancient philosophic systems, you would have found that they are far more substantial than you seem to imagine; and, in fact, that it is more easy to contemn them blindly, than fairly to refute them.

So thinking, I therefore inform myself concerning both these doctrines, and I take care to know the extent of their meaning; and my finding concerning them is this: first, that they are paradoxes of that kind, of which there are several, that go in pairs, the one of them serving as a place of retreat when we are in conflict with the absurdities of the other. At such a time we look about for any way of escape. Thus, when I am beaten off from atheism, which is the denial of the INFINITE, and the ONE, I rush into the arms of the other, which is the denial of the finite; and yet when there, I find only a momentary breathing time; for I quickly feel that atheism is in fact an easier, or more somnific philosophy to live under than pantheism. Besides, this oscillative antagonism between incompatible paradoxes is only a sample of several which are known of old, to breed inveterate discords in the house of abstract speculation. It is thus that I may be bandied about between idealism and materialism;—between a world without substance, and a world that is all solid. If the abstractive faculty mistakes its function in the intellectual economy, then an eternal jar is the only consequence;—and better were it to lodge out of doors, among the herd, than to be inmate in a mansion where husband and wife are wrangling, and striving for the mastery, every day, all the year round.

But this is not the whole of the reason why, after due inquiry, I should turn away the ear, for ever, from the contradictions of these abstruse speculations. They do not touch, or in any way affect, the matter in hand. I am in search of a religion at the impulse (mainly) of my instinctive belief of the reality of the moral system of which I am a member. Now this belief in conscience is not an opinion which I may continue to profess, or may cease to profess, in consequence of the reading of a book, or the hearing of a course of lectures. It is a permanent element of human nature:—it is common to mankind in all times and countries. This instinct flushes the cheek of every sensitive child, and it prevails over the laborious sophistications of the philosopher. This belief is cherished as an inestimable jewel by the best and the purest of human beings;—and it is bowed to, in dismay, by the foulest and the worst:—its rudiments are a monition of eternal truth, whispered in the ear of infancy:—its articulate announcements are a dread foredoom ringing in the ears of the guilty adult. You say you can bring forward a hundred educated men, who, at this time, will profess themselves to be no believers in a moral system; but I will rebut their testimony by the spontaneous and accordant voices of as many millions of men as you may please to call for, on the other side.

Therefore, as it concerns the liberty I feel myself possessed of, for accepting the religion of the Scriptures, notwithstanding the contradictions of pantheists and atheists, the state of the question is this:—pantheism and atheism cannot both be true, but they may both be false; and the residual probability of the truth of the one over the other is, at the most, quite an inappreciable quantity, when it is brought to weigh against a universal instinct of nature—a prime element of the human structure—an impulse, and an involuntary persuasion which, if indeed it might be wholly deadened within us, would leave man on a level with the brute, and men incapable of any social form of existence.

But in the second place, the Scriptures, Jewish and Christian, are denied to be, in any special sense, a revelation, or message from God, by those who assail the proper evidences supporting their claims as such. This kind of contradiction I at once admit to be pertinent to the question in hand, and, therefore, to be deaf to it would be not merely highly unsafe, but unreasonable.

If in this Essay I were undertaking the defence of my Biblical faith, as against all comers, it might be required of me to bring into view, in order, and to refute, *seriatim*, the several counter-pleas which, in these times, have been urged as the grounds of their non-belief by notable writers. Instead of attempting any such operose task as this, I am attempting nothing more than a setting forth, for my individual satisfaction, the grounds on which I receive and bow to the canonical writings, and accept the profound mysteries they may contain, as— ὁμολογουμένως—a message and a law, sent to me from heaven.

Now with this view, I may at once release myself from the imagined obligation to examine with care and labour those schemes of anti-Christian opinion which the authors of them have abandoned as impracticable and nugatory, or which their successors, labouring on the same field, and animated by the same zeal, have treated with contempt, or which they cease to bring forward. On this safe ground, therefore (after knowing what these cast-off arguments are) I dismiss the entire mass of anti-Christian ribaldry and impertinence which satisfied the reckless impiety of Europe during the times of Voltaire and Rousseau. In like manner, and with a consciousness of security, I cease to concern myself henceforth, any more, with that scheme which, in Germany, for a length of time, was accepted as a sufficient explication of the historical enigma concerning the origin of the evangelic memoirs; the story being admitted as mainly true, and the writers honest;—but the supernatural portions were alleged to be misconceptions on the part of these rude and uninstructed persons. This theory has long ago given way to a more strict critical method: —it is abandoned, and in its place there has come up— to be wondered at for a moment—a theory of the Gospel history, boldly conceived and elaborately set forth, but which, under the weight of its own marvellous improbability, has silently gone down:—the mythic "Life of Jesus"—is a scheme which I can never make to consist with facts that are as certain in my view, as are the events of my own life, last year. This mythic theory is a mass of incoherences; it has however been serviceable in purging the atmosphere of the effluvia of the decayed schemes of the preceding time.

Moreover, the prodigious painstaking, and the ingenuity, and the tempered virulence of this last attempt to rid the world of Christianity, have given evidence of the extreme difficulty of the task which those undertake who, on the ground of historic criticism, labour to disengage what is, in their view, credible in the Gospel history, from that which they are predetermined to reject as incredible. The human mind, advantaged by all imaginable aids of learning, has exhausted its forces in the endeavour to rend the supernatural from off its attachments to this history.

The state of the case, then, is this:—modern criticism, historic and literary, leaves me in undisputed possession of the books (with two or three exceptions) that are included in the Canon—the Bible, as I have it. There is not, so far as I know, at this time afloat, any accepted and available anti-Christian solution of the enigma regarding the origin of Christianity: non-belief, at this moment, has come to a stand-still; for it has no fresh solution of this enigma in readiness. Then there is this significant indication of the relative merits of the anti-Christian argument, namely, this—That every recent writer (of any mark or note) who has signalized himself on that side, and who has set out with a professed willingness to admit as much of Christianity as he can, has receded further and further from his first position:—he is seen labouring to ascend a slippery incline, but at every step he slides back, and it is not long before he comes to a breathing place—on the dead levels of material atheism, where alone a man may believe that he has no further to go.

For myself, instead of finding the supernatural element in the Biblical writings a difficulty, I should be met by a difficulty most perplexing, if I were required to receive the religion which I am in need of, apart from any supernatural sealing of the documents containing it, and destitute of an authentic signature. Such a sealing, or (might I use the word) such an endorsement, would be needed even if the revelation related to nothing higher than mundane opinions, or every-day rules of conduct; for I must possess the means of distinguishing these enactments from other opinions and rules—like to them, but not the same.

When, however, I find that the principal subject of this written or documentary revelation transcends, immeasurably far, the range of human thought, and that it carries me in meditation within the circle of an economy of which I have no knowledge by any other means, then, and in that case, I not merely expect, and desire, and need also, a sure and ample attestation of it from on high; but this attestation, of whatever sort it may be, stands forward as a part and a sample of that which is so attested. I mean to say that those visible acts of power which indicate the Divine Presence, are always less than the message itself; and in hearing and accepting the message, I have already given in my assent to the attendant miracle.

It depends entirely upon the position which I take whether miracles, such as those of the Gospel history, shall stand before me as matters not to be submitted to, if by any means I may evade the disagreeable necessity of doing so; or, as congruous accompaniments of a dispensation which is to connect this present world with another—a world in which what here I call miracle, is there order.

It is, therefore, without repugnance that I admit the supernatural element of the religion which I welcome as the gift of Heaven. But now—the attestation admitted—what is it to which it should be held to attach? What is it to which the Divine signature is indeed appended? This is a question which at all times claims an answer, and which especially demands an answer at this present moment.

SECTION III.

In accepting the Scriptures of the Old and New Testaments, as conveying a Divine Revelation, and as entitled to a deference which I yield to no other writings, ancient or modern, I am confronted by a question to which some sort of answer must be given. Is it *everything* which I find enclosed between the two boards of my Bible, that I receive and bow to, as sent to me from Heaven, and as sanctioned by supernatural attestations?

Controversy is rife on this point; and I find honest and well-informed men giving discordant replies to the question; and these replies are uttered often with an eagerness, and even an asperity, which is usual in religious controversies when, on both sides, there is a consciousness of some incompleteness or incoherence in the solution that is given of the problem in debate. With the one purpose in view, which has been professed in this Essay, it would seem that I should hold off from ground whereupon so many combatants are in conflict. Nevertheless, as I think, there is a standing room even here, whereupon a belief may be made to rest—" controversy apart."

The discussion which is still open and undetermined on the subject of the "Inspiration of Holy Scripture," is the inevitable, as it is the *proper* consequence, *first*, of the greatly advanced state of the art of criticism, and pre-eminently, of Biblical criticism. The assiduity, the intelligence, the improved methods, and the enlarged means, which give to this science or art its present high condition of effectiveness, and of certainty, have drawn thoughtful and well-informed men forward insensibly to take their stand upon an arena, whence some of them, as it seems, would gladly find a way of retreat; but this cannot be.

This controversy, in the *second place*, is a result, in a general way, of that tendency toward systematic completeness, or, as one might call it, *forensic determination*, which is a prominent characteristic of these times. We hear this utterance on all sides—"You say you believe this and that concerning the Canonical writings; tell us, then, *precisely* what it is that you intend, and what it is that you believe; and why you believe it." Nothing else ought to be looked for, in these times, than the putting of a question of this sort to those who profess aloud their submission to the sole and supreme authority of these writings.

But there is another, and a less ostensible moving force to which this present controversy owes much of its depth and meaning. Religious thought has made a marked advance in these times. Religious *fervour*—declining, has, at each retreating step, measured the space through which religious *sensitiveness* has moved forward; and at this moment we are driven at once to wish that our personal devotion was more cordial than it is, and our relative sympathies much less alive, than they are; or such as they were in years past. This progress—and *progress it is*, could not have any other result than to give point, or let me say, *poignancy* to many questions, that occur in the course of Biblical exposition. A style of apologetic commentary which the readers of Matthew Henry, and of Thomas Scott also, were content with, does not satisfy the nicer feelings of the religious community at this time. From this discontent, whether it be articulate, or stifled, there arise endless discussions—questionings that are never brought to an issue, concerning the extent and the conditions of that inspiration of Scripture which, in general terms, we all acknowledge.

An ill consequence of this present undetermined state of our belief concerning "inspiration" is, a habit it gives rise to, on the part of the authorized expositors of Scripture, namely, that of quashing intelligent inquiry, as the symptom of "an unrenewed nature;" or of evading it, by means of explanations which are satisfactory neither to the speaker himself, nor to his hearers.

What can be done to bring things into a more auspicious position? I will not presume to answer this question; but, instead of doing so, set forth what to myself is solid ground of belief—"controversy apart."

As well rid the question, at this point, of such things as admit of no question, or of none among honest and well-informed men. It is certain that Biblical criticism must pursue its course, and must ply its tools in its own manner, hereafter, as in the time passed. It must do so freely and manfully, and it must be exempt from that intimidation with which some mindless and superstitious men are fain to arrest its further progress. The stipulation which we insist upon, in giving this free scope to erudite criticism, is only this—that it shall be ingenuous, not petulant or captious; that it shall be serious in a religious sense, and not animated by a covert desire to make out a case against the Bible, and for the vexation of the religious commonwealth.

Criticism employs itself in making sure the genuineness of books—in restoring the text of such books, so far as the means of doing so safely, are in our hands. Within the province also of criticism, or of its cognate expository methods, it comes to inquire concerning the canonicity of books singly considered, and thus to draw a line that shall be exclusive of all writings in behalf of which no claim can be made good, of their direct connection with the supernatural attestation that gives *authority* to the books included in the canon.

But it is not within the province of criticism to sit in judgment upon portions of canonical Scripture, on the plea that such portions contain what we do not find it easy or possible to reconcile to our notions, either of the Divine Attributes, or of the abstract fitness of things. Rationalism, in the modern sense of the phrase, is the doing this. The rationalist provides himself with a theology to his liking, before he opens his Bible, and to this theology of his own, all things which he may find there must give way. From any such boldness as this I am held back, *first*, by the consciousness of the limited range of the human mind, universally, as related to the subjects of religious thought; and then by my individual consciousness, and experience also, of infirmity of judgment, and moreover, by a recollection of·those distortions of the intellect which have had their rise in the moral sentiments, and which may be far greater than I am distinctly aware of.

On these grounds, therefore, and for other reasons of a similar kind, I reject rationalism; yet in doing so, I do not abrogate reason—reason in its freest exercise, I take with me; but it is reason in *listening* and learning —it is not reason in *dictating*.

On the other hand, in the daily opening of my Bible, I put far from me that faulty practice which, while it professes itself to be the antagonist of rationalism, is, in fact, nothing better than another phase of the same arrogance, and the same presumption. What I mean is the technical dogmatism which insists that the teaching of Scripture shall, in every case, show itself to be—part with part—in accordance with a predetermined scheme of doctrinal synthesis. The dogmatist is indeed willing to bow his *reason* to the authority of Scripture; but he will not submit his scheme of interpretation to that authority: for this scheme, though he will not allow it, is dearer to him than truth:—his logic is his idol.

In seeking for truth, and in seeking for it in my Bible, and in labouring to possess myself of so much of this inestimable good as my individual infirmity, and the narrow limits of my spirit may be capable of, and in desiring a peaceful and uncontroverted holding of this truth, I have to look out for a principle, or practical rule, that shall meet the conditions under which religious truth offers itself to me in a *written* revelation—a message from Heaven, which has been consigned to a collection of books.

At the outset, when I give place, even in the most trivial single instance, to criticism, and when I ask aid from those who are accomplished in this line, and when I accept from them any proper correction of the document—for example, the emendation of a passage that has, in whatever manner, become faulty—when I do this, I acknowledge that the Bible in my hand is not an audible utterance of syllables and words, from the skies. But then this admission includes, by necessity, another admission, namely, this—that the Divine impartation of religious truth has become commingled with the human impartation of it;—or such a conveyance of it as is liable to the ordinary conditions, or, as we may say, to the *accidents* that attach to all things mundane—namely, accidents of the hand, of the eye, of the ear, of the memory; as well as what depends on habits of verbal exactness, and on the technical habitudes of individual human minds.

A consciousness of this intimate combination of what is human, with that which is Divine, in the canonical Scriptures, has given rise to many imaginary perplexities; and these have suggested various "Theories of Inspiration," such as might serve, either to remove the difficulty a little further off, or to conceal the extent of it from our troubled sight. These palliative schemes have been founded upon the supposition that there are several species, or several *degrees* of inspiration;—as, for instance, that of an indefinite control—that of the suggestion of thoughts merely, and that of the suggestion of the very words. But no such distinctions as these, nor any others which a taxed ingenuity may devise, yield me the aid which they promise. For, in the first place, I find no indication of them in the books themselves:—there is no precautionary notice to this effect, such as I find on the margin of some patristic volumes,

Cautè lege. These modern devices are arbitrary, and they are not susceptible of proof. Whether any such distinctions are true, in fact, or not, I can never know.

But in the second place, even if I believed these distinctions to be well-founded, and they may be real—it would remain for me to apply them to the books, severally, or to particular chapters, or to paragraphs, or to single verses, at my discretion; and while so employed, what would take place is obvious:—The scheme itself, or this hypothesis of a differential inspiration, is, as I may say, a *remedy* to be employed according to the urgency of the case:—it is an anodyne, to be used by the patient, *pro re natâ;* and in the use of this, as of every kind of alleviation, I shall insensibly go on from a rare, to a frequent recurrence to the dangerous preparation. I shall be tempted intemperately to avail myself of the saving hypothesis, until at length my Bible has become, like the Bible of the rationalist, a book of leisurely reference, but a book of no authority; and therefore, it will cease to yield me what I am in search of—a religion in which I may find *rest.*

There is a path before me that is less embarrassed than this, and much less perilous too. I put far from me the arrogance of the dogmatist who, " wise beyond and above what is written," has fixed the limits beyond which the DIVINE NATURE—the INFINITE, may not stoop in its correspondence with the finite nature. That this condescension may go far, is a fact that is made conspicuous in the very conditions of a *written* revelation; and this fact I fully recognize in allowing criticism, in its own way, to do its office. But I recognize this fact or principle to a further extent, when I allow historical criticism at all to discuss or consider questions concerning quotations of the ancient Scriptures in the Christian Scriptures; or concerning the exactness of any single historical statement.

To these extents modern Biblical criticism is allowed to go, without rebuke; or without rebuke from reasonable and instructed men. But where are we to stop? Should *historical* criticism also be left to take its course without prohibition? Or should any liberty at all be granted to *logical* criticism?

I find that if I were to go about to frame an answer to these questions, this answer must be made to rest upon the above-mentioned dogmatic ground of my presuming to know the limits which the Divine Wisdom must prescribe for itself in holding communion with man. I tremble to think of attempting to define these limits, or to make any such conditions; I define nothing, I insist upon no terms, I plant no hedge of my own around the Almighty; and therefore I am not careful to give any reply to the aboved-named questions.

But if not, then do I not set wide open the door of rationalism?—nay—I close it fast, and for ever. What I insist upon is a firm, and a thoroughly rational hold of the proper historic evidence attesting the supernatural element of the revelation which is conveyed in the canonical writings. So far as I have seen, it is the want of any such peremptory conviction, and of this clear-headed and firm-handed grasp of the facts of the Bible history—it is a confused, and a wavering, and an ill-digested belief in the reality of that history, whence come the pious alarms, and the jealousies, and the petulant outcries of unthinking religious persons, who denounce as a heretic every man who knows more than they know, and dares to say it.

Let criticism upon Holy Scripture make "full proof of its ministry:"—let it do its office without fear or intimidation: criticism, literary, historic, and logical (if there be room for this). If criticism becomes captious, irreverent, sinister in its aims; if it shows itself to be irreligious at heart, then I cease to listen to it. But so long as it is right-minded, and ingenuous, and is regardful of our first principle—that we have in hand a supernatural revelation—so long as criticism is thus minded, I welcome its advances:—it can do me no possible harm:—it may render me inestimable services; and while it walks by my side, I have no tremours, as if phantoms were at hand.

I read my Bible by the lamp of criticism as often as I may think it useful to do so. But I read my Bible daily, in the clear daylight of its own effulgence. Shall I ask for a rule, for a formula, like those of a schoolbook, according to which I am to discern between the Divine and the human in Holy Scripture? Idle pedantry were this, and how superfluous! I need no rule, when I walk forth, under the splendour of noon, and gaze upon the visible manifestations of the wisdom and goodness of the Creator. I fall into no errors in setting off the works of man, which mix themselves with the works of God, in this prospect. I know *these* at a glance, by their familiar characteristics. I pass my judgment upon them freely:—meantime that which indeed is Divine in the objects around me has its own inimitable aspect—its own indubitable characteristics—the things of God speak aloud their authorship: I am troubled by no perplexities. I ask not the help of the interpreter to make me sure that the works of God are indeed—the works of God.

If this be metaphor, it is more than metaphor, for the instances, although they are two in form, are identical in substance. You may demand in the one case, or in the other, a sharply defined discriminative test, by application of which I may preclude all chance of mistake, nor ever incur the risk of attributing to God, that which belongs to man—or the contrary. All such alarms are unnecessary:—a daily and devout perusal of Holy Scripture brings with it its own discriminative faculty—a perception, or I might call it, a *tact*, a taste, and a sense of congruity which will seldom lead an intelligent Christian man astray. Or such errors as he may fall into will not, in any appreciable degree, affect the large result of his consciousness of religious truth.

SECTION IV.

At the instigation of the moral sense, and upon the demand of emotions that are instinctive and universal, and at the prompting of forebodings which philosophy can neither disperse nor satisfy, I have come to seek for an authenticated religion—a religion countersigned in Heaven. I have found it in the Scriptures of the Old and New Testaments. And it is not only that I am willing to receive my religious beliefs from the Bible, for I ought to say that—after an industrious inquiry concerning this attestation, the liberty to hold myself loose from it, is gone! It is a necessity of a fully instructed reason that binds this belief upon me. It would be a less correct expression to say—after due inquiry, I *consent* to retain my faith in Holy Scripture; for the strict statement of the case is this—after inquiry, renewed often and at different epochs of life, and after listening to many pleadings on the other side—after this, it is not that I hold the Bible; it is the Bible that holds me. Any other statement of the case, or any softening of it, to save my pride, is—a delusion.

Of what sort, then, is the reply which I gather from my Bible to what must be my foremost question, as it is my chief anxiety? How is it as to the reality of the moral system? How is it as to the truth of the universal instincts of mankind concerning good and evil, praise and blame, reward and punishment? How is it concerning my prospect of well-being or of ruin in a future life? These questions, or any others virtually contained in these, are soon answered.

Holy Scripture, from its first pages to its last, is a spreading forth of the rudiments of the moral economy. The reality, and the unalterable permanence, and the inexorable force of whatsoever has a moral meaning—this is the import of all things therein contained, whether it be history, or formal teaching. Whatever I read in direct propositions, and whatever I gather by inference, has this same meaning. And there is a consecutive accordance of innumerable affirmations of the same truth.

Book after book, page after page, verse after verse, assumes as certain the reality of whatever is of a moral quality. Ordinarily this is assumed, and on a few occasions it is declared in form; but never is it argued as if it were questionable, or as if it had ever been questioned: never is it *excused;* never is an apology offered in behalf of what it may imply. Nowhere do I find any covert indications given me of a path of abstract thought in following which I may—if by constitution of mind I need it—work out the problems of the moral universe for myself.

Instead of this, I am met at the outset by the fact that, the one oriental family, to which, at the first, were "committed the oracles of God," was, throughout the period of its national religious existence, conscious only of the concrete forms of thought, and was wholly unconscious of its abstract or philosophic forms. This "election" doubtless had its psychological significance; and when I look into PHILO I see a curious instance of that torturing of the national intellect which could not but take place when the Jew aspired to think and write as the Greek.

Throughout the Scriptures the FIRST TRUTH in theology is conveyed *in terms of the moral system;* and very rarely in any other terms; nor ever in those of abstract thought. It might have been allowable, forty years ago, on the part of hopeful intellectualists, to imagine that a scientific theology would, at length, be educed, and set forth in propositions of a purely theoretic order. But no one can now entertain this hope who has followed the course of what is called metaphysics, throughout that period, and up to this present time. The result of the earnest endeavours of the choicest minds of Germany, France, and England, is this —to demonstrate the fact that a religious revelation of the INFINITE and ABSOLUTE BEING is not possible in any other mode than that which is employed by the inspired writers—the earlier of them, and the later.

And not only have these writers given to the world the only possible revelation of the DIVINE NATURE, but they have, at their first essay, reached the highest possible expression of it. That it is so there is at hand a very significant proof. Vast—prodigiously voluminous, is that amount of commentative labour of which the Jewish and Christian Scriptures have been the text. In attempting to compass, in thought, this body of expository industry—evoked in the course of more than two thousand years—the mind is quite overwhelmed and lost. That portion of this perennial toil which may now be extant upon our shelves, is nothing more than a fragmentary sample of the entire mass; for besides this specimen, treasured in books, *extant*, there is the greater mass, once consigned to books, but long since gone down to the abyss. Yet even if all were now before us which the pen had for a while conserved, we should need to add the far larger quantity—and much of it not less worthy of preservation, which has uttered itself within halls and churches, from week to week, throughout this great extent of time, but which has not outlived its own echoes. Thus has the human mind exhausted itself in the ever-to-be-renewed labour of spreading out to view the utmost meaning of Scripture—Scripture as the expression of what man may know, or conceive of, concerning GOD.

What, then, is the upshot? Has the original revelation become an obsolete rudiment, giving place to what all must now accept as an improved expression of the same elementary principles? Nothing of this sort has taken place; but instead of it, there has been, from time to time, an emphatic return to the purely Biblical expression of the highest truths, after each ephemeral enterprise, to give to these truths what was thought to be a more exalted, or a more refined expression of them, has had its season. If it were not beside my purpose, I should find it easy to bring forward as many as seven distinctly-marked and well-recorded endeavours of this sort, which have flared up for a while, and presently have gone out: and now, at this time, the decisive tendency of the best-trained minds is to return, with a zest, as if impelled equally by religious feeling, and by correct and cultured taste—to what?—to the Biblical expression of the highest truths in theology.

It must not be pretended that this adhesion of all minds to the Bible, and to its style, is the mere consequence of an opinion of its sacredness and authority. It is not so. Nothing is more certain in human affairs than this, that a better, or a more fully-developed form of what is substantially true, displaces, or supersedes, the more ancient or crude form of the same truths. In the long run, that which is antiquated and imperfect gives place to that upon which the men of a later time have laboured to good purpose. Tried by the test which this fact supplies, I return to my proposition—That the Bible writers have given to the world, not merely the only possible revelation of the Divine Nature, but have given us this revelation in its most mature form, and in that condition which we must continue to receive; or if not, must reject, not only revelation altogether, but theology also.

So much of the knowledge of God as I may be capable of admitting, I therefore look for in my Bible; and I cease to look for it from any other quarter—I mean from any conceivable future achievements of the human mind. The Scriptures thus accepted, become to me the source of religious truths, or, as we say, doctrines and preceptive principles of all kinds. These principles and doctrines I am compelled to think and speak of *distributively*, or according to an artificial order or method;

yet while doing so, I well understand that doctrines and precepts, the several articles of a creed, and the several rules of conduct, are not many items, but one Divine element, diversely uttered, to suit the limitations of reason, and the changing occasions of life.

Thus, *by necessity*, we think of the Divine Attributes, and, in doing so, stumble upon perplexities which, though they are unreal, are not to be evaded. Just at this point a knowledge of abstract science, or intellectual philosophy, may be serviceable; for it may enable me to set myself clear of *each special perplexity*, by finding that it resolves itself into the one master problem of the relation of the finite to the INFINITE. If the problem which stands foremost in philosophic thought were solved, none of the included problems would thenceforward give us any trouble: thus, therefore, I may remove from the roadway of the religious life difficulties which belong to another path, namely, the path of ultimate abstractions.

On this ground, therefore, I accept from Scripture what I first need, while in search of a place of rest;—namely, a confirmation of the instinctive belief in the reality of the moral system, and of my relationship thereto, and of whatever consequences, however formidable, which this relationship may bring with it. Thus far it is not *rest ;* but disquiet that attends me.

SECTION V.

Let it be that criticism has taken its course upon the text of Scripture without restriction, and free from intimidation; but in the exercise of this liberty it must not arrogate what can never belong to it, nor assume a right to stand between me and the product of my Bible-reading at large. There must be—a definite result, thence to be derived:—there must be *a main intention* in the Scriptures:—along with many things that are incidental, there must be that which is principal, that which is of the highest moment—that for the sake of which, and to teach it, the Bible has been given me; and which I shall not fail to find there, unless by grievous fault or negligence, on my own part.

At this point I wish, beyond mistake, to feel that I have a sure path. If the various writings making up the Biblical Canon were miscellaneous summaries of religious sentiment, and of didactic ethics—then, and in that case, they would not have needed the attestation of miracles: the supernatural accompaniment would have encumbered, more than it could recommend, such a revelation. But I do find this accompaniment, and therefore I look for that which must need it, and which I could not accept with an assured belief of its Divine reality, unless it were so attested.

In seeking, then, for that which I may receive as indeed *the principal intention* of Scripture, and as the final cause of its miraculous accompaniment, I take for my guidance two rules, the first of which is this—That as this revelation offers itself to me as a good—a boon—a conveyance of inestimable benefits—a gratuity, not merited or claimable by me, it must undoubtedly have been given in all sincerity; and it must suppose a correspondent ingenuousness and uprightness on my part, who am to be the recipient of so free a gift. That reverent regard with which I may seem to listen to a message from Heaven is little better than a disguised impiety, unless it springs from a full confidence in the good faith of HIM who speaks. As to the perplexities that have troubled me in my religious course, most of them have arisen from an unconscious distrust, or want of confidence in the good faith of HIM who speaks. If questioned on this point, I should have repelled the imputation—"Do you indeed mistrust the MOST HIGH?"— No: how can you impute to me such folly, and such impiety? So I might retort; and I may believe that the imputation is groundless. Nevertheless the suspicion which I disown in formal terms, creeps upon me when I am not thinking of it.

Those especially who have lived among books, and who, as a habit of their intellectual life, have been used to put themselves into the position of an opponent, so as to give the fullest weight to a contrary opinion—such persons find it difficult to read their Bible in undiverted remembrance of what it is, namely—a Divine Message. And yet I take it as such at the moment when I assent to its supernatural attestations. This proper recollection, therefore, is the reason of my first rule, in the reading of Scripture—That, as it is given me for my benefit, it must be given in all sincerity by HIM whose air I breathe, and who sends me, daily, my daily bread. It is clear that unless I am warranted in reading my Bible with this feeling of a pure religious ingenuousness, a written revelation can be of no service to me: otherwise read, it must keep me for ever on the rack of doubt and uncertainty: far better be rid of it altogether. This therefore is my determination, namely—To seek the PRINCIPAL INTENTION of Scripture, in a perfect confidence that it has been *worded in good faith*.

The second rule, available in the reading of Scripture,

and which is no less certain in my view than the first, is this—That the inspired books will not teach, or in any way suggest, a sense that shall be directly at variance with the most conspicuous purport, or foremost axiom of the whole revelation.

This rule, certain as it is, might easily be misapplied. It does not mean this—That my individual reason, or that human reason at large, should assume the right to accept, or to reject, what is affirmed in Scripture, because it is conformable, or not conformable, to its previous conclusions. Nor does this rule mean, that I should resist any Biblical doctrine on account of its apparent contrariety to other Biblical doctrines. The first of these errors is that of the rationalist; the second is that of the dogmatist;—and both errors spring from a similar misapprehension as to the powers, and the range of the human mind, in relation to religious principles.

The rule means this—That the Scriptures will not, whether on the very same page, or on pages remote from each other, bring the primary sentiments of the religious life into a position of irreconcileable conflict, so as that no other release from distraction of mind can be found, except that of a state of indifference, or religious unconsciousness. The instance is near at hand. I have no choice but this:—I must either attribute to certain conspicuous, and often-cited passages in the Gospels and Epistles *their plenitude of meaning*, in conformity with the laws of language, and the admitted principles of textual criticism; or if I refuse to do this, then I must seek an assuagement of the most distracting perplexities in the stupefaction of the religious emotions, and in courting whatever diversions I can find in a sensuous, or a frivolous life, or in a cold intellectualism. Is it not so? The Bible—the Old Testament, and the New—is a continuous and stern condemnation of the ancient error of the nations in their polytheism; and it is a rebuke of that inveterate perversity which transfers to a created power—seen or unseen—that regard, and that trustful confidence, which is due to the ONE, the SUPREME BEING. To err on this ground is perdition: to be rent by ambiguous influences, or counter-motives, is wretchedness;—or it is so unless I seek relief in indifference. But the import of the evangelic, and of the apostolic writings is to this effect—that the highest religious regard, and a full and trustful confidence, are due to HIM, personally, who is therein set forth as the Deliverer of men—the CHRIST—the Saviour of the world.

It would be most difficult—it would be impossible—for me to maintain, in my thoughts and feelings, a distinction, setting off the latria from the hyperdulia, on this ground, even if I were aided in attempting it by any apostolic explanations, and were impelled to do it by solemn and reiterated cautions. But there are no such aids given me—there is not one such:—there are no such cautions appended to passages which seem to demand them:—there is not one such. There is no phrase which elsewhere in Scripture is appropriated to the highest religious uses, that does not find a place also among those exhortations, the intention of which is to fix the thoughts upon the power and grace of the Saviour Christ. Instead of a caution, where it should come, if it ought to come at all, what I find is emphasis—intensity—accumulation of epithets;—the purpose of all being such as can find its reason in nothing—short of the unconditioned meaning of those passages which bring the PERSON—the CHRIST, into view, as the object of worship—even of the highest worship of which the human spirit is capable.

That it should be so is indeed—ὁμολογουμένως—a "great mystery." How does it transcend all faculties of human thought to grasp it, or to find its solution, or to bring it within the compass of any known analogies! Nevertheless it *is* the mystery, and it is the condition of the only possible religious existence. Clearly it is so, for the uniform testimony of experience, within the Christian community, is to establish the law that every attempted abatement of this belief, whether by theologic speculation, or by the application of exceptive criticism to single passages, takes effect upon the religious life— to lower it, to render it ambiguous, and perplexed, and feeble, and to induce a temper that is captious, and fastidious, and distrustful. The product of such attempts has, in every instance, been a religion, the characteristic of which is the irreligiousness of its tone, and of its language.

An instructed Christian man, when he accepts, as indeed true, that which the apostolic writers plainly affirm concerning the Person of Christ, will not fail to look back through the course of time, and inquire in what manner this same Biblical testimony has taken effect upon religious minds, from the first years of Christian history, to these last years. It is not in distrust of the Scriptures that I may wish to make this inquiry; it is more in distrust of myself, and it is as prompted by a proper diffidence that, when a truth so transcendant is put in my view, I should seek to know how it has been regarded by those who, in long series, have gone before me. I profess to believe in "the holy Catholic Church," and "the communion of saints:"—I believe, therefore, that Christianity has realized itself, from age to age, in the mind and affections of a great company of men, variously trained, and variously minded in all things; but yet of one mind as to their acceptance of whatever may be the principal meaning of the Scriptures.

Thus thinking, I look back and find that the orthodox faith, concerning the Person of Christ, has sustained itself in its controversy with each successive denial of it, by a direct appeal to the apostolic writings, on this principle, that Scripture has been worded in good faith, and that our part is to read it with a corresponding. ingenuousness. On the other hand, those who have laboured to establish an abated, or a contrary belief, have been thrown upon the resources of their individual skill and ingenuity; and although these might seem to avail them in single instances, it could only be by destroying our confidence in the good faith, or the intelligence of the Apostolic writers. In reviewing the history of the controversy concerning this—"the great mystery of godliness"—from the ante-Nicene age to this, the same characteristics of evasiveness and of subtile ingenuity attach to the side of (what is conventionally called) heresy; and yet with this difference, that whereas the early opponents of orthodoxy, when compelled to shift their ground, still betook themselves to positions within the pale of Biblical authority—their successors, in later times, have receded, from point to point, more and more remote from that authority. At the present moment those who maintain orthodoxy, do so in maintaining also the integrity and the simplicity of the Scriptures:—those who assail and reject what they designate as—a "dry

Athanasianism," in doing so, disallow the Apostolic commission to teach men, as with authority from Heaven.

At this time I should scarcely find an ingenuous opponent who would not allow that the question of orthodoxy has resolved itself into *the previous question* concerning the Evangelic and Apostolic writings as determinative in religious controversy. No voice is now heard in court as representative of those who, in times gone by, have pleaded for an intermediate belief concerning the Person of Christ. All argumentation of this order has long ago gone to wreck;—there is therefore, on the one side— this orthodox belief—and on the other side—what is it? If in candour and sincerity I ask myself what there is— I can find no answer which saves the authority of the Scriptures, or which distinguishes them in any sense from other records of human opinion. Christianity, as a revelation—means nothing, if it does not mean the faith which has been professed in all times by the great body of Christian men.

SECTION VI.

As is the recipient, such must be the product of any teaching. Especially does this condition take effect when truths that are as much beyond the grasp of the most capacious minds, as of the meanest, are symbolized in words, and condensed in propositions. The difference will be this, that what is so embodied carries a meaning to the one mind which moves it to its depths; while to another mind the same form of words is nothing more than what the ear admits—"a form of words"—a dead letter, or a letter that killeth—a word that *deadens* even what might have seemed to be alive.

"A dry and wordy Trinitarianism" is, in fact, a creed which, by some accident of a man's position, has come to lodge itself in a "dry and wordy spirit:" the aridity, the stiffness, the wordiness, are all in the soul; they are neither in the propositions, nor in the things spoken of. If the orthodoxy which I profess is to me a barren formula, I ought to know that the very same state of the feelings which forbids my receiving light, and life, and comfort, from my confession of faith, sheds darkness also, and discomfort, upon every element of the religious life. Yet there is something more than mere lifelessness, which intervenes between me and a cordial acceptance of what should next follow in constituting a Christian belief; for there is a repugnance, the existence of which, whether it be latent or avowed, will not fail to betray itself.

I believe in "the forgiveness of sins." Yes, assuredly; I *must* do so; for we are all in fault; and I too am so, no doubt:—I do not profess to be better than others; but if I am to accept pardon, I ought to know the conditions; and I should take time to consider the terms of peace: I should stipulate on the ground of my just pretensions. Few of us would choose to put feelings of this sort into words; and yet there are few who could truthfully declare that no such feelings had ever found a lurking-place in their hearts. A consciousness of such risings of nature might suffice, even without the citation of texts, as proof that man is indeed "far gone from original righteousness;" and that the whisperings of a disturbed conscience prevail to hide from him the humiliating reality of his own moral condition. If I take up in turn the several pleas, many as they are, which, in all time, have been urged as conclusive objections to the Biblical doctrine of the pardon of sin:—each of them has its source plainly in those delusions of self-love, which, while acknowledging an obligation to the requirements of impartial justice, insist upon terms, as if there were a counter plea which ought to be listened to.

But now, if I put far from me, and reject, and refuse, every such suggestion of pride, and if, in a mood which undoubtedly must be proper to me, I take up the Scriptures, assured as I am that there is therein conveyed a message of grace—*worded in good faith*—if so, then a question cannot arise as to the import of the many passages that bear on this principal subject. No shadow of doubt attaches to that often-recurrent affirmation concerning the purpose of the death of Christ—suffering—as suffering to save, when He "made His soul an offering for sin." Already I have accepted from the inspired writers their ineffable doctrine concerning the Person of Christ; but this doctrine finds its complementary truth in that which I now accept as also the meaning of the same writers, concerning the purpose of His death. The first truth demands the second, nor can it find its interpretation in the *teaching* merely, or in the Divine example of virtue and wisdom; nor otherwise is it to be understood than as it is related to His vicarious death upon the Cross. It is here, and it is at no point short of it, that the troubled human spirit finds rest. It is at this point, where the speculative reason consciously meets a limit it can never pass—it is here that the meditative mind—the awakened moral consciousness, acknowledges its home. Here the soul may abide:—here may man tranquilly, if not joyfully, await the final issues of the future life. Here, without dismay, is it possible for the kindling immortal spirit to look on to the dread moment of its summons into the Divine Presence.

I revert to what I have just before said of the Biblical mode of conveying to the human mind so much as may be conveyed concerning the Divine Nature. This teaching is most often in terms of the moral economy;—never is it attempted in those of abstract thought, or of philosophy. The inspired writers, in giving expression to human conceptions of the Natural Attributes (so we speak!) of God—His creative power and wisdom, His omniscience, and omnipresence, and the like, do so in phrases that are manifestly tropical, and such, that, in fact, they are never misunderstood, unless by infants, or by adults, infantile in mind. I thus read—" The eye of the Lord is in every place, beholding the evil and the good." But is this mode of teaching theology a *condescension*— is it an accommodation, having in view the benefit of the unphilosophic multitude? This may have been imagined, and though not giving words to so supercilious a feeling, I might have thought that—if a Bible, or if a supplementary theologic treatise had been granted, *for me*, and for a few others, of my class—men trained in abstractions—in that case, WE, enjoying *a book to ourselves*, and flattered by the gift, should have found the elements of theology conveyed in terms familiar to our habits of thought, and less rude than are those of the Scriptures at large. No such upper-class treatise as this —no such book for the privileged intellectualist, is included in the canon : it is not there; nor could it in the nature of things have been provided for me ; for there is no mundane dialect which could have been made the medium of it: there are none, born of women, who could have worded it; there is no college of philosophers competent to any such task as that of framing a theology in abstract terms of the finite reason. I take my Bible in hand therefore, not as if it were a book which, being graciously intended for the unlearned multitude, I may be willing to read *condescendingly:*—not so, for the Bible gives expression to the knowledge of the INFINITE BEING, in that mode which is demanded by the universal limitations of the human mind. Let me not practise any fond illusion upon myself in this matter. And undoubtedly it is better for me, as for others, that the conveyance of the first truths in theology should be made in those terms that are *manifestly tropical*, and which I must know at once to be allusive and analogical, than that it should be given in terms that would seem to have been carefully and artfully concocted, but which, by their very avoidance of tropes and figures, would seduce me into the notion that I was receiving from them *a direct* knowledge of the INFINITE and the ABSOLUTE BEING. In *so* reading a hyperwrought theology, I should be led away upon a path of positive and dangerous error. In reading the Scriptures *such as they are*, the INFINITE and SUPREME is symbolized to me in a mode which, while it secures the religious end intended, suggests no error of a speculative kind. As for instance:—it is good and needful for me to be told, by authority, that " the eyes of the Lord are in every place, beholding the evil and the good." But now let me go to work, and attempt to put this truth concerning the Divine Omniscience into the most approved form of philosophical expression; let me condense it, and let me expand it, and let me fence it off from its contraries, on every side. I shall not have finished my task until I have gone deep into that rayless abyss in the midst of which a true theology, and a ghastly atheism look so much alike, that I am in danger, every moment, of mistaking the one for the other. Again, it is highly serviceable to me—in truth, it is a necessary condition of the religious life—that I should have a firm belief in the efficacy of prayer, and in the reality of that Providential Government of all things, which is the complementary Biblical doctrine, involved in the belief that prayer is efficacious. The two beliefs, while they spring up irresistibly in the human mind, are assumed as certain on every page of the inspired writings. Innumerable passages give expression to these two elements of piety. But in every instance they are conveyed *in the terms of the finite*, both as to the suppliant recipient of favours, *and not less so*, as to the Hearer of prayer, and the Giver of good things. I ought, with especial care, to keep in view this fact at this time, inasmuch as a nugatory philosophy has gone so far to entangle these religious elements with abstractions wherewith they have no inner connection—no connection at all.

This, then, is the ground on which I accept, from the inspired writers, what they teach concerning the death of Christ—dying as the Saviour of the world. I find it is not in figures of one kind only that the meaning of Scripture on this momentous subject is expressed; but in figures derived from three or four sources. Whatever there may be in the transactions of our social existence which may be made convertible to the purpose of teaching so transcendant a doctrine as that which it so much concerns us to learn, is, either by Christ Himself, or by His inspired servants, so made available for this purpose.

When I examine this symbolic phraseology in detail, it becomes evident that there is not one of these tropical terms which I can imagine to be, by itself, adequate to the occasion on which it is employed. If it were indeed adequate to its subject, there would be no room for other terms, or symbols; but there are several others; and each must find its place in the teaching to which I am to listen.

But what is the treatment which I should give to these symbols? Am I at liberty to say—These are figures, they are metaphors, in the oriental style, and as such, if I am in search of their exact import, they must be shorn of much of their apparent value. The very contrary of this should, as I think, be the rule of interpretation in the case. Oriental writers do indeed indulge themselves in the use of extravagant similes when they are framing adulations for the ear of potentates; but this is not the style of the Biblical writers; and when they are teaching theology in terms and phrases proper to the finite mind, which are the only terms available, or, indeed, *possible*, they accumulate such figurative terms as *substitutes* for *terms of the Infinite.* Thus, in teaching what they teach concerning the Divine Power—they say of the Most High, such things as these: That HE taketh up the isles, as a very little thing; that with HIM, the mountains are only as the small dust of the balance; that HE stays the raging of the sea, and says to its proud waves—Thus far shall ye go, and no further. They say of God—That HE spreadeth forth the heavens as a tent to dwell in; and that as a garment, some time hence, He shall roll them together. These figures, ought they then to receive a retrenched interpretation? Ought they to be denuded of their oriental garb? Not so, for if I am willing to take up David's genuine theology, and to read it off in the light of my modern astronomy, then I shall find that these symbols—true and sublime as they are, demand now, an interpretation which immeasurably surpasses what was included in the largest conceptions of the Hebrew king; these metaphors are cumulative terms of the finite, employed for teaching me truths, concerning the INFINITE, which could neither be taught, nor learned, in any other manner, whether by me, or by the loftiest and the largest of human minds. Nay, if on this arduous ground I might allow myself to speculate at all, I should incline to believe that, in an upper world, and in the schools where immortal intellects receive their training, the theology current among them is, from its beginning to its end, delivered in tropes and figures, which are known and acknowledged to be such: the difference between the teaching on Earth, and the teaching in Heaven, being this—that whereas we, in the dark, are for ever beating about among our abstractions, and are vainly labouring to stretch them out to the dimensions of the Infinite, they in Heaven have long ago come to understand that all such endeavours are a folly. The abstractions of the finite reason become delusive fictions when they are put forward as applicable to the INFINITE: whereas the figures and (as they might be called) the fictions of a symbolic style are lights on the highway of eternal truth, when we take them for what they are—our *only* guides on that road.

Let me now apply these maxims of Biblical interpretation—I venture so to think of them—to the Biblical style in teaching me all I can learn in this world, and perhaps in another, concerning what is technically called the doctrine of the Atonement. Take one instance out of many. CHRIST, as teacher of a new morality, or of a morality newly illustrated by His own practice, is spreading out to view that self-renunciation of which His coming into the world was the brightest example. He says—"Even as the Son of Man came into the world, not to be the receiver of services, but that He might Himself render services to others." Thus far the terms are literal, and they are such as manifestly exhaust the subject to which they are applied; for the words find a full interpretation within the circle of the duties and offices of common life. But then there is an appended clause:—the teaching, in relation to the immediate occasion, was completed at the semicolon; yet it receives a supplement; it is as if, when the purpose of Christ's coming into the world were brought within the field of vision, it was not possible to stop short in the mention of what was only an adjunctive purpose—the giving an example of self-denying beneficence; not so, for this Teacher of men came principally as their Deliverer; and in this capacity He came "to give His soul a redemption-price for the many." Now the terms of this appended clause are not intelligible in a literal sense: manifestly they are tropical:—they lead *outward*, beyond that home-circle within which the terms of the first clause complete their intention. There was nothing which met the eye of those who were spectators of the Crucifixion, that could correspond with the terms of this subjoined clause: a sense more remote—a sense occult is to be inquired for. There is a transaction, the parties concerned in which do not make their appearance on this stage: the principals are not here visibly present. Christ's death, as a *martyrdom*, was a visible event; and those of the bystanders who were capable of learning the lesson, might learn the whole of it as they stood.

It is, then, as if in these eight words—καὶ δοῦναι τὴν ψυχὴν αὐτοῦ λύτρον ἀντὶ πολλῶν—a momentary uplifting of the veil of the great world were taking place: and in this moment (begun and passed in the twinkling of an eye) there had stood in view the long line of the captive human race:—the Tyrant—enemy of God and man—with the chain in his hand:—the laying down of a price which he would, but which he dares not refuse:—then the dropping of that chain from his reluctant grasp, and—the release of uncounted millions!

All this is figure; but it is figure which has its intention, and which touches more nearly the truth of the things in prospect than any form of words could do which, discarding metaphor, should aim to be literal and exact. In changing its terms, and in seeking aid from other sources among the things of earth, the Biblical style keeps steadily in view its single purpose, namely, to suggest a belief concerning the death of Christ which shall quite exclude the notion (otherwise probable) that the crucifixion was a martyrdom merely. It would be safe to seek for instances in the Apostolic writings; but those occurring in the Gospels may be regarded as having a peculiar emphasis.

"The Good Shepherd giveth His life for the sheep"— He layeth down His soul for them. Metaphor again, and it is indeed a brief utterance; but yet the terms, few as they are, open up, as before, the unseen world; and the same persons, and their conflict, are dimly revealed; and the centre fact is the same—the crucifixion; and the price offered to the Tyrant is the same; for it is the soul of the Deliverer that is the price of the redemption of the captives. And the metaphor is such as to preclude all risk of its being interpreted in a literal sense. And it is because the doctrine, and the facts, which are thus symbolized, so immeasurably transcend the powers of human language to express them, and so far transcend the range of human thought to grasp them, that both the doctrine, and the facts, are everywhere consigned to figures, and to such figures as could not, except as perverted by the superstition of a dark age, have received a literal interpretation. Understood as a system of figures, Christ's teaching, on various occasions, constitutes a uniform doctrine concerning the one purpose of His death. Even those variations in the wording of His last utterance at the Supper, as reported by the three Evangelists, may well be understood to convey a further precaution, intended to guard against the dangerous mistake of interpreting literally that which so far exceeds any power of words. It is evident that, in the conveyance of what should be understood in a literal sense, on a subject like this— namely, the purpose of the death of Christ, there could have been only one form of words by which so momentous a doctrine could be certainly made known. But a *figurative* conveyance of it may admit of many variations without damage to the meaning; inasmuch as, at the best, such language can be taken for nothing more than an approximate expression of an ineffable truth.

Throughout the Apostolic writings every utterance bearing upon the same subject is concentric with Christ's own words, when His death, and the manner of it, and its purpose, are in His view. This purpose I can no more misunderstand than I can misunderstand those many passages occurring in the Psalms, and the Prophets, which symbolize the power, the providence, the wisdom, the omniscience, and the compassion of God. The terms are various, the metaphors are drawn from every available source; but the final intention is put beyond the reach of mistake, unless when a perverted reason resolves to take to itself the false, and to cast away the true.

More than three or four passages in the Apostolic Epistles might suggest an inquiry concerning the purpose of the Saviour's descent into Hades—the Sheol—the prison of spirits. But that which more concerns me is—the triumphant return of the Deliverer from that prison-house. It is not among shadows, obscurely spoken of, that I am left to seek the assurance of safety which I need, when on the border of the world unknown. A firm assurance of the forgiveness of sins, and of every other benefit which now in this life, and in the future life, is embraced in the Christian scheme, is brought to rest upon a fact concerning which I may possess myself, *if I need it*, of incontestible historic evidence, namely—the Resurrection of Christ. Yet are those to be accounted happy whose personal consciousness of their individual membership in Christ carries them clear of any such necessity! To feel this necessity is a penalty that must be paid by the educated, as the price of their prerogatives.

SECTION VII.

The Resurrection of Christ—a principal event, it must be, in the history of the human family; and as this event is cognizable through the medium of those ordinary evidences which put us into correspondence with history at large, it might well claim the place due to it as at once the instance, and the proof, of a destiny so much higher than mortality could otherwise aspire to. Thought of in this way, this event might seem itself to pass over from the region of theology, and to attach itself to the philosophy of human nature. But no such transference as this can, in fact, be allowed; for the Resurrection of Christ has another, and a higher intention than that of enlarging our conceptions of the destiny of the human species: it is the governing event in an economy which is *purely spiritual;* and it will withdraw and withhold our thoughts from whatever belongs to a lower order of ideas.

What is it then that I intend by this phrase—a phrase so vaguely employed often—the spiritual economy? It is that recovery, and it is that discipline of human souls *individually*, which is the leading subject of Christ's last discourse with His disciples before His hour of suffering. He there speaks to them of the advent of the COMFORTER, the Spirit of Truth, who should "abide with them for ever," and should "teach them all things" —in a word, should open up anew the communion of man with God, and bring it to rest upon a new foundation. This spiritual economy is not declarative, nor is it universal, like that of the moral system, which embraces all beings that are rational and accountable; but it is a dispensation that is strictly individual, and the benefits of which are imparted in a sovereign manner, wherever they are bestowed at all. It is a dispensation of grace connected always with the life, the death, the resurrection, and the mediation of Christ, as the Saviour of them that, throughout all time, shall hear His voice and follow Him.

If, while this present life is running out, I am seeking assurance, and if I need a steadfast hope as to the future life, neither of these blessings can ever be attained on the field of discursive and unauthentic meditation; for that field, on every side of it, borders upon an abyss—dark and unknown. Hope, and peace, and assurance, must come to me from above, and they must so come as that I may be able, at all times, to connect them with that which is well-defined, and is warranted, and is approvable to reason and conscience. That Divine Energy to which I am taught to attribute whatever, in a genuine sense, is good within me, conforms itself to the terms of the written Revelation which is in my hand. The spiritual life is a discipline, and an exercise, and a commencement, every rudiment of which, and every possible condition of it, has already been noted, and put into terms, and set forth in instances, within the compass of the inspired writings. Apart from this verbal and this definite guidance, and from this authentic teaching, I may conjecture anything, and imagine what I please; and after making excursions, to the right and the left, far into the illimitable gloom, I shall return to question all things, to doubt everything, and to sicken of all. There could be no rest, on this ground—*ground* it is not, but a region of dreams, wherein the human mind has never attained to what it needs—peace in prospect of the future.

Within the compass of the inspired writings I find that which meets and satisfies the wants of the soul in its yearning to hold communion with God—the Father of spirits, and to be assured of His favour. In the Gospels and Epistles I am fully instructed as to the *terms* of this communion; but it is in the devotional portions of the Old Testament, and there only, that I find the expression of it. I need both; and it is a circumstance full of meaning that, whereas in the New Testament the conditions of peace between man and God are set forth with the utmost explicitness, little or nothing is added in them, either in the Gospels or the Epistles, as a pattern or exemplification, or as the formulæ of this newly-opened communion. In the New Testament there is history, and there is doctrine, and precept; but there is no spiritual liturgy; there are no models at large of evangelic meditation; there is no new recension of the worship of the ancient Church: as well the public prayer and praise, as the solitary wrestlings of the soul with God, which served the faithful in the earliest times, the same must serve us also in these last times.

What should be the inference from this noticeable fact? It is this, that as to the communion of the human spirit with the Father of spirits, it had already received its character and style, and it had attained its highest expression, and it had reached its most mature form in the Psalms, and in the theologic and devotional passages of the Prophets. It is thus, in fact, that the devout in all ages have taken up, and have employed these sublime passages, and these odes, and these meditations. But then these ancient formulæ of devotion—these model expressions of the throes of the spiritual life, were given to the pious among the Hebrew people while they were still uninformed, explicitly, concerning the future life. This fact imports much. Thinking just now only of the devotional Psalms, and of some passages in the Prophets, it is to be noted that these voices of the soul, moved to its depths, and giving emphatic utterance to its yearning for the enduring favour, and fruition of the presence of God, are drawn forth by nothing more momentous than the changeful experiences of the ordinary lot of man—man whose days are so few—man, in his brief time of frailty and sinfulness—man in his passing hour of sickness and destitution—his hour of faintness and thirst in the wilderness, when pursued by the cruel, and betrayed by the false, and cast down by troubles that shall see their end at sun-rise, and chilled by a cloud that is even now moving off from the heavens! It is as thus disciplined among the things of this short day of life, that the soul is brought into correspondence with the Infinite, the Eternal, whose favour shall be endless.

Here then is a result that is vastly out of proportion with the occasions whence it is educed. Here is a discipline, looking on to a remote futurity, which futurity has barely been announced! Here is a training for an endless life; but the endless life itself is, at the best, dimly foreshadowed only. The trial begins and ends in a day—a year, or a threescore years and ten; and the learners in this school are spending their days of vanity or pain as a tale that is told; and while they are thus chastened every morning, and sore troubled every evening, they are learning those lessons of immortal wisdom which bespeak a destiny whereof nothing more than an ambiguous whisper has come, once and again upon the ear. Here then, in considering the conditions under which souls were trained, of old, I learn what it concerns me to understand, as to the DIVINE METHOD, always the same, for the spiritual discipline of the human spirit.

Now—and under the conditions of the Christian system—just as it was under the ancient system—the soul is wrought upon intensely, and it is profoundly moved by the things of the hour and of the day; from which transient interests it would fain, but cannot do so, disengage itself. Why not treat, as they deserve, these trials of the moment—come and gone, while we smart under the lash? Why not contemn these cares and pains? How wise were it to contemn them! We think we will do so to-morrow; but to-morrow shall see our stoical resolves shattered, and we in school once again. But in this school of to-day I am learning lessons which, *so far as appears*, I shall have no occasion to put in practice when the time comes that I have thoroughly well learned them.

So it was with the long series of those to whom the Scriptures of the Old Testament were given:—they were in training for a life hereafter, which life had not been *so* revealed to them as that the hope of it should distinctly utter itself in their religious language, either of solitary meditation, or of discourse, one with another. And thus it is now, even under the brighter light of the Christian revelation: the Divine Method is substantially the same. Although the announcement of immortality is now distinct, and the conditions of its attainment are set forth in the clearest manner, yet little more is given than some dim indications of what that life eternal is to be, in preparation for which the discipline of the present life is—what we find it to be. The arduous services, and the trials of principle, and the bold enterprises of that future cycle of æons shall be such—how can it be supposed otherwise—they shall be such as shall exhibit, and shall justify the wisdom that has ordered the training which fills the years and days of this present life.

That I should well learn the lesson of this life, but that while learning it I should not know its meaning—this is the purpose of Him who appoints it; therefore, it is upon the learning of this lesson that my best thoughts should be concentred, and I ought to be content to look on, seeing in front of me the thick folds of a veil that is never lifted. And yet this veil, impenetrable as it is, is it not figured with symbols *on this side?* Certainly it is so; nor need there be hesitation in attempting to decipher these hieroglyphics, for whatever is spread out before the eye of man is doubtless intended for his perusal. But ought it not to be believed that, at this time, if not ages ago, the entire sense of Scripture has been laid open? What can there now remain, in these days of Bible exploration, to be brought up from the depths? An answer to this question, intended to check presumption, I find at hand, *first* in this fact, which obtrudes itself in reviewing the course of religious thought through the lapse of centuries—that what have been the allowed limits of thought in one age, have not been its limits in another: these limits, in fact, are found to be variable, from time to time: the subjects of religious inquiry are in a course of shifting from one period to another. The indifference, and the inobservance of this present time, on some subjects, may thus be brought into comparison with the vivid intelligence, and the active curiosity of times long gone by, and now almost forgotten. The individual reader of the Bible ought indeed to be cautious when he is tempted to set his single opinion in opposition to the mind and judgment of the Church universal; but he need not be troubled with diffidence when he puts small value upon the opinion of the time now passing, if it stands opposed, as it may, to the opinion of times passed.

But again, a reply to the above-named repressive query may be found in noticing that inattention to the meaning of certain signal passages in the Old Testament, and in the New, which prevails at this time—whether it be the pulpit, or the press, that is thought of. In public and in private—in the family and in Church—the Bible is read—by the chapter:—it is doled out in lumps: it is recited, and it is heard, as if it had long ago spent its force; it is insisted upon with emphasis at points only: it is disregarded throughout those flat places upon which no intensity of the present moment happens to fall.

Moreover, in what relates to the future destiny of the human family at large, there are other influences which come in to intercept the course of a free interpretation of the inspired writings. We hear it said—"Do not open up such and such subjects:—you will unsettle the minds of people." Meantime Christianity itself is weighted down in the secret musings of thousands of thoughtful persons. But beyond this, the incubus of systematic Theology sits heavily upon religious thought, and stifles Biblical inquiry. Such and such beliefs—plainly as they may stand out upon the surface of the Scriptures—how shall they be reconciled to our other beliefs, which are equally certain, or more so? What will become of our doctrinal forms?—nay, how shall we save the credit of our theological synthesis?—how—unless we pass over in silence those things which this synthesis will never avail to bring into their place in our divinity scheme. Besides, if you admit into your religious system this and that, you surrender our controversial stronghold:—you open a way, and the enemy will come in!

Allowance should be made for these fears, groundless as they are; for it can be no wonder if even men of intelligence give way to alarms at a time when a lawless and arrogant scepticism has made deep inroads upon the Christian convictions of multitudes, as well among the educated, as among the uneducated. It may seem the duty of wise and discreet instructors to throw their whole weight on to the conservative side, in religious opinion. But there are moments when nothing is so perilous as a blindfolded persistence in conservatism. We know it is so in politics, and is it not so in religion also?

Conservatism in the seniors passes into some form of worldly discretion, or of sheer indifference, or of tacit infidelity, when it is taken up by their sons and successors. The transmutation is a silent process—no one speaks of it; no one denounces it; but it is in the course of this very process that Christianity subsides into its periodic condition of powerless formalism. Thus it has been—how many times—in the course of eighteen hundred years? It cannot be told how often this cycle has been run through; but this may be affirmed, that, at whatever point of Christian history we make our entrance upon the scene, the rise and the fall—the time of power, and the season of slumber, are just then taking their turn. False religions slumber for centuries, when once they have spent their primeval forces; but the Christian force suffers abatement for short seasons only;—itself lives, it awakes, it walks forth:—it has renewed its youth, and it gathers souls anew.

So it shall be yet again: national events may come in

to give an impulse to the minds of men:—there may come a season of suffering perhaps; but the new life of a period of restoration takes its rise in the spirits and hearts of a few—a two, or three. So it has always been. Greater than any " tendency of events" is the mind of this and of that man—born, and taught, and moved onward from above. But although the movement be individual, and thus must defy human forethought, yet does it stand related to the things of the time, when it occurs. It is on *this* ground, therefore, that the characteristics of the next coming Christian renovation might be predicted; and thus one might presume to predict for the Church of the next age a reaction from the formalism of this.

There is an outer-work that must precede an inner Christian movement. There must be a clear ground of reason on which the convictions of the few who think must be made to rest. In the coming time those many forms of anti-Christian opinion which have flared up in these last times shall have collapsed, or have fallen in upon that one mode of thought which alone is logically possible on the side of disbelief. Even now those who have followed the course of thought on that side from year to year will be ready to acknowledge that there is no holding—there is no ledge for the foot—anywhere upon the slope toward material atheism, or that extreme creed which satisfies a sensuous and sensual fleshliness. As to any scheme of pantheism which hitherto has been imagined—it is a figured gauze—stretched over the mouth of the bottomless pit.

The basement work, in preparation for a season of Christian renovation, must be carried yet some way further. In a remarkable manner the course of inquiry of late years has tendered to the clearing up of antiquity on all sides—to the certification of history, at all points, and to the consequent verification of those methods of argumentation, by means of which a solid road athwart the gloom of ages has been formed, and is safely trodden. The issue shall be a realizing confidence in the truth of the Evangelic Records—simply thought of as history. This renovation is now greatly needed. The myth-whims, and the cobwebs of German "profound thought" are an amazement to English minds that have made acquaintance with the realities of the Apostolic period, and these fancies will be gone as mists, at the dawn of the next day-time of religious feeling.

The basement work in preparation for such a time must include also some reforms in halls of philosophy. Accomplished and well-intending men will come at length to acknowledge the impassable limits, and the impotency of abstract thought, as related both to the unknown, and to the INFINITE in theology. Such men will sicken of the infructuous toil of attempting to teach Christianity philosophically, or of teaching atheistic philosophy, Christianly. What is it that has come, hitherto, of these misdirected endeavours? They have not given us either a Christian metaphysics, or an intelligible anti-Christian metaphysics. Christian belief is expressible in Biblical style, and not in any other style; yet this is not because there is not, in the upper heavens, a philosophy proper to it; but because, for conveying its axioms, no dialect on earth has any terms.

Nugatory disbeliefs wound off, and done with! nugatory Christianized philosophies spun out, and done with! Biblical criticism become religious, because admitted without jealousy :—Holy Scripture become resplendent; or, as one might say, incandescent, throughout, and taking effect upon all minds—and then it need not be thought a chimerical supposition that the Divine intention of the inspired writings should be accepted on all sides, and that (let church organizations be as many as we please) Christian doctrine should be received in its integrity, humbly, cordially, everywhere, and " without controversy," by all!

In this Essay I have endeavoured to set forth—step by step, a course of thought, in following which a position of religious rest, or of a tranquil, if not joyful looking forward into the unknown future may be attained. A position much in advance of this point of rest is no doubt attainable; and the simple-hearted Christian man, whose life and temper are in accordance with Christian precepts, may assuredly reach it without presumption. If at this time I am stopping short of this further and warrantable stage in the Christian life, it is on this account—namely, that I am supposing the case of those —and there are more than a few such—whose habits of thought may be of a kind that debars them from any such tranquil enjoyment of a cloudless faith. It is the enviable happiness of some—of many—to have read their Bible from their youth up, and to have read little else. But I am now thinking of those who—often and often, have trod the round of meditation, and who, after deriving from Christianity itself exalted conceptions of the Divine Attributes, have imbibed from it also a sensitiveness which is incompatible with that tone of enjoyment which gives animation to the piety of some around them. Let it be granted that there is a fault— and it may be a serious fault—on the part of any who thus come short of this animation, and who, when challenged to be glad, and to lift up the head, find it difficult to disengage themselves from meditations that come on as a cloud, from remoter sources, and which settle down upon their prospect. The sensitiveness and the disquietude which I am here speaking of are recent developments of the Christian consciousness; and they are of that sort which attends deep changes in modes of thinking that have not reached their end or purpose: no doubt they *shall* reach that end, if not now, yet in the times of our successors.

In looking back upon any period we please in centuries past, there are to be seen Christian men—many or few—doing honour to their profession as laborious and self-denying benefactors—the dispensers of benefits, bodily and spiritual:—wherever want, and pain, and woe were abounding, men have been at hand who have learned from Christ the first lesson of His new law of love. All was right thus far; nevertheless one may be amazed to find, along with this active Christian element —the absence of that meditative sensibility which, in these times, so deeply moves many minds, in relation to the human family at large.

Christian charity, in these times, seems as if it would reverse the order of beneficence, as given us in the Apostolic precept—" Doing good to all men—specially to them that are of the household of faith;" for now it is as if we read it—" Specially to them that are *not* of that household." Doubtless there is a deep meaning in this revulsion of feeling; and we may take it as a silent preparation for a new and amazing development of the powers of the Gospel to restore all things. At this time it is not only the present condition, but the destinies of the unblessed, the unprivileged, the lost, the visibly non-elect of the thousands near us, and afar off, who are dwelling in the outer darkness of hopelessness, as to this life and the future—it is these, and their wretchedness, that fix the thoughts of the meditative few who muse and spend their days in sadness. Meantime the enterprising and the better-minded are up, and are busied in all practicable schemes of reformation. Concerning such schemes, if wisely ordered, there can be no controversy; for how thick soever may be the darkness into which we have lately learned to look, it must be well to carry into it a lamp; and whatever may be the miseries of the pit, it must be a good work to carry help to our fellow-men there that have never had a better home!

On this path, as on every other, the blessed Book which has been given us from above holds toward us the same method:—it solves no problems—it satisfies no impatience, it gives no philosophy of pain and of sin:—it abstains even from affording a gleam of light—off the narrow way which the individual Christian man is to tread. None of these things do the inspired writers do for us; but yet that narrow way is well defined, and as to the mystery of the evil and the suffering of which lately we have learned to think so much, we must seek no solution of it, or ask—How is it so?—Why should it be so?—What will be the end? There is no response! Heaven will not be inquired of by us as to any such matters.

Let it be so; for the work before us is free from a shadow of doubt. As to our troubled thoughts—an anguish as they are to some—this disquiet may be the prognostic of a time coming when the power of the

Gospel to bless the human family shall be so amply developed as shall at once overpass all controversy within the Christian pale, and put to silence for ever all gainsaying from without.

SUPPLEMENTARY TO THE FIFTH ESSAY.

A DISTINCTION which should always be kept in view has not been duly presented in the Essay—" THEODOSIUS: —Pagan Usages, and the Christian Magistrate." What we should intend by these "Pagan Usages" with which the "Christian *Magistrate*" may have to do, are not the immoralities of men individually—abounding, as they do, everywhere, and which it is the office of the minister of religion to rebuke, and which he must aim to remove by persuasions addressed to the consciences of men singly :—these are not what we mean ; for with these —*as sins*—it is not the office of the magistrate to concern himself. Pagan usages (we are thinking of such as are *immoral*) are national customs, and legalized practices, and *institutions* which, being of ancient date in a country, are recognized as *allowable*, or are cherished as *good;* at least they are subjected to no general reprobation ; but perhaps they are gloried in, and are upheld by the public arm, and are endowed by the public funds.

Now as to such usages—such institutions, and such legalized crimes—abominable as they may be—this is to be noticed concerning them—and never should it be forgotten—that Christianity abstains from naming, or denouncing, or prohibiting them :—it is silent because it takes quite another course in ridding the world of them : it *does* at length rid the world of them : but this happy issue it brings about in its own manner. It becomes us to understand what this method is—for, if we mistake it, we shall be likely to fall into the impious practice of pleading the silence of the Gospel in behalf of the worst abominations.

When a crime of any sort has passed into its fixed form as an INSTITUTION—when a sin has come to stand upon the fair side of a people's statute-books—when the Devil has been called in to prepare the rough draft of a liberal enactment, then—we shall look in vain for texts in which such crimes of a state are denounced, or are even named. The Gospel, as it addresses no offer of salvation to nations, so does it preserve an ominous silence concerning their sins.

But this boding silence—is it approval? none will think so but those whose reason is fast going—where their conscience has long ago gone—to ruin. What then are these Pagan usages? What are these NATIONAL INSTITUTIONS which Christianity does not name, and does not denounce, but of which, at length, it rids every country where it gains the ascendancy? They are these nine following:—I. Polygamy. II. Infanticide. III. Legalized Prostitution. IV. Capricious Divorce. V. Sanguinary and grossly immoral Games. VI. Infliction of Death or Punishment by Torture. VII. Wars of Rapacity. VIII. Caste; and, IX. Slavery.

Each of these immoralities was practised, and was more or less distinctly existing as a social Institution—a usage—of the neighbouring nations in the time of Christ's ministry. In fact, each of them had then a place even in Palestine, so far as that it must often have come before Him;—and was an immorality perpetrated under His eye. Yet one only of the nine on this list did He name, and denounce—that is the fourth: and the reason of the preference given to it we might easily find. But were the eight approved? It is madness to think so—it were blasphemy to say it! With each of these non-mentioned immoral usages Christianity, in its progress among the nations, came into conflict at an early time; and then, *in its own manner*, by enlightening the individual conscience, it either abrogated them entirely, or it greatly mitigated the evil of each of them. Some of these usages disappeared silently, very soon after the moment of the imperial conversion: others fell from their place as applauded customs, and quietly subsided into a position of tolerated evils—condemned, yet winked at. Each of them, among modern nations, vanishes wherever Christianity prevails, and is free to speak its mind. To this averment there is not—there never has been—an exceptive instance. Certainly the worst of the nine—SLAVERY—is not an exception: how could it be so, for it includes, and it gives its eager support to, at least, *seven* of these enormities out of the nine:—it does so as thus—Slavery has had its commencement in the most atrocious of all the forms of aggressive and lawless war: slavery perpetuates the most odious of the distinctions of caste: —slavery enforces its initial wrong by giving a brutal licence to punishment by torture. And as to that circle of crimes which are the attendants of slavery, in vitiating the relation of the sexes—slavery is the soul of each of those abominations with which the brutal lust and the demon-like cruelty of man have ever blighted what God has blessed. Slavery does indeed exist in countries where Christianity is blasphemously professed;—but in no country does slavery maintain itself in which the Gospel takes effect upon the consciences of men.

BIOGRAPHICAL SKETCH.*

ISAAC TAYLOR was the son of the late Rev. Isaac Taylor, a dissenting minister at Ongar, in Essex, and brother of Jane Taylor, whose " Contributions of Q. Q." are well known. He was born about the close of the last century, and, we believe, educated privately under the immediate superintendence of his father. He was originally destined for the dissenting pulpit, and commenced a course of preparatory study; but he soon relinquished the idea of becoming a minister, and turned his thoughts to the bar. His connexion with the legal profession was not of long duration. He betook himself to literature, and for many years lived in retirement at Stanford Rivers—a beautiful rural retreat in the immediate vicinity of his native place. In this secluded spot he wrote and published anonymously "The Natural History of Enthusiasm," and other works, some of which have had a fair share of popular favour, more especially among the enlightened and thoughtful of the various dissenting communities. His other principal works are "Ancient Christianity," published periodically, and manifesting an intimate acquaintance with the writings of the early fathers—an attempt to meet the Tractarians on their own ground, and to prove that some of these ancient writers were not so immaculate, either in doctrine or morals, as to entitle them to the blind adherence claimed for them by their modern eulo-

* From "Men of the Time." Kent & Co London 1859.

gists—"Elements of Thought," a small treatise which is used as a sort of *vade mecum* by students entering upon their philosophical studies in dissenting colleges— "The Physical Theory of Another Life," in which he indulges in speculations respecting the material condition of man and other created beings in a future state. The mental characteristics displayed in this and his other works gave rise to a highly amusing and interesting article from the pen of Sir James Stephen, in the "Edinburgh Review." Mr. Taylor, however, was comparatively little appreciated as a writer until it became known that he was the author of "The Natural History of Enthusiasm." He had been for some time before the public *in propriâ personâ*, but failed to elicit that attention to his writings which their intrinsic merits deserved. His circuitous style and Coleridgean manner of viewing the various subjects on which he wrote proved a great barrier to his popularity. His classical learning, his philosophical acuteness, and his general culture, were never called in question; but the laboured obscurity of style, and his indefinite mode of expression, proved substantial obstacles to his literary fame. "The Natural History of Enthusiasm," however, was very differently received by the religious public. It was fortunate in the time of its appearance. It was issued when the excitement and enthusiasm connected with Row and Irving were at their height. Mr. Taylor's philosophico-religious turn of mind, his previous studies, and even his peculiarities of style, enabled him to treat this subject in a manner agreeable to all professors of religion, of whatever sect or denomination. Young men preparing for the ministry began to imitate the idiosyncrasies of its style, and some with greater success to imbibe its unsectarian spirit. His other works on kindred subjects, "Fanaticism," "Spiritual Despotism," "Loyola and Jesuitism," "Wesley and Methodism;" the series of sacred meditations entitled "Saturday Evening," and "Home Education;" have all been well received, although their popularity has been by no means equal to that which "The Natural History of Enthusiasm" has all along maintained. In addition to his gifts as an author, Mr. Taylor possesses a certain amount of mechanical genius, which, we believe, he has turned to some profitable account in originating various designs of a useful and ornamental character. It may not be uninteresting to add that his habits are simple and methodical; although a "recluse," as he somewhere in his writings styles himself, he is said to be an expert and eager angler, and fond of healthy and manly sports. He spends his Saturday mornings in directing the games of his children, while his Saturday evenings are devoted to meditations of a religious character, similar to those which appear in the work under that name; and on Sundays he occasionally preaches, although a layman, to the great delight of those who are fortunate enough to hear him. His books have all, or nearly all, been republished in America, and have had an extensive circulation in the States as well as in Canada.

A CATALOGUE

OF THE

WRITINGS OF ISAAC TAYLOR.

Ancient Christianity,
 And the Doctrines of the Oxford Tracts for the Times. Fourth Edition, with Supplement, Index, and Tables. 2 vols. 8vo., pp. 550 and 700. London, 1844.

Ancient Christianity,
 And the Doctrines of the Oxford Tracts for the Times. Supplement, including Index, Tables, &c. 8vo., pp. 142. London, 1844

Spiritual Despotism.
 Second Edition. 8vo., pp. 504. London, 1835.

Fanaticism. 8vo.

Natural History of Enthusiasm.
 Eighth Edition. 8vo. London.

Saturday Evening.
 Sixth Edition. 8vo. London. 12mo., pp. 379.

Home Education.
 Crown 8vo. London, 1838.

Physical Theory of Another Life. 8vo.

Four Lectures on Spiritual Christianity,
 Delivered in the Hanover-Square Rooms, London, March, 1841. 12mo., pp. 203. London, 1841.

Writings of Isaac Taylor.

Elements of Thought;
Or, Concise Explanations, Alphabetically Arranged, of the Principal Terms Employed in the Different Branches of Intellectual Philosophy. Seventh Edition. 12mo. London.

An Essay,
Introductory to a New Edition of Pascal's Thoughts. 12mo.

Transmission of Ancient Books
To Modern Times. 8vo.

Essay
On the Application of Abstract Reasoning in the Christian Doctrine. Originally published as an Introduction to Edwards on the Will. 12mo, pp. 163. Boston, 1832.

Wesleyan Methodist;
A Review, published in the Edinburgh Review.

Introductory Essay
To a Translation of Pfizer's Life of Luther.

Loyola and Jesuitism
In its Rudiments. 12mo, pp. 416. London, 1850.

Process of Historical Proof. 8vo.

Balance of Criminality,
Or Mental Error. 12mo.

Jane Taylor's Works.
A New Edition. With a Life and Notes. 5 vols. 12mo.

Wesley and Methodism.

Josephus, The Works of.
A New Translation, by the Rev. Robert Traill, with Notes, Explanatory Essays, and Pictorial Illustrations. Edited by *Isaac Taylor*. Royal 8vo. London, 1847.

Writings of Isaac Taylor.

Restoration of Belief.
The Restoration of Belief. 12mo., pp. 381. Cambridge, 1855.

World of Mind.
The World of Mind, an Elementary Book. 12mo. London, 1858.

Logic of Theology.
Logic of Theology and other Essays. 12mo., pp. 384. London, 1859.

Ultimate Civilization.
Ultimate Civilization, and other Essays. By Isaac Taylor London, 1860.

www.ingramcontent.com/pod-product-compliance
Lightning Source LLC
Chambersburg PA
CBHW062001220426
43662CB00010B/1197